Cooperative Strategy

Cooperative Strategy

Competing Successfully Through Strategic Alliances

Pierre Dussauge
and
Bernard Garrette
HEC-School of Management, FRANCE

JOHN WILEY & SONS, LTD
Chichester · **New York** · **Weinheim** · **Brisbane** · **Singapore** · **Toronto**

Authorised adaptation from the French language edition Dussauge and Garrette, 'Les Stratégies d'Alliance', published by Les Editions d'Organisation.

This edition extensively revised and updated published
1999 by John Wiley & Sons Ltd,
      Baffins Lane, Chichester,
      West Sussex PO19 1UD, England

      National   01243 779777
      International (+44) 1243 779777
      e-mail (for orders and customer service enquiries):
      cs-books@wiley.co.uk
      Visit our Home Page on http://www.wiley.co.uk
              or http://www.wiley.com

Other Wiley Editorial Offices

John Wiley & Sons, Inc., 605 Third Avenue,
New York, NY 10158-0012, USA

WILEY-VCH Verlag GmbH, Pappelallee 3,
D-69469 Weinheim, Germany

Jacaranda Wiley Ltd, 33 Park Road, Milton,
Queensland 4064, Australia

John Wiley & Sons (Asia) Pte Ltd, 2 Clementi Loop #02-01,
Jin Xing Distripark, Singapore 129809

John Wiley & Sons (Canada) Ltd, 22 Worcester Road,
Rexdale, Ontario M9W 1L1, Canada

Library of Congress Cataloging-in-Publication Data

Dussauge, Pierre.
  Cooperative strategy / Pierre Dussauge and Bernard Garrette.
     p. cm.
  Includes bibliographical references and index.
  ISBN 0-471-97492-7 (alk. paper)
    1. International business enterprises. 2. International economic relations. 3. Government business enterprises. I. Garrette, Bernard. II. Title.
HD2755.5.D873 1999
658'.049—dc21

98–53082
CIP

British Library Cataloguing in Publication Data

A catalogue record for this book is available from the British Library

ISBN 0-471-97492-7

Typeset in 11/13pt Garamond by Dorwyn Ltd, Rowlands Castle, Hants
Printed and bound in Great Britain by Biddles Ltd, Guildford and Kings Lynn
This book is printed on acid-free paper responsibly manufactured from sustainable forestry, in which at least two trees are planted for each one used.

Contents

Foreword

C.K. Prahalad
Harvey C. Fruehauf Professor of Business Administration
The University of Michigan Business School, USA

As we approach the next millennium, managers will be confronted with a rapidly changing competitive landscape. Competitive discontinuities—abrupt changes such as deregulation, globalization, digital convergence and the emergence of the Internet—will change the rules of the game. Managers will have to learn to compete differently. One major area of difference in the future of competitive dynamics is the growing role of partnerships and alliances.

The alliances of the future are not just a replication of the traditional joint ventures in the extractive industries. The purposes, costs and risks of these emerging forms are different. Managers need a robust framework for navigating through these uncharted waters. This book provides a basis for securing the competitive high ground.

The emergence of "new rules" of competition is never instantaneous. Cracks in the established "rules" are broken slowly. The early warning signals have been visible for some time. While managers have experimented with a wide variety of forms, there have been but few attempts to codify our experience thus far and extend the lessons to the future. This needs an astute combination of detailed case studies and an ability to generalize from the specifics. That is what Pierre Dussauge and Bernard Garrette do in this book.

They start with the development of a rationale for alliances as a basis *for a multi-company strategy as well as a basis for interfirm collaboration.* Alliances create this new competitive and organizational context; cooperation between separate legal entities with their own strategies and goals and at the same time the need to collaborate to pre-empt others, to gain access to unique resources, to create virtual size and scope in the market place, to reduce and focus investments, and to gain market entry.

The rationale is followed by a *typology of alliances.* This is an important contribution. Alliances have multiple facets and the dynamics are not the same in all of them. The stability of the relationship, the capacity for leverage and the costs and risks of managing these relationships depend on the type of alliance. A vertical alliance (e.g. supplier relationships) is different from a cross-industry alliance (e.g. bio-tech sector). The purposes of alliances vary as well and influence the industry dynamics. The goals vary from sharing supply to creating virtual scale effects, to seeking complementary assets and skills.

Collaboration and competition coexist in these alliances. Value creation is different from value extraction. The outcomes for the firms in the alliance are not all uniform. The evolution of outcomes has a logic associated with it—how the alliance was formed and how the players prepared for extracting value.

Pierre Dussauge and Bernard Garrette have successfully consolidated in this book much of the wisdom on alliances and cooperative strategy. They have pushed our knowledge of alliances a big step by moving beyond the case studies and by building managerially relevant models.

As managers and firms search for ways to compete effectively and to create the future, they will have to learn new ways to leverage their resources. This book provides an invaluable source of ideas and practical guidance in their search.

Introduction

During 1993 Microsoft's market value became greater than that of IBM. Such an event would have been unthinkable just a few years before, given IBM's total dominance of the computer industry. Yet, at the end of the 1970s, when they chose a small company— Microsoft—to be their partner in developing the operating system for their PCs, Big Blue's senior executives little imagined that their decision was, in fact, paving the way for such a dramatic reversal of fortunes. Allied to IBM, Microsoft was able to create and impose the international standard for personal computing and, on this basis, to become the world's undisputed software leader. Its control of PC operating systems in fact turned out to be the company's main asset for dominating the market for applications software.

When Rover, the flagship company of the British motor industry, teamed up with Honda, it thought that this decision would offset the fact that it had fallen somewhat behind in upgrading its range of vehicles. About 10 years later, in 1992, the group's senior executives were proud to claim that the alliance had reached its objectives while remaining perfectly balanced. To prove their point, they emphasized the existence of cross-holdings between the two groups; as one top manager put it: "Honda now owns 20% of Rover's equity while we own 20% of Honda" . . . Honda-UK that was, however! A new development occurred in January 1994 with BMW taking over Rover, under Honda's very nose. Thus, this 15-year-long "trial marriage" ended in a merger with an outside competitor. Honda, which seemed durably in control of its alliance with Rover and was using its partner as its bridgehead into Europe, saw its entire European strategy called into question.

These two examples demonstrate how alliances, formed initially to solve an immediate problem, can have major strategic consequences in the long term. It is therefore not enough, when engaging in cooperative strategies, simply to review the explicit objectives, as they are stated at the outset, pursued through an alliance; managers must in fact try to anticipate all the possible, and sometimes unwanted, consequences of the partnerships they set up and make sure that these consequences are not detrimental to the long-term interests of the company.

Anticipating the outcomes of alliances is of vital importance, notably when they involve the transfer of technology and know-how between the partner companies. This concern led General Electric, which had teamed up with a French company, SNECMA, to produce the CFM-56 aircraft engine, to seal the most sophisticated parts of the engine in order to prevent its partner from gaining access to them. But it is not enough to try to limit one's partner's access to sensitive know-how; companies must also take best advantage of the alliance to extend their own competencies. The case of the NUMMI joint venture, set up by General Motors and Toyota to produce small cars in the USA, is highly significant in this respect. Toyota successfully managed the careers of the Japanese executives who had worked for NUMMI; these executives were later given the responsibility of setting up and managing Toyota's plants in the USA. Thus they were able to make full use of their experience with NUMMI, notably in managing American employees, negotiating with local unions and dealing with North American suppliers and subcontractors. In contrast, the General Motors executives who had worked for NUMMI were frequently assigned positions where they were unable to give the company the benefit of their understanding of Japanese management and production methods.

These problems in the management of alliances derive from the fundamentally ambivalent nature of this type of relationship. The allied companies are constantly obliged to trade off their own interests against those of the partnership. For instance, the partner firms in the Airbus consortium were surprised to find out that CASA, the Spanish partner in the venture, had agreed to act as a subcontractor in McDonnell-Douglas's MD-83 program, an aircraft that was to compete directly with their own Airbus A320. A few years later, the press revealed that another Airbus partner, the German company DASA, was negotiating with Boeing for a share in a project to develop and manufacture a 600- to 800-seat jumbo jet, while Airbus was working on a competing project.

If managers are still looking for methods and models to help them manage their alliances, public authorities are also unclear about what attitude to adopt when confronted with these new strategies. Thus, while the Regional Development Department of the European Commission was paying subsidies to Ford and Volkswagen to encourage them to set up a joint production plant in Portugal to manufacture minivans, the Competition Department of this same Commission was scrutinizing the potentially anti-competitive—and consequently illicit—aspects of this partnership.

More fundamentally, when a company enters into multiple alliances, its very contours become increasingly blurred. For example, the senior managers of Philips' household appliances business, associated in a joint venture with Whirlpool, found themselves faced with a thorny problem of loyalty: should they protect the interests of their former company (Philips) or work primarily for the benefit of the business, irrespective of its owner? The problem was all the more difficult to resolve as Philips had announced its ultimate intention of withdrawing from the venture in favor of Whirlpool. Similarly, executives of Matra-Hachette found it difficult to accept the fact that the Espace minivan—which their company had designed and manufactured, but which was sold under the Renault brand—was considered by the general public to be a Renault product.

When carried to their extreme, collaborative strategies can empty the partner firms of their industrial substance, by transferring most of their business to joint ventures. Thus Aerospatiale, a large European aerospace company, gradually divested most of its manufacturing activities in favor of multiple alliances forged in all its businesses: the Airbus and ATR consortia for aircraft; the Eurocopter and Euromissile joint ventures set up with DASA for helicopters and missiles respectively; Ariane for space launchers, etc. As a result, in the mid-1990s, about 80% of Aerospatiale's sales were derived from collaborative projects undertaken in partnership with other companies. In certain cases, the firms that had initially formed the partnership ultimately become mere shareholders and all but disappear in the shadow of their joint venture, which takes over all operational activities. Who still recalls that Shell or Unilever were both started as joint ventures set up by Dutch and British firms?

These examples—which could be extended almost indefinitely considering how widespread alliances have become in recent years—illustrate the variety and saliency of the problems raised by this new type of industrial organization. Thus, when they consider engaging their company in alliances, senior managers invariably have to face the following dilemmas:

- Is an alliance really preferable to independent growth?
- What firms will turn out to be suitable partners?
- How should the partnership be organized?
- Is a simple agreement sufficient or should a joint subsidiary be set up?
- Will all the partners benefit equally from the alliance? Might there not be winners and losers?
- How long will the alliance last? Should termination be planned from the very beginning?
- Is it possible to cooperate loyally while still preserving the vital interests of the company?
- How can the company effectively protect its technology and know-how?
- Do alliances hinder or eliminate competition? Are certain forms of collaboration illicit?

It is impossible to provide a single answer, valid for all alliances, to each of these questions. Not all alliances are the same. A simple collaborative agreement between an original equipment manufacturer (OEM) and its subcontractors, a joint venture with a local partner to expand into a developing country, and a partnership between major global competitors for the joint development and production of a new car or aircraft correspond to extremely different circumstances. Strategies must therefore be tailored to each main type of alliance. This book presents an analytical framework making it possible to provide answers to the questions listed above, taking into account the specific characteristics of each individual alliance.

The book is organized on the basis of this framework, presented in Figure I.1, which enables readers to find their way in the text and

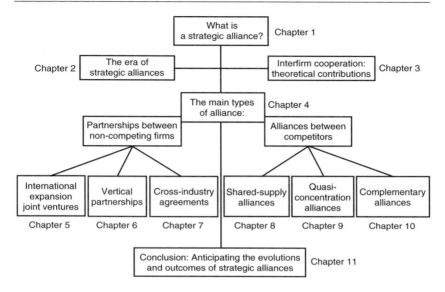

Figure I.1 Book outline

to choose the themes and chapters corresponding more particularly to their specific interests and to the particular alliances with which they may be confronted.

Chapter 1 is aimed at defining precisely what we understand by "alliance" and at describing its specific characteristics. This is made necessary by the fact that alliances are too often confused with more conventional interfirm strategies, such as mergers and acquisitions. Indeed, it is the very specific nature of alliances that makes them so difficult to manage. In Chapter 2, we analyze the reasons for the recent burgeoning of alliances in virtually all industries and regions of the world. This will enable us to identify the strategic motives which, over the past few years, have driven ever-increasing numbers of companies to engage in collaborative strategies. Readers interested in a more theoretical analysis of alliances should turn to Chapter 3 for a review of the approaches developed on this subject.

Chapter 4 deals with the heart of our problem. In distinguishing alliances between rival companies from partnerships between non-competing firms, it presents a typology of alliances that should enable readers to identify the specific form of cooperation with which they are confronted. They will then be in a position to turn directly to the chapter or chapters corresponding to the situations of greatest concern to them. Each of the following six chapters describes one of the main types of alliance, providing a detailed analysis and presenting guidelines for suitable action.

Chapters 5, 6 and 7 analyze partnerships between non-competing companies. Chapter 5 focuses on joint ventures designed for international expansion, frequently set up by multinational corporations that decide to team up with a local partner to start operations in a new market, mainly in developing countries. Chapter 6 is devoted to vertical partnerships between suppliers and customers, operating at different stages in the production process. Chapter 7 deals with cross-industry agreements. These relationships are formed to exploit technological or commercial synergies, or to help one of the partner firms diversify into the other's business.

Chapters 8, 9 and 10 are devoted to strategic alliances between competitors. Chapter 8 analyzes shared-supply alliances in which the partners develop and manufacture common components, which each then incorporates into its own specific products. Chapter 9 studies quasi-concentration alliances in which the allied companies develop and produce together a single common product. Chapter 10 deals with complementary alliances. These partnerships bring together rival companies into an alliance where one firm will market a product initially designed by the other.

Finally, an original study on the evolutions and outcomes of strategic alliances is presented in Chapter 11. It reveals that the various types of alliances described in this book follow different patterns of evolution and lead to quite dissimilar outcomes. Therefore, correctly identifying the type of alliance a firm is about to enter is critically important. Indeed, it makes it possible to anticipate, before the alliance is actually formed, what its evolution, its outcome and its consequences are likely to be.

We suggest that readers wanting a rapid and synthetic view of the subject start with Chapters 1, 4 and 11. On this basis, and depending on their particular interests, readers looking for a more detailed presentation of a particular type of alliance may then choose among the other chapters as outlined in the preceding paragraphs.

1

What is a Strategic Alliance?

The proliferation of strategic alliances is one of the most striking changes that has occurred in the business environment over the past 10 or 15 years. Hardly a day goes by without the media reporting the signing of some agreement between two or more firms.

Strategic alliances involve all kinds of companies and take extremely diverse forms; they are forged by very large, frequently multinational, corporations as well as by small companies. All, or virtually all, industries—both in manufacturing and services—as well as all regions of the world, have been affected by the rapid growth in interfirm collaboration. Collaborative agreements—frequently lumped together under the generic term "alliance"—cover a host of substantially different situations and forms. Some of these have been with us a great many years, while others have only emerged more recently; they range from outlawed collusion and cartels through marketing arrangements, joint ventures, licensing agreements, joint research . . . to major international programs such as Concorde or Airbus.

The extreme diversity of interfirm cooperation requires that we begin by defining as precisely as possible what we mean by alliances in order subsequently to identify their essential characteristics. This will form the subject of the first part of this chapter. We shall then review the different legal frameworks adopted for alliances, before studying how they are perceived and regulated by public authorities, focusing more particularly on differences between the USA and Europe.

ALLIANCES: A SPECIFIC FORM OF MULTI-COMPANY STRATEGY

Strategic alliances are fashionable. They are discussed in board-rooms around the world and mentioned constantly in the media. What the term actually means, however, is rarely defined precisely. For some, strategic alliances link companies and subcontractors together in what is described as "extended companies" or as "con-stellations of firms" (Lorenzoni and Ornani, 1988); others use the term to distinguish "friendly" mergers or acquisitions from "hostile" takeovers. The acquisition of minority cross-holdings is sometimes viewed as a sign of an alliance in the making. Certain analysts will still only consider alliances "strategic" if they lead to the creation of a legal entity, a joint venture—in other words, a shared subsidiary distinct from the parent companies (Harrigan, 1985). For yet others, strategic alliances are pacts with no clearly identified aim linking large conglomerates to one another; these "mega-deals", as they are sometimes called, are based primarily on the bond of friendship and mutual trust existing between senior executives from both companies. It would seem that clarification is called for.

A Definition of Strategic Alliances

The term "strategic alliance" cannot, in our opinion, be applied to any kind of interfirm links, but should be reserved for a special type of relationship which, in particular, makes these alliances so diffi-cult to manage. The key element in the notion of alliance—as understood in these pages—is that each firm involved in the part-nership remains independent, despite the agreement linking it to its partners. In other words, in alliances, the partner companies join forces in pursuit of common goals without losing their strategic autonomy and without abandoning their own specific interests (Child and Faulkner, 1998). Figure 1.1 presents a diagram of this particular type of relationship.

Conversely, merging or acquired companies relinquish their in-dependence and give birth to a new entity pursuing a single, co-herent set of goals. Though in practice the pre-merger companies may well continue to exist as legal entities, and may even maintain

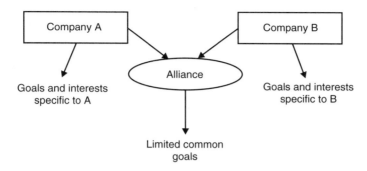

Figure 1.1 Representation of an alliance

separate identities and cultures, they have become part of a larger corporation; the merger or acquisition *per se* implies that the original entities are answerable to a single chain of command, that they are subject to a central decision-making center and that, as a result, they lose all autonomy in the choice of their objectives and definition of their strategies. Figure 1.2 offers a representation of mergers and acquisitions as opposed to alliances.

If we adopt the preservation or loss of strategic autonomy as a criterion to distinguish alliances from mergers and acquisitions, it is abundantly clear that the association between Daimler-Benz and Chrysler in 1998 was not an alliance but a merger, considering that both companies eventually intended to form a single corporation under a single chain of command. In contrast, the agreement between British Airways and American Airlines concerning the coordination of their routes, schedules and reservation systems was

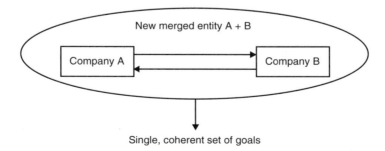

Figure 1.2 Representation of a merger

definitely an alliance, similar to many others set up in the air-travel industry between US and European airlines. In the case of British Airways and American Airlines, both companies remained independent and each pursued its own strategy, but benefited from the advantages conferred by the cooperation agreement that linked them to one another. In the automobile industry, where alliances as well as mergers have been legion over the past 20 years, the acquisition of Citroën and Chrysler-Europe by Peugeot, that of Seat and Skoda by Volkswagen, and that of Jaguar by Ford are mergers, while the agreements between Ford and Volkswagen, between General Motors and Toyota and between Chrysler and Mitsubishi are alliances. Citroën is now a brand name and division of the Peugeot SA corporation, just as Seat is a subsidiary of the Volkswagen Group and Jaguar is a subsidiary of the Ford Motor Company. In contrast, GM and Toyota on the one hand, Chrysler and Mitsubishi on the other, joined forces to produce small vehicles for the American market, yet they all remained independent car makers.

This criterion of the continuing autonomy of the partner companies confirms that the Airbus consortium is undeniably an alliance, since the companies that are members in the consortium— Aerospatiale for France, British Aerospace for the UK, DASA for Germany and CASA for Spain—are independent aircraft manufacturers pursuing their own agendas that even produce mutually competing aircraft: CASA's CN 235, British Aerospace's ATP and the ATR aircraft involving Aerospatiale are three regional transport airplanes competing in the market for 35- to 70-seat aircraft. All four companies decided to work together on Airbus; without, however, merging or even proceeding with the acquisition of cross-holdings in each other's equity.

Our definition of strategic alliances is designed to emphasize the specific nature of alliances while distinguishing them from other forms of interfirm relationships. Thus, in this book we take the view that:

> strategic alliances are links formed between two—or more—independent companies which choose to carry out a project or specific activity jointly by coordinating the necessary skills and resources rather than:
>
> - pursuing the project or activity on their own, taking on all the risks and confronting competition alone;
> - merging their operations or acquiring and divesting entire business units.

The Specific Features of Alliances: Multiple Decision-making Centers, Constant Bargaining and Clash of Interests

The main characteristics of interfirm cooperation stand as a direct corollary of the definition given above. By bringing together several companies which, despite the agreement between them, remain independent entities, alliances imply first of all that multiple decision-making centers will be involved in the choices to be made about the joint project or activity. This multiplication of decision-making centers makes alliances considerably more complex to manage than organizations with a single chain of command. To become effective, every decision requires the agreement of all the partner companies involved.

The example of Airbus is eloquent in this respect. Following the outstanding success of the A320, a 150-seat, short-to-medium-range aircraft, the consortium partners decided to develop a larger 200-seat version—the A321—which first flew in 1992. Some of the partners then wanted to follow up with a smaller 120/130-seat version of the same aircraft to offer customer airlines a broader range of airplanes to choose from. Despite the interest expressed by a great many airlines for this A319 project and promising sales prospects, it took several years to decide to launch production owing to the opposition of certain partners; this procrastination allowed the competition—notably Boeing with its 737-500 model—to enter this particular market niche earlier. A company acting alone would have been able to make the decision to launch the program much more rapidly.

In certain cases, the lack of agreement between the partners can even paralyze the alliance for considerable lengths of time or lead to ill-conceived compromises. Thus, in the case of Concorde, the Franco-British supersonic jet, the aircraft that was finally developed was a compromise between the initial French plans for a medium-haul jet and British plans for a very long-distance airliner carrying fewer passengers. While both these projects enjoyed a certain coherence, most experts deemed the final compromise ill suited to the market's needs, as did the airlines themselves. Indeed, the aircraft's range barely allowed it to cross the North Atlantic without refueling and prevented it from flying non-stop over longer distances where supersonic speed would really have been an advantage, while its seating capacity of about 100 passengers made it extremely difficult to cover costs over shorter distances (Hochmuth, 1974).

Because it entails the simultaneous authority of several partner firms, interfirm cooperation leads more often than not to a virtually unending round of negotiations. After a merger or acquisition—or more generally within the framework of a single enterprise—all divergence of opinion about choices to be made and strategies to be implemented can be arbitrated by the senior management, which is in a position to impose whatever decision it deems most appropriate. In an alliance, however, one of the parties cannot, in theory at least, force the others to accept any particular solution. And even if this were the case—if, for example, the management of the activity or joint project has been entrusted to one of the partners—it would be extremely ill-considered on the part of the dominant partner to impose too many of its own decisions against the wishes of the other allies. This would probably lead the dominated partners to withdraw from the agreement, resulting in the collapse of the alliance.

By the very nature of interfirm cooperation, negotiation is a key aspect in the management of alliances. In the case of Concorde mentioned above, most of the managers who took part in the project report that the slightest decision about the design of the aircraft or any of its components gave rise to endless haggling. The engineers from Sud-Aviation on the one hand and those from the British Aircraft Corporation on the other were thoroughly convinced—out of corporate loyalty or mere chauvinism—that their respective solutions for solving whatever technical issue was being discussed were the best by far. Choosing between the French and British options then became a major problem. Innumerable committees and commissions were set up to make decisions and protracted negotiations ultimately took up a substantial proportion of the time devoted to developing the aircraft.

The second main characteristic of interfirm cooperation is related to the potentially conflictual nature of the interests and objectives embodied within it. The partner companies, which remain independent entities, continue to pursue their own agendas of interests and objectives. They have managed to agree on a set of more or less explicit targets which the alliance was set up to attain, but these common goals are not the only objectives pursued by the partners and at times they may clash with the more fundamental objectives of one or more of the allies (Khanna, Gulati and Nohria, 1998). The Airbus A319 project mentioned above provides a good case in point. If British Aerospace and DASA were particularly reluctant about building an aircraft of this kind, it was not because they had no faith in its chances of commercial success but because it came into direct competition with aircraft of their own. The A319 threatened to lure customer airlines away from the BAe 146, a four-engine jet seating 80 to 100 passengers manufactured by British Aerospace. Similarly, the presence of the A319 on the market would have made the launch of the Fokker 130—a projected 130-seat airliner derived from the Fokker 100 which the Dutch manufacturer had been selling since 1988—a much more hazardous enterprise. When one recalls that DASA acquired Fokker in 1992, it is easier to understand its reservations about plans for the smaller Airbus. DASA, like British Aerospace, had a direct stake in Airbus's success and could only hope for the success of the European consortium—provided, however, that this success did not run counter to other interests it considered of even greater importance.

In general, clashes of interest such as these between the partnership and the allies will occur whenever the alliance does business with its different partner companies. If, for example, each of the allies sells its services to the consortium, each will be tempted to bill these services at the highest possible price. The performance of the consortium will suffer but, by adopting this behavior, what an ally loses as a shareholder in the consortium is more than offset by what it gains as a supplier. If all the partner firms start to play the same little game, the alliance turns into a financial disaster—even if the losses incurred are largely recouped by the partners through overbilling—and, even more significantly, it rapidly becomes unmanageable. It was in order to preclude this kind of abuse that General Electric and SNECMA, which joined forces to manufacture the highly successful CFM-56 aircraft engine, devised a special system for allocating work and sales that prevented either of the allies from seeking to promote its own interests at the expense of their common objectives (see Box 9.1 in Chapter 9).

Are Alliances an Unstable Type of Organization and a Hazardous Strategy?

The specific characteristics of strategic alliances (multiple decision-making centers, constant bargaining, clashes of interest) inevitably make cooperation an unstable form of industrial organization (Arino and de la Torre, 1998). This observation is confirmed by several statistical studies of alliances. In one such study, which examined the fate of 880 alliances, K.R. Harrigan found that only 40% survived four years in existence and that fewer than 15% lasted longer than a decade (Harrigan, 1988). Other research has shown that more than two thirds of all alliances encounter serious problems during their first two years in existence (Bleeke and Ernst, 1993). And other studies highlight the fact that more than 50% of all joint ventures with shared management disappear or are completely reorganized within less than five years of their creation (Killing, 1983). These high mortality rates seem to confirm the mostly cautious, if not openly hostile, opinions expressed by managers themselves about the alliances in which they have been involved. It should, however, be pointed out that the end of an alliance does not imply the demise of the business in question. On the contrary, in three-quarters of cases the termination of a joint venture leads to its takeover by one of the parent companies (Bleeke and Ernst, 1993).

The fact that alliances usually have a short lifespan and frequently end up with the activity in question being taken over by one of the allies has led certain analysts to use the metaphor of the Trojan horse to describe the relationship between partners within an alliance (Mankin and Reich, 1986; Hamel, Doz and Prahalad, 1989; Hennart, Roehl and Zietlow, 1999). In their opinion, alliances are temporary arrangements in which one of the partners manages to strengthen its position at the other's expense. Without denying the fact that certain alliances do, indeed, lead to highly unbalanced outcomes such as these, we consider it excessive to apply the Trojan horse metaphor systematically to all interfirm cooperation of this kind. Evidence shows that not all alliances evolve in the same way and not all of them lead to the same outcome. The point of view defended in this book is that an alliance lasts for a longer or shorter period of time, produces more or less balanced or un-balanced benefits for the partner companies and leads to one outcome rather than another depending on the type of cooperation to which it corresponds.

The instability of alliances, stressed by a great many experts, is not a drawback in itself. One of the specific features of alliances is that, unlike permanent industry consolidations carried out through mergers or acquisitions, they allow for a certain degree of reversibility in strategic choices. It follows that some instability is a logical consequence of this reversibility. When an alliance is formed, the partner firms may in fact be seeking some degree of reversibility. When entering or withdrawing from a given business, for example, a firm can use collaboration as an initial step towards full entry or exit, while still maintaining the option of deferring complete acquisition or divestment, if both partners so decide.

At the end of the 1980s, Eridania-Beghin teamed up with three partners: Johnson & Johnson, James River and Feldmuehle. Its intention, from the very outset, was to withdraw gradually from the paper industry in order to refocus its operations on the agro-food business. Eridania-Beghin set up three subsidiaries, specializing respectively in cardboard for packaging, magazine paper and personal care products; each partner then acquired 50% of the equity in one of the newly set-up subsidiaries. The injection of funds from the partners into the three paper subsidiaries provided them with the resources they needed to develop their activities, while enabling Eridania-Beghin to devote the greater part of its own funds to the expansion of its agro-food businesses and, in particular, to the acquisition of Cerestar, Central Soya, Italiana Olii e Risi and Lesieur, among others. After a few years, Eridania-Beghin withdrew entirely from the three joint ventures. The cooperation phase enabled the purchasing partners to acquire commercial know-how specific to the European market and to gain a clearer idea of the value of the businesses they were acquiring. For Eridania-Beghin, the arrangement enabled it to participate in developing its paper businesses at a lower cost and, at the winding up of the alliance, to sell its stakes at a higher price. The transfer of skills organized by Eridania-Beghin was paid for through the greater value of the assets ultimately divested. What is more, both parties involved could renegotiate the date at which the deal was to be concluded, making it possible to postpone Eridania's complete withdrawal or even to reverse the initial decision. Compared with the complete and immediate sale of Eridania's "paper" businesses, these alliances afforded advantages linked to their unspecified length and their reversibility. In a very similar fashion, Philips and Whirlpool formed a joint venture which resulted, after several years of existence, in the complete acquisition of Philips's appliance business by Whirlpool. The transition phase allowed for the Michigan-based company to acquire knowledge about the European market, progressively to substitute the Philips brand with Whirlpool and to gain a clearer appreciation of the real value of the assets it eventually acquired.

Therefore termination of an alliance through acquisition of the joint venture by one of the allies, which could be interpreted as strongly favoring the acquiring partner, may well have been planned from the beginning by both companies. For one partner, therefore, the alliance provides a means to gain access to or to strengthen its position in a given market; and, for the other, a way to withdraw gradually from that same business.

THE LEGAL CONTEXT OF INTERFIRM COOPERATION

The complex and ambiguous nature of alliances is reflected in the diversity of the legal forms they can be given, as well as in the significantly different regulations adopted in the USA, Europe and Japan to control their creation and to limit their anti-competitive impact.

The Legal Forms Given to Alliances

Interfirm cooperation and alliances, as examined in this book, differ from incorporated companies in that they do not enjoy any clear legal definition. As we have seen in the first part of this chapter, what defines an alliance is not any particular legal status but the nature of the relationship formed between the allied companies. Thus, if it is easy on legal grounds to distinguish between, for example, a public limited company and a private limited company or a limited partnership, nothing makes it possible to identify an alliance from the same strictly legal point of view. Alliances will then by necessity make use of the traditional legal forms available in contract and company law to be given a legal status.

It should be emphasized first of all that an alliance is necessarily based on an agreement between the partner firms; cooperation is thus founded on a contract between these partner firms, whether this contract is explicit or tacit, written or not. From the legal point of view, therefore, every alliance is a contract. Indeed, a great many alliances are organized exclusively on the basis of a contract, or of a series of contracts, between the partner companies without leading to the creation of any specific legal entity.

In certain cases, however, the allies may consider it desirable to endow the alliance with a legal status distinct from that of the partner companies. They will then set up a legal entity, an equity joint venture. From the legal standpoint, such a joint venture must be given the status of a corporation in harmony with the law of the country in which it is registered.

In 1967, France created a legal construct well suited to interfirm cooperation: the *Groupement d'Intérêt Economique* (GIE, or Economic Interest Grouping), providing for the creation of a legal structure with no equity. A GIE is empowered to sign contracts but the partner companies remain jointly liable for the commitments made. The GIE is also transparent for tax purposes; the profits or losses generated by its activities only become taxable when they are consolidated in the accounts of the partner companies. The legal status enjoyed by the French GIE was considered to offer sufficient advantages to justify the creation, in 1985, of a similar legal status at the European level, the European Economic Interest Grouping (EEIG).

One of the problems to arise as soon as a legal structure is set up within the context of interfirm cooperation is the question of how to allocate ownership and power within the new entity. Some experts recommend evenly balanced joint ventures with all the partner companies owning equal shares (Kogut, 1988), while others see in this equality a source of potential conflict, paralysis and inefficiency (Harrigan, 1988). This issue will be examined at greater length in Chapter 5, devoted to international expansion joint ventures.

Lastly, it should be stressed that when an alliance does indeed lead to the creation of a separate legal entity, this structure does not necessarily cover the entire scope of the cooperation between the firms involved. It is not uncommon, for instance, in alliances formed between several companies to design, develop and manufacture a product together that a specific structure is set up to take care of all marketing activities (sales and after-sales in particular). In the examples we have already mentioned, this is true in particular of Airbus and CFM. In the case of Airbus, the entity responsible for all commercial contacts with the customer airlines was, until the late 1990s, a GIE incorporated under French law, Airbus Industrie; for CFM, two companies have been set up—one under French law and the other under American law—to market the jointly produced jet engine from General Electric and SNECMA.

The fact that the scope of the legal entities set up is restricted to sales in both these examples (as in a great many others) obviously does not mean that cooperation focuses exclusively on this aspect. It was simply felt unnecessary to set up a joint venture for the other activities of these alliances, a contractual agreement being deemed sufficient. This clearly confirms the point emphasized above that alliances should not be confused with their legal structure. Joint ventures frequently do not embrace the entire scope of the cooperation and, in practice, merely cover a part of the alliance. This is why studies devoted to joint ventures alone fail to take into account all the different facets of cooperation. These studies overlook all alliances that have not led to the creation of a joint structure and, in those cases of cooperation that they do examine, ignore all aspects of the collaboration between the partners falling outside the scope of the joint venture.

If there exists no legal form specific to alliances, and no legal definition of interfirm cooperation, the legislation regulating the activities of these alliances can hardly avoid being rather vague itself.

Regulations Governing Alliances and Cooperation

If public authorities are concerned about controlling the creation and activity of alliances, it is because they fear that these alliances will inhibit competition. Yet, because there exists no easily applicable definition of alliances, interfirm cooperation tends to be regulated in most countries via more general legislation concerning competition, restrictive practices, concentration and monopolies. On this basis, alliances between competitors that are primarily aimed at coordinating pricing policies, for example, or vertical relationships resulting in discriminatory practices are almost always considered illegal.

In practice, those alliances most suspect in the eyes of anti-trust agencies are alliances between rival firms. In most countries, agreements aimed at setting prices, limiting production or carving up a market are forbidden. When scrutinizing agreements between companies that actually intend to do business together, the authorities will usually refer to regulations governing industry concentration. However, the fact that there exist no convincing theories about the effects produced by intercompetitor alliances leads to a certain ambiguity, both in the regulations adopted and in the practices of the agencies responsible for enforcing these regulations. In certain cases, alliances between competitors are treated more leniently than mergers and acquisitions; in other cases— particularly in the USA—they are treated more harshly.

Two contradictory approaches may be observed within the European Union: on the one hand, steps are taken to control alliances and prevent them from hampering competition; on the other hand, European authorities encourage pan-European cooperation between companies and expect it to enhance the competitiveness of European firms *vis-à-vis* their foreign rivals. Except when they are R&D agreements, alliances are governed by the provisions of the Treaty of Rome concerning the rules of competition (articles 85 and 86, in particular) and by the regulations on concentrations (no. 4064/89) adopted in 1989. The latter explicitly consider alliances operating on a permanent basis and having all the functions of an independent entity as outright concentration (Sachwald, 1994). Although their aim is to maintain and enhance competition, these regulations nevertheless explicitly allow that a cooperation agreement restricting competition may be authorized if, at the same time, it produces a positive economic impact—notably, if it improves production, if it favors technological progress and if consumers ultimately share a substantial part of the related benefits.

In practice, the department responsible for the European Commission's competition policy seems to have adopted a relatively flexible attitude towards alliances. For example, it ruled against

Matra when the latter took legal action against the alliance set up by Ford and Volkswagen for the joint production of a minivan that directly competed with the French company's Espace. The whole debate was somewhat ironic, however, considering that the Espace was itself produced by Matra and Renault in collaboration and that Ford and Volkswagen had received a large subsidy from the European Commission to build the factory that manufactured their joint vehicle in Portugal. In contrast, the acquisition of the Canadian aircraft manufacturer De Havilland by the ATR consortium, formed by Aerospatiale and Alenia, was rejected on the grounds that this acquisition would have given the new group a 50% share of the world market, and 65% of the European market, for commuter aircraft. The Commission, however, was not against the alliance between Aerospatiale and Alenia as such, but against the acquisition of a third firm by the allied companies even though the company in question was not European and the greater part of its business was generated in North America. It is also interesting to note that, in this case, the European authorities considered the ATR alliance as a fully fledged company to which the regulations governing concentrations could be applied, even though the only legal entity set up in the context of this alliance was a GIE with responsibilities limited to sales and after-sales.

Collaboration in R&D, however, is exempt from the regulations limiting interfirm agreements. This freedom to enter into R&D agreements with competitors without having to obtain prior approval goes as far as joint exploitation of the results of research conducted together. This exemption from the general rules that is granted to research activities is justified by the desire to promote innovation and technological development in Europe, and it was felt that innovation and technology would benefit more from greater interfirm collaboration than from stiffer competition. The special treatment reserved for R&D alliances may even include the provision of financial support. The European Union has, over the years, set up a whole series of programs, such as ESPRIT, JESSI, START and EUREKA, that are aimed at stimulating joint R&D in Europe and heavily subsidize R&D projects submitted by consortia of firms originating from several different European countries.

In the USA, the legislation governing alliances between competitors is much more restrictive than in Europe. Not only are concentrations more tightly regulated in the USA than in Europe, but also the attitude of the Justice Department—the body responsible for enforcing anti-trust laws—is, *ceteris paribus*, less favorable to alliances than to mergers and acquisitions. Thus, the Justice Department seems to approve mergers and acquisitions between competitors, which it feels it can accurately evaluate (with such tools as the Herfindahl–Hirschmann index that measures concentration in a given industry on the basis of the distribution of market shares), more readily than alliances, which it has a harder time assessing (Jorde and Teece, 1992). It is significant, for example, that the Justice Department only examines cases of mergers and acquisitions when the aggregate market share of the companies concerned exceeds 20%. Under this threshold, mergers may be carried out without having to obtain prior approval. Alliances between competitors, on the other hand, must be approved by the Justice Department irrespective of the market share of the partners. Even regarding collaboration in R&D, the freedom granted to companies in the USA is considerably smaller than in Europe. It was not until 1984 that a law (the National Cooperative Research Act) authorized competing firms to conduct research together (Link and Bauer, 1989). The NCRA is extremely restrictive, however, since it only authorizes R&D agreements that remain pre-competitive, i.e., that do not extend to the joint exploitation of research findings. Thus, the NCRA explicitly forbids all joint production and marketing activities based on the research jointly carried out and even specifies that the agreements must in no way alter competition in downstream activities.

In Japan, the attitude of public authorities regarding interfirm cooperation seems very close to that prevailing in Europe. There exists no legislation specific to alliances; these are governed by the traditional anti-trust laws—notably, by the Anti-monopoly Act dating back to 1947. The agency responsible for enforcing these laws, the Fair Trade Commission, has adopted an extremely tolerant position regarding collaborative agreements. Alliances between competitors enjoy a treatment at least as favorable as actual industry concentration and are approved by the FTC in a virtually automatic way if the combined market share of the various companies involved is no greater than 25%. R&D agreements, deemed to promote general economic and technological progress, are almost always approved even when they provide for the joint commercial exploitation of research findings and involve companies with substantial market share. Indeed, agreements of this kind are frequently encouraged and coordinated by the Ministry of International Trade and Industry (MITI) itself, which sees them as a means of strengthening the competitiveness of Japanese industry in certain areas.

All in all, the contrasted policies of the anti-trust agencies in Europe, the USA and Japan, as well as the absence of legislation specific to alliances, confirm the lack of consensus on a precise definition of this form of economic organization as well as on its impact on competition. In order to clarify this second point, we shall examine in Chapter 3 the main theoretical contributions to the understanding of interfirm cooperation. Before this, however, we shall attempt in Chapter 2 to assess how widely alliances have spread throughout the global economy and in what industries and regions of the world they are most prevalent. We will also try to understand why we have been witnessing such a proliferation of alliances since the beginning of the 1980s.

2
The Era of Strategic Alliances

Considered unusual—indeed suspicious—just a few years ago, alliances are now a fact of life in most industries. They have become an essential component in the strategies implemented by most global companies. It would be a mistake, however, to assume that collaboration between firms is a radically new development in business practices; historians could confirm that firms have worked together ever since companies first came into being. But the dominant forms of cooperation have changed over the years and alliances, as we know them today, have become increasingly visible and complex.

Without going back to the dawn of economic history, it can be noted that international cross-licensing agreements were a widespread form of cooperation as early as the 1930s, notably in the electrical equipment and chemical industries (OECD, 1986). In the wake of the Second World War, the process that led many large corporations to expand internationally gave rise to a large number of agreements. To start operations in foreign countries, multinational enterprises set up a large number of joint ventures, subsidiaries whose ownership was shared with local partners (Franko, 1971; Stopford and Wells, 1972). It was the 1980s, however, that witnessed the development of real strategic alliances. Unlike earlier forms of cooperation, these strategic alliances bring together global companies that cooperate in certain areas while they continue to compete in other parts of their business; they involve leading-edge technologies and advanced capabilities, and are formed to fulfill strategic objectives rather than merely to comply with restrictive local legislations (Porter and Fuller, 1986; Morris and Hergert,

1987). Thus, in recent years, limited and peripheral agreements have given way to partnerships that are an integral part of the long-term strategies of the allied companies.

FROM TRADITIONAL JOINT VENTURES TO STRATEGIC ALLIANCES

The first studies to focus on interfirm agreements were conducted in the 1960s by academics interested in the development of joint ventures. These studies examined interfirm cooperation from two clearly distinct standpoints, giving rise to two different streams of research (Porter and Fuller, 1986).

The first stream of research studied the process whereby large corporations became multinational, focusing on international expansion joint ventures (see Chapter 5). These ventures were jointly owned subsidiaries set up in association with local partners, the objective of which was the penetration of new geographic markets. The joint ventures' activities were usually restricted to marketing and, in some cases, to manufacturing a selection of the multinational's existing product line in the host country.

The second stream of research was driven by anti-trust concerns and focused on joint ventures set up by domestic firms taking concerted action in their home market. Most of this work has examined joint ventures set up by two or more US firms and has attempted to assess their impact on competition.

By the middle of the 1980s, the two above-mentioned streams of research began converging on the topic of "strategic alliances". Indeed, the multinationalization process in many large corporations was relying more and more on alliances with other global competitors rather than on joint ventures with minor local partners; at the same time, these global alliances between major competitors raised the same anti-trust concerns as domestic collaborations. This extended view of alliances completely renewed the approach to interfirm cooperation. Instead of limiting its focus to equity joint ventures, it examined all the different forms of collaboration between firms, regardless of their legal status, and centered on their strategic implications for the involved firms, as well as on the specific management issues they raise.

Joint Ventures and Multinationals

One of the most extensive studies on joint ventures and multinationalization was carried out in the context of the Harvard Multinational Enterprise and the Nation State Project; it led to the compilation of statistics on 187 American multinationals and their subsidiaries worldwide (Curhand, Davidson and Suri, 1977). The main conclusion to be drawn from this mass of data, which covered a period of several decades extending into the 1970s, was that the propensity of multinational enterprises to set up joint ventures increased considerably over the years (Stopford and Wells, 1972). The proportion of joint ventures in the total number of foreign subsidiaries created by the 187 firms in the sample rose progressively from around 20% at the beginning of the century to 45% by the 1960s. More recent studies have shown that this trend continued well into the 1980s, with the absolute number of joint ventures and their share in the total number of subsidiaries created abroad both increasing. However, these studies seem to indicate that the propensity to create joint ventures is somewhat cyclical, some periods appearing to be more favorable to the formation of these shared-ownership subsidiaries than others (Hladik, 1985).

A more in-depth analysis of the data gathered during the Harvard Multinational Enterprise and the Nation State Project revealed a fundamental change in the scope and activity of joint ventures starting in the mid-1970s. The activities of many joint ventures were no longer restricted to the local marketing of products already developed and manufactured by the multinational parent company; the scope of their activities was expanded to include the development of new products and they also began exporting to other countries. More precise studies on this subject showed that 20% of all joint ventures carried out R&D activities in 1982, as compared to a mere 8% in 1974 (Hladik, 1985). What is more, approximately 50% of the joint ventures set up after 1980 exported products outside their host country, while this proportion was only 25% for the joint ventures created between 1974 and 1979 and was insignificant before that. Thus, joint ventures of a new type, similar in many ways to the strategic alliances formed more recently, began to appear among conventional joint ventures.

Overall, the statistics clearly show that international joint ventures gradually moved away from the traditional model—according to which they were mere channels for exports—and evolved towards greater strategic autonomy, to the point even of competing with the activities of their parent companies. Thus, the origin of current strategic alliances can be traced back to the evolution of international joint ventures set up by multinationals to penetrate new markets. This does not mean, however, that traditional international expansion joint ventures are doomed to extinction. On the contrary, multinational corporations continue to create new ones, particularly in developing and Eastern European countries where local legislation often requires that a certain percentage of the equity of foreign subsidiaries remains in the hands of local shareholders.

Joint Ventures and Competition

While the initial goal of studies on international joint ventures was to understand the different ways in which companies could expand internationally, the aim of research on domestic joint ventures was primarily to evaluate their potentially anti-competitive impact. Most of the studies carried out in the USA in the 1960s and 1970s tended to show that agreements associating domestic firms usually had a clearly collusive purpose and negatively affected the intensity of competition (Pfeffer and Nowak, 1976b). It also emerges that, in a majority of cases, these joint ventures were set up by rival firms—a fact that seems to support a collusive interpretation. Analyses of a radically different nature, however, began to appear towards the end of the 1970s. A number of analysts began pleading in favor of alliances, arguing that they could in fact be formed in order to pursue perfectly legitimate objectives and could actually foster economic progress (Berg and Friedman, 1981; Berg, Duncan and Friedman, 1982). A great many joint ventures, it was argued, appeared in fact to be set up to pool and acquire expertise, making it possible to better innovate and, ultimately, to better satisfy customer needs. Therefore, by forming alliances companies were not necessarily trying to set higher prices, increase short-term profits or reduce risk; they might instead be looking for a more efficient alternative to in-house R&D.

This discussion on the competitive impact of joint ventures and alliances is important both for government decision makers and for managers, because it creates a distinction between value-creating partnerships and anti-competitive agreements. Collusion obviously has a negative impact on customers—who are its immediate victims—but it also has a sterilizing effect on the companies involved which, protected by the illicit agreement, tend to become less competitive, particularly *vis-à-vis* their foreign rivals. Alliances, on the other hand, allow the partner firms to make the very most of their complementarities, and make it possible to enhance the value offered to customers and to increase the competitive edge of the allied companies (Doz and Hamel, 1998). Engaging in such strategic alliances and leveraging the complementary capabilities of partner firms makes it possible to concentrate most of a company's resources on its core capabilities, thus reinforcing its position in relation to both its partners and its direct competitors (Yoshino and Rangan, 1995).

What Makes Alliances "Strategic"?

Since the mid-1980s, confining the interpretation of interfirm cooperation to alternative modes of international expansion on the one hand, or to potential collusion on the other, has become inadequate. It would not make sense to analyze the European Airbus consortium, the General Motors/Toyota alliance or the IBM/Toshiba agreements as either mere collusions or as export-boosting arrangements; this would fail to capture the full extent of what these partnerships are trying to achieve.

In traditional international expansion joint ventures, one of the parent companies—the local partner—plays a rather passive role. In strategic alliances, on the other hand, the partners' contributions to the venture tend to be reciprocal and the relationship is more balanced, which creates management problems of a completely different nature.

In collusive agreements, the alliance is defensive and intended to ward off some of the threats created by competition. In contrast, true strategic alliances are aimed at creating and enhancing the competitive positions of the firms involved, in a highly competitive environment.

An alliance can therefore be described as "strategic" when it contributes significantly to the strategies pursued by the partner companies, and when it involves pooling and combining the partners' capabilities. It should also be emphasized that, unlike traditional joint ventures that are always separate legal entities, strategic alliances are not characterized by any particular legal status. It is more the nature and scope of the projects, and the expertise brought in by the different partners, which make alliances "strategic".

Most analysts seem to agree that real strategic alliances, as we have just described them, started to proliferate in the early 1980s. Research using earlier data fails to reveal any clear trend (Ghemawat, Porter and Rawlinson, 1986), while more recent studies show a rapid and steady growth in the number of alliances formed after 1982 (Morris and Hergert, 1987). The rapid increase in the number of collaborative agreements at the beginning of the 1980s can be summed up by a single statistic: from the late 1970s to the early 1990s, the number of major alliances formed each year by American, European and Japanese companies was multiplied by a factor of 30 (Collins and Doorley, 1991).

A PANORAMA OF INTERFIRM COOPERATION

There are many misconceptions about strategic alliances. It is often said that Japanese companies excel at forging alliances and at taking best advantage of the partnerships in which they participate. One also often reads that cooperation is particularly well suited to high-technology sectors because it makes it possible to combine leading-edge capabilities and create radical innovations. It is often argued that alliances are second-best strategic options, suitable only for smaller or weaker competitors playing a catch-up game. . .

These perceptions are not all necessarily wrong, but they may well give a distorted view of reality by highlighting a few isolated cases. The results of several statistical studies devoted to interfirm collaboration show that alliances are not formed primarily where one would expect them to be and that the "champions" of cooperation are not always the firms that one would predict.

Table 2.1 Geographic origin of companies involved in alliances

	Harvard database (Ghemawat et al.)	INSEAD database (Morris and Hergert)
USA	38%	30%
Japan	14%	12%
Western Europe	23%	47%
Other developed countries	6%	
Developing countries and Eastern Europe	19%	11%
Total	100%	100%

Source: Morris and Hergert (1987); Ghemawat et al. (1986)

The Geography of Alliances

As shown in Tables 2.1 and 2.2, most alliances are formed between companies within the so-called Triad (North America, Europe and Japan ((Beamish and Killing, 1997a, 1997b, 1997c)). It should nevertheless be pointed out that firms coming from newly industrialized nations (South Korea in particular) or from Eastern Europe are making rapid progress in the worldwide networks of alliances by building agreements with Western partners.

The first conclusion to be drawn from an analysis of the available information is that European companies play a predominant role in alliance networks (Urban and Vendemini, 1992). Despite some discrepancies between the various sources, it appears that a majority of agreements include at least one European company. It also appears that European firms tend to forge alliances more often with other European companies or with American partners. If Europe is analyzed country by country, we also note that the most active European companies are of British and French origin. The role of Japanese companies, frequently emphasized in more qualitative work on cooperation, seems on the other hand to be more limited than expected. In particular, the figures seem to reject the idea that Japanese firms make massive use of alliances to "colonize" Western economies (Mankin and Reich, 1986; Hennart, Roehl and Zietlow, 1999). In addition, the under-representation of intra-Japanese alliances in the data is somewhat intriguing, given that research on Japanese companies unanimously emphasizes their propensity to cooperate (Gerlach, 1987). As for the over-

Table 2.2 Breakdown of alliances by nationality of partner firms

Intra-Europe alliances	31%
USA–Europe alliances	26%
Europe–Japan alliances	10%
USA–Japan alliances	8%
Intra-USA alliances	8%
Europe–rest of the world	7%
USA–rest of the world	4%
Other combinations	6%

Source: Morris and Hergert (1987)

representation of intra-Europe alliances, three convergent explanations can be put forward:

- It should be pointed out first of all that a vast majority of intra-European agreements are international. The fact that Europe is a fragmented market obviously accounts for the large number of alliances formed by European firms from different countries. The growing internationalization of the economy—a general phenomenon—has obviously had an impact on alliance formation in Europe, whereas it has not led US companies—which all operate in the same unified market—to partner with one another.
- In addition, many leading European firms are often dominant players in their home country but are in fact only medium-sized competitors in the global arena. British Airways, for example, is by far the largest European airline but is only about half the size of American Airlines or United Airlines. In semiconductors, the leading European manufacturers (Siemens, Philips or ST Micro-electronics) are dwarfs when compared to Intel, Motorola, Samsung or Hitachi. In automobiles, Volkswagen, the European leader, produces only 3.5 million vehicles annually, while General Motors produces 7 million, Ford 6 million and Toyota 5 million. Forming alliances within Europe is a way to overcome this handicap.
- A further explanation, linked to the different political and legal contexts mentioned in Chapter 1, could also be offered. Although European law governing competition largely draws its inspiration from American anti-trust legislation, it is interpreted in a way that makes it more tolerant of alliances than its American counterpart.

Table 2.3 Alliances per industry (American study)

Sectors	Industries	% of total	% per sector
Primary	Agribusiness	4%	9%
	Metals and minerals	8%	18%
	Energy	13%	29%
	Construction	3%	7%
	Textiles, clothing and leather	2%	4%
	Paper and wood products	2%	4%
	Chemicals	13%	29%
	Total primary sector	45%	100%
Secondary	Computers and semiconductors	6%	15%
	Other electronics	4%	10%
	Other electrical	2%	5%
	Automobiles	5%	13%
	Aerospace	2%	5%
	Other machinery	12%	31%
	Other manufacturing	8%	21%
	Total secondary sector	39%	100%
Tertiary	Transportation	2%	12.5%
	Communication, publishing, leisure	2%	12.5%
	Distribution	3%	19%
	Finance	4%	25%
	Other services	5%	31%
	Total tertiary sector	16%	100%

Source: Ghemawat, Porter and Rawlinson (1986) p. 353. Reprinted by permission of *Harvard Business Review*. Copyright © 1986 by the President and Fellows of Harvard College, all rights reserved.

The Industrial Context of Alliances

As shown in Tables 2.3 and 2.4, interfirm cooperation is not specific to so-called high-technology industries, even though such industries have indeed witnessed the formation of a relatively large number of alliances.

The automobile industry appears to be very alliance intensive (Nohria and Garcia-Pont, 1991). It has seen the formation of numerous horizontal alliances between car manufacturers (GM/Toyota, Ford/Mazda, Renault/Volvo, etc.) as well as the creation of a multitude of vertical partnerships between car makers and parts manufacturers. From 1970 to 1988, the number of alliances formed annually between car makers alone increased by a factor of five (Sachwald, 1992).

Table 2.4   Breakdown of alliances in manufacturing industries (European study)

Industry	% out of 839 cases
Automobiles	24%
Computers	14%
Telecommunications	17%
Aerospace	19%
Other electronic/electrical equipment	13%
Others	13%

Source: Morris and Hergert (1987)

The large number of alliances in aerospace also deserves special emphasis. These cooperations are frequently under-estimated in American studies because they chiefly associate European firms. In addition to their relatively large number, it should be stressed that most of the alliances in this industry are very large projects (such as Airbus, Tornado, etc.) requiring massive investments, and that these joint projects account for a significant portion of total activity in this industry. The impact of just one of these alliances in aerospace can outweigh all the alliances forged in most other industries. It also seems that, unlike in most other industries, cooperation has been a widespread practice in aerospace for almost 40 years, the first major joint developments dating as far back as the late 1950s (Dussauge and Garrette, 1995).

In the area of information technology and telecommunications, studies reveal that the number of collaborations rose by a factor of five between 1980 and 1990 (Cainarca, Colombo and Mariotti, 1992). This rapid growth was largely due to the decision made simultaneously by several large firms in this industry, hitherto pursuing extremely independent strategies, to create networks of alliances. Thus IBM, AT&T, Olivetti and Toshiba each forged more than 100 agreements during the 1980–90 decade (Garrette and Quélin, 1994).

In contrast, the study of primary-sector industries—such as mining and petroleum, metals and chemicals—suggests that inter-firm agreements are a much older form of relationship in these businesses and that they have not grown particularly in more recent years (Stuckey, 1983).

WHY ENTER INTO ALLIANCES?

The recent and rapid growth in the number of strategic alliances can be explained by various changes in the international business environment; in particular, the globalization of trade and the acceleration of technological progress seem to be major driving forces that have led firms to enter into significant numbers of cooperative agreements.

Globalization

The globalization process that most industries have been undergoing is forcing many companies to expand internationally as rapidly and extensively as possible. Alliances are one of the means through which this can be done. Globalization in the telecommunications services industry, for example, has led to the formation of numerous alliances; Deutsche Telekom, France Télécom and Sprint, in particular, created Global One to better address the needs of their international corporate customers. As the case described in Box 2.1 makes clear, alliances are not a panacea, however; while they do help the partner firms globalize, they also create specific management problems.

Box 2.1 Global One

The need to provide services to customers on a worldwide basis has led all major telecommunications companies to form strategic alliances. In Europe, the first such move was made in 1987 by Deutsche Telekom, the third largest worldwide operator, and France Télécom, the fourth largest, when they created their Atlas joint venture. In the following few years several other major alliances were formed in the same industry: British Telecom bought 20% of MCI, AT&T joined with several companies in a worldwide alliance called World Partners, Unisource was created in Europe as a joint venture between the Swedish, Swiss, Spanish and Dutch telephone companies, etc.

In order to better compete with these global networks, Deutsche Telekom and France Télécom announced, in June 1995, the creation of Global One, a 50–50 joint venture between Atlas and Sprint, the third largest US operator and the twelfth largest worldwide. The combined revenue of the three firms was over $73 billion, more than twice the size of the BT–MCI alliance. The new venture was set up to "offer worldwide telecommunication solutions for companies." In February 1996, Deutsche Telekom and France Télécom bought 10% each of Sprint's equity for a total of $3.5 billion.

Based in Brussels, Global One started its operations with 3000 employees, 1200 switching centers around the globe, and an expected $800 million in annual revenues. Global One offered integrated worldwide telecommunication services to multinational companies. In its very first month of existence, and even before it had received final European Union approval, Global One had already signed contracts with such global customers as LVMH and UPS.

By 1998, however, the results of this cooperation were very disappointing: accumulated losses were much higher than expected, and the venture had already laid off 180 of its employees; 60% of France Télécom's employees on assignment to Global One had asked to return to their job at France Télécom. One of Global One's main problems was that France Télécom and Deutsche Telekom tended to compete with their own joint venture and kept international contracts to themselves. France Télécom, for example, directly signed partnership agreements with local telephone operators in Mexico, Indonesia and Argentina without involving Global One.

One of the main drivers of globalization is the fact that customer needs and preferences throughout the world are rapidly converging. This in turn makes it possible to produce so-called "global" products, i.e., products uniformly suited to all consumers, irrespective of their nationality. Such an opportunity, seized by certain competitors, becomes a threat for the others. Globalization, by expanding the market for products designed from a global perspective, makes it possible to produce in larger quantities and therefore leads to increased pressure on costs. In this context, international alliances can offer an effective way to globalize more rapidly and therefore enhance a company's competitiveness. While making international acquisitions is both costly and risky, while setting up a network of wholly owned foreign subsidiaries is long, expensive and hazardous, while licensing agreements provide very little control, alliances can allow the partner companies to pool resources in order to produce a global product and distribute it worldwide. Partners in a strategic alliance can thus acquire an international dimension very rapidly by working together. Such a strategy is perfectly suited to products such as aircraft, VCRs or computers. For instance, the network of alliances and licenses that Matsushita established throughout the world was instrumental in the success of its VHS standard, allowing it to diffuse this standard worldwide more rapidly than Sony's Betamax system and Philips's V2000. As a result, the VHS standard was eventually adopted by all VCR manufacturers, including Philips and Sony.

However, if the trend towards globalization is obvious for many product categories, it does not affect all industries to the same extent. Alongside truly global industries, multidomestic businesses continue to exist; for such businesses, adapting to the local context is more important than standardizing internationally. Cooperation can also prove effective for this purpose, although its rationale is quite different. In this case, the objective is no longer to pool resources to produce global products and diffuse them worldwide as rapidly and extensively as possible, but to leverage the complementary capabilities of partner firms originating from different parts of the world in order to offer products and services adapted to the different geographic regions.

Consider the example of encyclopedia and dictionary publishing. Producing a bilingual dictionary requires a very fine knowledge of at least two totally different cultural contexts. It would be virtually impossible for a British publisher to develop an English–French or an English–Spanish dictionary using teams of writers and translators all based in the UK. That is why a significant presence in both countries is critical. Some publishers have therefore set up local subsidiaries or acquired existing firms in those countries that correspond to the languages with which they deal. Larousse, a French publisher of dictionaries, thus acquired Chambers in the UK and also created Larousse de España *ex nihilo.* Such a policy, however, is extremely costly and the related investment is difficult to recoup. Many other publishers have therefore formed alliances with foreign partners that can provide the knowledge they lack and can, in addition, actively participate in expanding the market for the jointly produced dictionary. HarperCollins, from the UK, has formed such a partnership with Le Robert in France, while Hachette, also of France, teamed up in a similar fashion with Langenscheidt in Germany and with the UK's Oxford University Press.

In short, the globalization argument is too often presented simplistically. If, in certain cases, alliances enable companies to keep pace with the international standardization of a market, they are also frequently used in other situations to widen, and differentiate, the range of products and services by adapting them to the idiosyncrasies of local markets.

Technical Change

The cost and complexity of new technology are increasing extremely rapidly. Between 1970 and 1990, R&D expenditures rose three times as fast as spending on fixed assets (Collins and Doorley, 1991). This is why companies—including leading companies—in industries where technology is a major source of competitive advantage can no longer, on their own, meet all the costs or develop all the different capabilities required for a totally independent strategy (Hagedoorn, 1993; Hagedoorn and Schakenraad, 1994). The sheer scale of the resources necessary encourages firms to collaborate. Indeed, cooperating enables partner firms in an alliance to combine a wide range of different and complementary capabilities (Doz and Hamel, 1998).

The example of the automobile industry is particularly significant. Although before the Second World War, a firm like General Motors could possess in-house all the different technologies and skills ___ o build its cars, the sophistication of modern vehi- : manufacturers can no longer rely exclusively on ilities. This is why automobile manufacturers are ıstrial relationships with their subcontractors and d, through this process, are increasingly becom- ›signers and assemblers. The suppliers, in turn, can no longer be dealt with as mere subcontractors that are given to manufacture those parts that the car maker can't be bothered to produce. On the contrary, auto makers and their suppliers are setting up partnerships that enable them to specialize and, thus, to enhance the value of their respective skills. Substituting traditional arm's-length relationships with these new vertical partnerships is triggering a "cultural revolution" on both sides: suppliers must become capable of developing increasingly complex systems, and the customer firm must accept that the relationship with its upstream partners no longer corresponds to the traditional "procurement" function. Maintaining excellent partnership relations with suppliers has become a key strategic weapon that enables manufacturers to have access to all the technologies they need while achieving competitive costs and high quality. This issue will be further developed in Chapter 6, devoted to vertical partnerships.

Companies are also facing an increasing degree of technological uncertainty. With the increase in the diversity and complexity of technological know-how, the range of possible innovations based on this expertise is growing wider. While the range of possibilities offered by new research has been increasing tremendously, individual R&D programs are growing ever more expensive and the chances of achieving technically successful and commercially profitable results have become more and more uncertain. This is why cooperation is viewed as unavoidable in many high-tech industries: by dividing up the R&D work between the partner firms, it enables them to share costs, pool their expertise, and explore a greater number of avenues (Dussauge, Hart and Ramanantsoa, 1992).

Paradoxically, however, technological progress leads to a drastic reduction in the commercial life expectancy of many products. In consumer electronics and computers, for example, product renewal rates are so fast that most products become obsolete just a few months after having been launched; in 1992, Dell Computer was introducing new PCs every three weeks while the oldest product in its catalog was 11 months old. Other technologically intensive industries are faced with the same trend. It has been shown that the higher an industry's R&D expenditure/net sales ratio, the shorter the commercial lifespan of its products (Mytelka, 1984).

As a result, in order to remain competitive companies must devote ever greater resources to R&D, while the chances of recouping their investment grow smaller because of the products' shorter shelf life. Alliances provide one possible answer to this problem. They make it possible to expand the market and to introduce the product on a worldwide basis in a matter of months, or even weeks, in order to take better advantage of its narrow "window of opportunity". Thus, technical progress and the globalization of the economy combine and converge to create an environment very favorable to the formation of interfirm alliances.

Disenchantment with Mergers and Acquisitions

The 1980s were marked by an unprecedented wave of mergers and acquisitions worldwide. Unfortunately, the success rate of these operations has proved to be quite low. According to many analysts, 80% of the acquisitions carried out by American companies have not benefited the acquiring firms' shareholders and should in fact never have taken place (Lynch, 1993); more generally, three-quarters of all acquiring companies eventually come to feel that they paid too much for their acquisitions.

Acquisitions present two main kinds of disadvantage. The first is "indigestion". Once acquired, the day-to-day management of the target company is very often disrupted by the new parent company. Either its specific advantages are undermined by the trauma resulting from the acquisition, or its expertise is difficult for the acquirer to assimilate and use. A large number of innovative small and medium-sized companies taken over by large corporations are caught up in the bureaucracy of the buyer and lose the flexibility and innovative capacity on which most of their value was based, if they don't lose their best engineers and executives; this has happened, in particular, to numerous small biotech firms acquired by pharmaceutical giants. The second problem with mergers and acquisitions is that acquired companies more often than not include activities or assets of little or no value to the acquirer. It is not always easy to dispose of them without destroying a significant portion of the company's value.

The disenchantment that has followed many mergers and acquisitions seems to be one of the reasons behind the recent development of strategic alliances. Alliances make it possible to avoid the culture and organizational shock coming in the wake of a merger by proceeding step by step, and by gradually adapting the content and structure of the agreement. What is more, an alliance is, by definition, limited to a specific area of cooperation laid down in the agreement. The scope of collaboration may subsequently be extended, but those activities of no interest to one or the other of the partners can be excluded from the arrangement. This represents a substantial advantage over a merger.

The data and discussion presented in this chapter show that interfirm cooperation has not only increased dramatically in the last two decades of the twentieth century, but that it has also undergone radical changes. The tactical and limited goals typical of traditional joint ventures have given way to more strategic motives. In this new context, executives must significantly alter their behavior and their management approach in order to benefit fully from the specific advantages afforded by alliances. The following chapters will provide frameworks and tools for dealing with these new issues.

3
Interfirm Cooperation: Theoretical Contributions

Traditional approaches in economics and management have usually considered the firm as a clearly defined entity, the boundaries of which raise no particular problem. With alliances, the border between the enterprise and its environment is blurred; worse still, even the boundaries between the enterprise and its competitors frequently become ambiguous. Managers, and not only academics, are also being confronted with this eminently theoretical problem. For NUMMI managers, many of whom came from either General Motors or Toyota, the question of the boundaries of the firm was far from being purely theoretical. Indeed, because NUMMI was not an integral part of General Motors, nor of Toyota for that matter, and was not a stand-alone operation either, they were likely to be torn between contradictory loyalties. In their day-to-day work, some may have felt that they had to protect the interests of the parent company they came from, while others may have wanted to serve the best interests of the joint venture itself; some may even have considered that their primary function was to keep the GM–Toyota relationship as smooth and harmonious as possible.

This chapter presents a review of recent theoretical analyses of interfirm cooperation. It has two main objectives. First, its aim is to help readers interested in the conceptual aspects of the topic to find their way through a rapidly expanding body of literature. Second, it sets out to offer managers a perspective that will prove useful when trying to understand the nature and implications of the different types of alliances with which they may be confronted.

ALLIANCES AND THE BOUNDARIES OF THE FIRM: THE CONTRIBUTION OF TRANSACTION COST ECONOMICS

Because the central issue it tackles is that of economic organizations and their boundaries, transaction cost economics (Williamson, 1975, 1981) plays a central role in the analysis and interpretation of alliances. It offers a theoretical justification for situations where cooperation is preferable to mergers and acquisitions on the one hand, and to mere arm's-length transactions on the other.

The Fundamentals of Transaction Cost Economics

The basic idea underlying the transaction cost theory was formulated as early as 1937 by Ronald H. Coase, who was awarded a Nobel prize in 1991 for this. Coase put forth the proposition that markets and firms are two alternative and substitutable modes of organizing production (Coase, 1937). According to this theory, firms are created and grow by replacing the market in areas where the market is not fully efficient. In the market, production is regulated by price variations only. Within firms, price-based transactions are abolished and replaced by internal exchanges, coordinated by the entrepreneur who manages production. The problem is to determine when it is more efficient to organize particular exchanges within a firm rather than letting the market regulate them. This can be determined by comparing the costs of using the market—known as "transaction costs"—with the costs of organizing the same exchanges within a structured enterprise. Transaction costs stem from searching for a supplier or a customer, negotiating and drafting a contract, and finally from monitoring and enforcing it. All these operations, which are not linked directly to the production of goods, often prove to be lengthy, difficult, hazardous and therefore expensive, which may incite the parties to institutionalize their relationship and withdraw it from the market.

The basic theoretical contribution of transaction cost economics is the notion that using the market may be expensive, and that economic decisions can therefore not be made on the basis of production costs alone. This consideration is of critical importance, in particular in the case of make or buy decisions. The sum of production and transaction costs is what guides the choice of the adequate "governance structure", i.e., the market or the firm or, in simpler terms, external or internal sourcing. Williamson further enriched and developed the transaction cost approach by suggesting a series of factors that determine the existence and extent of these transaction costs (Williamson, 1979):

- the uncertainty surrounding the transaction that prevents the parties from drafting a comprehensive contract in which all possible events and situations are contemplated. In this respect, product design is less likely to be outsourced than manufacturing, because it is more difficult to lay out all the specifications of a product that does not yet exist than to provide a subcontractor with the blueprints of an existing design.
- the specificity of the assets put into place in order for the transaction to be carried out. If a supplier must make a specific investment to respond to the needs of a particular customer, this will create a "lock-in" situation: competition can no longer regulate transactions because the supplier can find no other customer for the goods produced with these specific assets, while the client will find no other vendor capable of supplying these goods. In this bilateral monopoly situation, opportunistic behaviors can develop. For example, the supplier may be tempted to increase its profit by charging higher prices or reducing quality, taking advantage of the fact that the client cannot switch to another source.
- the frequency of the transaction, which increases the problems mentioned above and also favors the creation of a permanent organization to manage the transaction instead of turning each time to the marketplace.

These three factors tend to increase transaction costs. If these costs are too high, the parties will tend to avoid the market and carry out the corresponding exchanges inside a single organization, provided that the organizational costs incurred are no greater than the transaction costs avoided. The limits of the firm are therefore determined in order to minimize both transaction and organization costs. This logic applies as long as the decision to internalize or externalize a transaction has no impact on the other costs borne by the firm, namely production costs. As this is generally not the case, the theory stipulates that firms extend their boundaries to the point that minimizes the sum of production and transaction—or organization—costs. Because they vary in opposite directions, reduced transaction costs can be offset by increased production costs, and vice versa. Market transactions will usually lead to lower production costs, because they make it possible to increase the quantities produced and obtain scale economies by lumping together the demand of several customers. But, in the market, transaction costs tend to rise owing to the phenomena described above. In contrast, internalizing exchanges makes it possible to reduce transaction costs, but in-house production limits scale economies because the company only serves a single customer—itself.

This theoretical framework is particularly suited to analyzing alliances, as these can be interpreted as hybrid forms in an intermediate position between arm's-length transactions carried out on the market and complete internalization within the firm. In the make or buy dilemma, alliances appear as an intermediate solution.

The Transaction Cost Approach of Alliances

The transaction cost theory suggests that alliances may be the optimal form of governance structure in certain situations (Kogut, 1988; Hennart, 1988). When neither the market (i.e., an arm's-length transaction between the parties) nor internalization (i.e., the organization of exchanges within a single firm) can minimize the sum of production and transaction costs, alliances offer a valuable alternative. Indeed, when the limited number of potential suppliers for a customer-specific product creates conditions favorable to opportunism, thus increasing transaction costs, and when internalizing production increases production costs too drastically, collaboration, which can be viewed as only partial internalization, may allow a decrease in both transaction and production costs.

The PRV (Peugeot, Renault, Volvo) alliance, set up in 1971 to produce V6 engines, illustrates this logic perfectly (see Box 8.5 in Chapter 8). All three manufacturers needed a V6 engine for their top-of-the-line models (Peugeot 605, Citroën XM, Renault Safrane and Espace, Volvo 740/940). None of these manufacturers expected to sell large enough quantities of these cars to cover the cost of developing and manufacturing a V6 engine efficiently on its own. Internalization was therefore not a viable option. On the other hand, procuring these engines from external suppliers would have been too hazardous. First, the only available suppliers for automobile engines were other car manufacturers, which therefore happened also to be competitors. Second, Renault, Peugeot or Volvo would have had to buy existing V6 engines, which may not have been perfectly suited to their requirements, as it was unlikely that any potential supplier would have been willing to invest in order to produce a specifically designed engine for them. Third, if they chose to purchase an existing engine from a competitor and design their cars on this basis, then they would have become captive customers and would have been vulnerable to price increases, quantity limitations, as well as quality problems. Instead, forming the PRV joint venture increased the output for the jointly produced engine, thus reducing production costs, while giving each partner control over specification and design issues, pricing, quality, quantities, etc., and thereby decreasing transaction costs.

Transaction cost economics thus provides a powerful framework with which to identify those situations in which alliances are more efficient than either turning to the market or internalizing transactions. Under this logic, alliances are solely viewed as an optimizing mechanism and it is assumed that, when firms choose to collaborate, it is only with the objective of minimizing costs. However, many alliances are more strategic in nature; they may also be aimed at enhancing the firm's competitive advantage. Thus, alliances are not only economic devices, they are also strategic moves aimed at outcompeting rival firms. The eclectic theory of international production broadens the transaction cost perspective and makes it possible to accommodate this strategic dimension of alliances.

Pushing this logic further, it can be argued that competitive advantage stems from the resources that firms have developed. In this perspective, alliances can also be interpreted as a means through which to develop new capabilities and acquire skills from the other partner. While in the transaction cost perspective, alliances are primarily viewed as a way of optimizing the use of available resources, they are seen as a source of competitive advantage in the eclectic approach of international production and are analyzed as a means through which to expand and diversify the firm's resource endowment in the resource-based view of the firm.

A STRATEGIC VIEW OF ALLIANCES: THE ECLECTIC THEORY OF INTERNATIONAL PRODUCTION

Competitive strategy is based on the idea that, in order to survive in the face of competition, a company must create and sustain durable and defendable competitive advantages. These advantages stem from distinctive skills and know-how which enable the firm to be more cost effective than its competitors or to produce specific differentiated products (Porter, 1985). Dunning's eclectic theory of international production expands on this basic concept by transferring it to an international setting and by incorporating some of the insights gained from transaction cost economics (Dunning, 1988).

The Three Sources of Advantage in International Expansion

The eclectic theory of international production stipulates that a firm can only grow its operations internationally if it can pull together three types of advantages: ownership-specific advantages, advantages derived from internalization and advantages related to localization.

Ownership-specific advantages, or O-type advantages, are in fact competitive advantages developed domestically. They derive from the ownership of exclusive resources (know-how, experience, brands, etc.) and must provide the multinational corporation with a stronger position than local competitors, which in turn benefit from a better understanding of the economic, political and social context of the targeted country.

Internalization advantages (I-type advantages) are created when the company itself is better positioned to exploit its O advantages on its own than any local firm to which they can be transferred—for example, through licensing or renting out assets. Internalization advantages can be assessed on the basis of transaction cost considerations.

When a firm benefits from O- and I-type advantages simultaneously, it can choose either to export its products or to set up a subsidiary in the targeted country. It will only choose the second option, and therefore create international operations, if the local political and economic conditions (production costs, legislation, size of the market, etc.) encourage it to do so. This is what determines localization advantages (or L-type advantages).

For a company to globalize, it must therefore (i) possess a specific competitive advantage (ii) that is better leveraged internally (iii) by physically setting up a number of assets in the host country.

Insights from the Eclectic Theory for the Understanding of International Alliances

Recent changes in the business environment, due to technological progress and to the globalization of the economy, have radically modified the conditions whereby companies create O-, I- and L-type advantages. This explains the proliferation of strategic alliances which are increasingly replacing more traditional forms of multinational expansion.

The increase in R&D costs, the emergence of new technologies and the faster pace of innovation, linked to the shorter lifespan of many products, make it very costly and difficult to create and maintain O-type-advantages. As discussed in Chapter 2, this evolution encourages firms to join forces and pool resources in order to compete successfully. These changes could obviously lead to mergers and acquisitions rather than to alliances. However, the analysis of I-type advantages leads to the conclusion that alliances are more suited to this new context than is complete internalization. Indeed, accelerated technical change and global competition create an uncertain and hazardous environment in which flexibility and reversibility are critical success factors. As alliances offer much greater flexibility than mergers and acquisitions, they are increasingly favored by firms.

Finally, the need to diffuse products globally as fast as possible implies that firms must create L-type advantages simultaneously in a very large number of countries. Doing this internally is both very costly and too slow. Collaborating with partners that benefit from these L-type advantages in their home countries therefore becomes an increasingly attractive option.

THE RESOURCE-BASED VIEW OF STRATEGIC ALLIANCES

Accessing Complementary Resources through Alliances

The traditional school of thought in business strategy holds that long-term survival and above-average performance are produced by competitive advantage. The resource-based view of the firm expands this approach by stressing that competitive advantage is not bestowed on firms by chance or created *ex nihilo* by management, but that it results from efficiently deploying a set of rare and valuable resources (Penrose, 1959; Wernerfelt, 1984; Barney, 1991; Conner and Prahalad, 1996). In this perspective, a firm is fundamentally characterized by an idiosyncratic portfolio of resources, rather than by its portfolio of products. Referring to the resource-based view, it has been argued that alliances are a means of combining complementary skills and resources held by different firms in order to exploit new business opportunities (Teece, 1986; Itami and Roehl, 1987; Grant, 1996; Mitchell and Singh, 1996; Singh and Mitchell, 1996). Firms that do not possess all the necessary capabilities and assets to develop a business successfully on their own can nevertheless do so by collaborating with partners which can contribute the resources they lack.

For example, Microsoft and Visa joined forces to develop systems that would allow for secure Internet transactions (see Box 7.1 in Chapter 7). To take advantage of the explosive growth in Internet shopping, Microsoft needed to combine its software development expertise with Visa's knowledge of the credit card transaction process. In the same way, Microsoft formed a 50–50 joint venture with NBC to create a global 24-hour news and information cable network, as well as a complementary interactive news service on the Internet. This venture combined Microsoft's Internet capabilities with NBC's experience in TV programming and broadcasting.

If alliances virtually always set out to make joint use of the partners' complementary resources, they may also, in certain cases, lead to skill transfers and capability appropriation between the partners. Indeed, in addition to combining complementary resources, another less innocent motivation of the parties may be deliberately to capture the partner's know-how (Hamel, Doz and Prahalad, 1989; Hamel, 1991; Doz and Hamel, 1998). Such a Machiavellian view of alliances corresponds to the Trojan horse metaphor already alluded to in Chapter 1. This perspective on alliances focuses on the strategy of each ally rather than only considering the alliance *per se*. Thus, wanting to examine the success or failure of alliances is somewhat irrelevant, the real issue being that of the success or failure of each partner firm within the alliance and thanks to the alliance. Similarly, considering the duration of an alliance as a sign of success is extremely questionable, because a long-lasting partnership may result from the dependency of one allied firm on the other rather than from a balanced and harmonious relationship between the partners. On the contrary, a break-up may result from one partner having captured the capabilities it was seeking rather than from tension and misunderstandings between the partners.

Outcomes of this nature are likely to occur because alliances not only allow the partner firms to combine resources, they also create conditions that are very favorable to interpartner learning.

Appropriating vs Accessing Resources through Strategic Alliances

As discussed above, alliances are a means for gaining access to complementary resources owned by potential partners; in many cases, these resources are combined within the scope of the partnership, but continue being owned and controlled by each partner. In other words, even though the partner firms leverage the existing complementarity between their business portfolios, their respective resource endowments are not affected by the alliance. In some cases, however, the alliance allows one partner permanently to acquire the resources contributed by its ally (Pucik, 1988; Ohmae, 1989; Hamel, 1991). Through this process, one partner expands its resource endowment and can therefore apply these newly acquired resources to other businesses or activities outside the alliance, with no contribution from its former partner. Using alliances to appropriate skills and capabilities rather than only gaining access to these resources is subject to the firm's ability to learn from its partners.

Research on interorganizational learning (Argyris and Schon, 1978; Fiol and Lyles, 1985) has shown that the acquisition of new capabilities is significantly facilitated by the existence, inside the learning organization, of a competence base that is closely related to the new knowledge being sought. In other words, a new skill can only be grafted successfully on to a closely related competence base (Moingeon and Edmondson, 1996). Firms operating in the same business inevitably share such a common competence base because they use similar technologies, satisfy identical needs, serve similar customers and offer substitutable products. Therefore, alliances between competitors are likely to create a context that is very favorable to interpartner learning (Hamel, 1991). Competing in the same industry, however, does not preclude each allied firm from possessing specific, idiosyncratic skills and capabilities. Competing firms with different and complementary resource endowments potentially have significant things to learn from one another in alliances.

Overall, the resource-based view of the firm and the organizational learning approach suggest that the alliances in which capability appropriation is most likely to occur are alliances formed by competing but nevertheless significantly different firms. One dimension along which competing firms differ significantly is that of their region of origin and of the main markets they serve. It can therefore be predicted that alliances associating competitors from different regions of the world tend to result in significant capability transfers. As it is between competitors that the consequences of technological leakage and skill appropriation are most dramatic, we consider that the Trojan horse metaphor primarily applies to these alliances between global competitors. This metaphor is particularly relevant in the case of most alliances set up by US and Japanese auto manufacturers. Through these alliances, the Japanese partners not only sold cars thanks to their US allies, they also acquired precious knowledge about the North American market, which made it easier for them eventually to set up wholly owned operations in the USA.

In some cases, the Trojan horse strategy is not based on appropriating resources possessed by a partner but on preventing the partner from developing or maintaining its own resources. By doing so, the partner is weakened and made permanently dependent on the partnership. Thus, companies can restrict their competitors' innovative capacity by cooperating with them (Contractor and Lorange, 1988). Providing them with pre-developed technology, for instance, can deter them from investing in in-house research and developing proprietary technology. Forming an alliance with an innovator can also be a way to prevent it from teaming up with another powerful competitor. This is one of the reasons why small, innovative firms working in biotechnology, for example, are subject to such attention on the part of large, front-ranking pharmaceutical groups. The goal of these large corporations is to conclude agreements with the best potential innovators before a competitor can do so. Similarly, by teaming up with Mitsubishi, Kawasaki and Fuji to produce its 777 model, Boeing may have been pursuing the implicit objective of preventing these Japanese companies, eager to enter the commercial aircraft industry, from forming an alliance with the Airbus consortium. As such, the alliance with the Japanese newcomers was potentially dangerous for Boeing because it could help the Japanese partners become future competitors; but an alliance between these same competitors and Airbus would have been more dangerous still.

A company can also fight a large rival by teaming up with a third competitor that it will reinforce, provided that this third company is more dangerous for the rival than for the company itself. For example, Caterpillar joined forces with Mitsubishi in the Japanese earth-moving equipment market in order to undermine the position of Komatsu, its main competitor worldwide. The alliance contributed to reduce Komatsu's market share and profits in Japan. Thus weakened on its domestic market, a vital source of cash used to fund its international investments, Komatsu found itself in a globally weaker position (Hout, Porter and Rudden, 1982).

Organizational Learning in Strategic Alliances

All alliances are not formed with such a Machiavellian objective. In some alliances, capability appropriation may not be an issue and may in fact be an explicit objective of the partnership. When this is the case, setting up a joint venture, i.e., a separate organizational entity, has been shown to be an effective mechanism through which to transfer complex skills and know-how. Indeed, the "organizational learning" theory stresses the fact that "tacit" knowledge, expertise that is excessively difficult to formulate, can only be acquired through a "learning by doing" process (Mowery, Oxley and Silverman, 1996; Doz and Hamel, 1998). As the know-how to be transferred is embedded in the organization that implements it, transferring the knowledge requires that the partners jointly replicate this organization. The creation of a joint venture, in which the partners work together, thus becomes a vital instrument for transferring tacit knowledge. For example, in the NUMMI alliance between General Motors and Toyota, the creation of a jointly owned plant was needed in order to replicate Toyota's manufacturing system in the USA. Indeed, one of the main objectives of the alliance was to transfer certain Japanese management skills to General Motors and, conversely, to help Toyota acquire knowledge about the US market. If the partners had only wanted to sell rebadged Toyotas through GM dealerships, a joint venture would not have been necessary. Cars assembled in Japan by Toyota could have been shipped to the USA for sale by GM dealers, or GM could have assembled the cars in the USA under license from Toyota. The only rationale for creating a joint venture in the USA was to give GM and Toyota the opportunity to work together.

The traditional view of interfirm collaboration primarily focused on the potentially collusive dimension of such agreements. Some analysts of business cooperation still hold that alliances are potentially anti-competitive in nature: "Hiding behind the new-fangled 'strategic alliance', do we find nothing other than the familiar evil of worldwide industrial cartels? Is cooperation and harmonization of interests among alliance partners simply collusion in a flimsy disguise?" questioned the president of Germany's anti-trust agency (Henzler, 1993). This perspective ignores the value-creating potential of most alliances formed in recent years. As discussed in this chapter, more up-to-date approaches on alliances highlight the benefits that are derived from combining complementary skills and assets possessed by different firms. In addition, both the transaction cost theory and the resource-based view stress the interpartner rivalry that exists within alliances rather than the anti-competitive impact that cooperation may produce.

Finally, it can be noted that each of the theories referred to above focuses more specifically on certain types of alliances: the transaction cost theory applies more readily to collaboration between suppliers and buyers, the theory of international production to international expansion joint ventures, the resource-based view to alliances between companies with complementary skills, notably global competitors. This suggests that a better understanding of interfirm collaboration may be gained from categorizing alliances. The following chapter presents a general typology of alliances.

4

The Main Types of Alliance

"Despite the very strong opinions often expressed indiscriminately on alliances and the broad generalizations made about them, inter-firm cooperation is in fact a highly heterogeneous phenomenon (Lorange and Roos, 1992). What does the multipurpose agreement signed by Ford and Mazda, which has eventually led to a virtual takeover of Mazda by Ford, have in common with the "USCAR" agreement by which Chrysler, Ford and General Motors jointly carried out upstream research of general interest for the auto industry (on fuel efficiency, recycling, protection of the environment, etc.)? How can the European Ariane consortium, which has invested billions of dollars in order to become a world leader in satellite launching, be compared with the simple mutual distribution agreement signed by Pernod-Ricard and Heublein in the alcoholic beverage business, each company marketing certain of its partner's brands in its home market?

It appears, in fact, that alliances can be divided into several clearly distinct categories. At a first level, it seems important to distinguish partnerships forged between companies from different industries—and which are not, therefore, in direct competition with one another—from alliances between rival firms, which raise specific problems, both from an anti-trust point of view and in terms of managing the relationship between the allied competitors. At a second level, within partnerships between non-competing firms, a useful distinction can be made between international expansion joint ventures, vertical partnerships and cross-industry agreements. As for alliances between rival firms, we suggest an original analytical model derived from extensive research carried out on a large sample of such alliances. This model shows that strategic alliances uniting rival firms can be divided into three main categories: shared-supply alliances, quasi-concentration alliances and complementary alliances.

This general typology of interfirm cooperation will be further explained and justified in this chapter, each of the subsequent chapters being devoted to the detailed examination of one of the types of alliance. We should emphasize at this point that our typology is not simply descriptive and theoretical; it is above all pragmatic and focused on the resolution of actual management problems. Indeed, we have noted that the strategic issues raised, as well as the solutions most appropriate to tackle these issues, vary considerably depending on the different types of alliance. The strategic issues specific to each type of alliance, and guidelines for dealing with them more effectively, will later be described in greater detail in the six chapters devoted to the various categories of partnership.

PARTNERSHIPS BETWEEN NON-COMPETING FIRMS

Partnerships between non-competing firms are formed, by definition, by companies belonging to different industries. This type of alliance is a means for the companies concerned to expand into areas new to them, areas in which the partner can make valuable contributions. These alliances are an alternative to more traditional forms of expansion: greenfield investment or acquisition. They can therefore be categorized on the basis of the area into which the firm seeks to expand.

Growth and Expansion Options

Growth and expansion options are usually grouped into three main categories:

- international expansion;
- vertical integration;
- diversification.

These three possible expansion options are represented graphically in Figure 4.1.

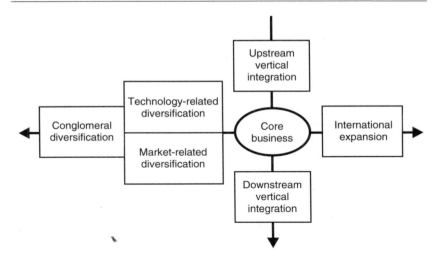

Figure 4.1 Alternative growth and expansion options

International expansion, first of all, is a strategic move whereby a company extends its activities into new geographic markets. Companies such as Procter & Gamble, Coca-Cola or McDonald's, after having established a dominant position in their domestic market, successfully internationalized, which resulted in their eventually having operations in most countries around the world.

Vertical integration corresponds to a strategy by which a company extends its activities upstream or downstream, in order to become its own supplier or customer. By acquiring a stake in Hertz, the world leader in car rentals, Ford took over one of its potential customers and gave itself the means to control a major outlet for its vehicles; it came as no surprise that most of the vehicles offered for hire by Hertz were Fords.

Diversification corresponds to a company's expansion into new businesses outside its industry of origin. General Electric's entry into television broadcasting with its acquisition of NBC is an example of such diversification, because television had very little to do with any of General Electric's other businesses (power generation equipment, lighting, jet engines, financial services, etc.).

Certain diversifications, like the GE/NBC case, lead the company towards industries unrelated to its initial business; this is conglomeral diversification. In other cases, the original businesses of the company and the diversification activity are based on a body of similar technology, or share a common customer base; this is related diversification—through technology or through the market. If several automobile manufacturers such as Ford, General Motors, Saab or Daimler-Benz have, at some point or another, diversified into aerospace, it was because they anticipated the existence of technological synergies between the two businesses. If Salomon, the world leader in ski bindings, diversified its activities towards ski boots and subsequently towards skis themselves, it was because of the commercial synergies existing between these three families of products.

These three strategic moves—international expansion, vertical integration and diversification—are traditionally carried out through either external or internal growth. In the first case, the company's entry into the new activity is achieved via the acquisition of a firm already established in the target industry. The diversifications of General Motors and Daimler-Benz into the aerospace industry were made via the purchase of Hughes Aircraft and Messerschmidt respectively. In the second case, the company makes a greenfield investment in the target industry or market and starts its operations there alone. Salomon developed its activities in the ski-boot and ski businesses by developing products in-house and marketing them through its existing distribution networks; in contrast, in order to diversify its activities towards golfing equipment, it bought Taylor Made, a company already specializing in this area. In order to start operations in Europe, American car makers chose external growth and took over local manufacturers (Opel and Vauxhall for General Motors, Taunus for Ford, Simca for Chrysler) while, more recently, Toyota, Nissan or Mazda opted for internal growth.

In this context, partnerships between non-competing firms offer companies a third alternative for pursuing these various expansion options. Partnerships between non-competing firms can therefore be categorized into three categories corresponding to the three expansion options. Figure 4.2 highlights this link between expansion options and types of partnership.

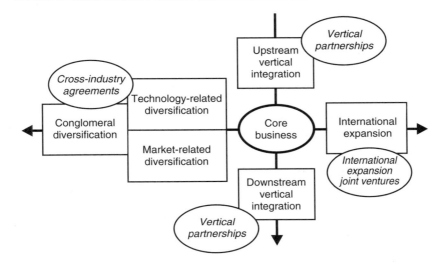

Figure 4.2 Expansion options and types of partnership

International Expansion Joint Ventures

International expansion joint ventures are formed by companies that originate in different countries; one of the partners has developed a product that it seeks to market in a particular country, and the other has privileged access to the country in question. The alliance opens a new market to the foreign partner and offers the local partner a product to distribute. To gain a foothold in Mexico, Renault set up with DINA (Diesel Nacional, SA), a Mexican company specializing in the manufacture of trucks, a joint venture named Renault Mexicana, whose role was to assemble Renault models locally, using components shipped from Europe, and to market them in Mexico.

The international expansion joint venture is, for the foreign company, an alternative both to establishing a wholly owned subsidiary in the host country and to simply exporting finished goods. For the local company, it is an alternative to importing foreign products and to developing similar products locally. In the example given above, Renault could have created a distribution network in Mexico from scratch or could have bought a Mexican company owning dealerships, provided that such a company existed. As for DINA, it could have tried to develop its own range of vehicles. Alternatively, Renault could have sold assembled vehicles to DINA which the Mexican company would then have marketed on its own account in Mexico. If, for the foreign company, choosing between these three options (exporting, forming an alliance or setting up independent operations in the host country) is a real possibility, for the local company, as illustrated in the DINA example, the choice is limited at the very best to an import *versus* cooperation dilemma. In a majority of cases, the local company possesses neither the technical expertise nor the resources to develop its own product. Indeed, international expansion joint ventures are almost always created by partner companies that have unequal skills and resources, one coming from a developed and the other from a developing country.

Several factors will, in certain circumstances, militate for the creation of international expansion joint ventures and favor cooperation at the expense of other forms of market penetration. First, the regulations of a great many countries, aimed at encouraging local production, make it difficult to import merchandise purely and simply. In order to carry out part of the manufacturing locally, the foreign company can either opt for an autonomous operation and set up a wholly owned local subsidiary or create a joint venture with a partner in the relevant country. In addition, local legislation frequently requires that national capital should have a controlling interest in all companies operating in the territory of the country in question, thereby making the creation of joint ventures with local partners virtually mandatory. For a long time, Mexico implemented a policy of this kind, both nationalist in nature and aimed at promoting local production. This is the reason that Renault, like all other auto manufacturers operating on the Mexican market, chose to team up with a local partner.

In other cases, it is not the legislation that imposes cooperation but the intricacies of the market, which only a local partner understands, that militate for the creation of international expansion joint ventures. In order to expand sales in China, Procter & Gamble decided to set up a joint venture with a Chinese partner, Guanzhou Lonkey Industrial Company. Procter & Gamble brought its technical expertise in manufacturing detergents into the partnership and Guanzhou contributed the best-selling brand in China as well as one of the most extensive distribution networks in the country. Similarly, in order to gain a foothold in Japan, a great many Western companies feel it necessary to join forces with Japanese partners owing to the complexity of Japanese distribution networks.

Although international expansion joint ventures are one of the older and more traditional forms of cooperation, they remain a common practice for developing business internationally. Chapter 5 is devoted to the analysis of their organization and management.

Vertical Partnerships

Vertical partnerships bring together companies that operate at two successive stages within the same production process; partner companies are therefore—or, at least, could well be—suppliers or customers of one another. By setting up Sextant Avionique, Aerospatiale and Thomson teamed up in a vertical partnership of this kind. These firms operate at different stages in the same production process: Thomson manufactures avionics and electronic equipment used by Aerospatiale in the aircraft and helicopters that it builds. Aerospatiale could have chosen either to procure avionics from one or another of the companies manufacturing electronic equipment, including Thomson, or to manufacture it on its own. It decided in fact to participate in the design and production of avionics through Sextant Avionique, a 50–50 joint venture between Aerospatiale and Thomson.

Vertical partnerships offer an alternative both to simple transactions between suppliers and customers and to full vertical integration. They are a form of partial vertical integration, since the company does not rely on the market for its supplies or for finding outlets to its products, nor does it integrate fully and become a competitor of its own suppliers or customers. In the same industrial setting, different firms can choose radically opposite strategies. Fast-food restaurants are a critical outlet for soft drinks producers. They account for a large portion of total sales and give the product a great deal of visibility. In order to better control this group of customers, Pepsi chose to fully integrate and acquired several large fast-food chains such as Pizza Hut, Kentucky Fried Chicken and Taco Bell, thus becoming the largest fast-food company in the world. Coca-Cola, in contrast, decided to form long-term partnerships with two of its main customers, McDonald's and Domino's Pizza; both chains carry exclusively Coke products and participate in joint advertising and promotion.

Vertical partnerships address the problem—now a classic in corporate strategy—of whether to make or buy. The question, in fact, is to determine, among all the various raw materials, components and supplies entering into a company's production process, which should be manufactured in-house and which should be bought from outside suppliers. The strategy and economics literature suggests a series of guidelines to help decide whether it is preferable to integrate the production of a given component within the company or, on the contrary, to rely on the market to procure it. In certain cases, however, it is possible to combine the incentives created by market relations with the high level of coordination provided by integration. It is in these situations that vertical partnerships appear as an appropriate option. We examined this issue from a theoretical point of view in Chapter 3, in the transaction cost theory section.

A critical issue in vertical partnerships is that of the relative bargaining power of the partners and, more importantly, of how this relative power may change over time. Vertical partnerships in the automobile industry, by transferring a large share of systems design and development from car makers to equipment manufacturers, have had two significant consequences. In the parts business, technological capabilities have become an increasingly critical resource and weaker competitors, unable to keep up in this area, have lost ground. As a consequence, larger competitors such as Bosch, Magneti-Marelli and Valeo in Europe, TRW, Allied Signal or Dana in the USA have benefited from the rapid concentration of the industry. Large suppliers have thus increased their power *vis-à-vis* auto makers. In addition, product innovation is increasingly created by larger equipment suppliers and is therefore available to all car manufacturers. This in turn has reduced technical differentiation between automobile producers and intensified competition in the industry.

We shall examine in Chapter 6, devoted to vertical partnerships, the situations in which they appear as a better choice than integration and market transactions. We shall then analyze how companies must adapt their organization to manage these vertical partnerships efficiently.

Cross-industry Agreements

Cross-industry agreements are cooperations formed by companies from totally different industries which seek to diversify their activities by leveraging their complementary capabilities.

BMW forged a major alliance with Rolls-Royce in aircraft engines, in order to make an easier entry into what was a new business for the German company—although BMW had manufactured aircraft engines before the Second World War—by taking advantage of the technical and commercial expertise of one of the world's leading aircraft engine manufacturers. As for Rolls-Royce, although this agreement favored the emergence of a new competitor, it also offered a chance of controlling the long-term development of BMW in the aircraft engine business. Through this partnership, Rolls-Royce was also able to complement its range of engines by having most of the development work on the new joint project financed by its partner. Cross-industry agreements are sometimes formed for this purpose—openly admitted or not—of facilitating the entry of one of the partners into the other's business. These alliances offer an alternative to the new entrant's diversification both via internal development and through acquisition of an existing competitor. Agreements of this type obviously raise the issue of the learning ability of the partner entering a new market and, at the same time, that of the established partner's ability to maintain a sufficiently rapid pace of technological innovation. It is in the interest of the former gradually to eliminate the expertise gap between the allies, while it is clearly in the interest of the latter to maintain this gap for as long as possible.

Cross-industry agreements are also formed when developments in two distinct industries lead to technological or commercial convergence. The development of optical processes for data storage encouraged Philips, one of the inventors of the optical disk system, and DuPont de Nemours, one of the world's chemical industry leaders, to create a joint venture, PDO (Philips–DuPont–Optical), to produce surface coatings for this technology. Another example is the technical convergence of data-processing technology and telecommunications since the early 1980s; the convergence of these two hitherto entirely distinct industries has led to a rapid increase in cross-industry agreements between companies from both sectors.

Table 4.1 Cooperation, internalization and market relations

	Non-competing firms			Competitors
	Multinationals and local companies	Buyers and suppliers	Firms in unrelated businesses	
Arm's-length relationship	Exports and imports	Transactions	—	Competition
Mergers and acquisitions	Local acquisitions	Vertical integration	Diversification	Industry concentration
Cooperation	International expansion joint ventures	Vertical partnerships	Cross-industry agreements	Alliances between rivals

In these situations of technological or commercial convergence, cross-industry agreements must enable both partners to diversify their activities simultaneously; they also represent an alternative to internal development or diversification via acquisition. Cross-industry agreements will be examined in greater detail in Chapter 7, focusing on how these alliances can be managed.

Table 4.1 compares partnerships between non-competing firms with alliances between competitors on the one hand, and with alternative arrangements (mergers and acquisitions, arm's-length transactions) on the other hand. Incidentally, it can be noted that in the case of cross-industry agreements, there is no alternative corresponding to an arm's-length relationship. It is indeed difficult to leverage potential complementarities between companies belonging to different industries on the basis of market transactions.

We are now going to examine alliances between rival firms and suggest a classification of these partnerships. A classification of this type is critical in understanding and managing the somewhat paradoxical situation created by such alliances. Indeed, if all alliances are difficult to manage and can have far-reaching consequences for the companies involved, alliances between competitors raise extremely specific problems due to the ambiguity of the relationship between the partner companies which, nevertheless, remain rivals. In alliances between competitors, each partner must be open enough to collaborate efficiently with its rival allies, while still concealing critical knowledge in order to protect its vital interests.

ALLIANCES BETWEEN COMPETITORS

The analytical model of alliances between competitors presented in this section is derived from a research project based on the statistical study of a large sample of such alliances. We considered it necessary to investigate empirically what issues these alliances raised and how they were managed, as well as the outcomes they produced; indeed, most analyses and prescriptions developed to date on the subject are strongly influenced by subjective perceptions, either favorable or opposed to collaboration between rivals. By actually studying a large number of cases, our research set out to resolve some of the contradictions found in the literature on strategic alliances between competitors.

The very existence of alliances between rival firms is paradoxical: competitors are expected to compete with one another rather than to join forces. Anti-trust legislation is there to remind managers of this, should they be tempted to forget it. However, far from being unusual, these alliances between rivals account, according to certain studies, for approximately 70% of all cooperation agreements (Morris and Hergert, 1987). One of the intrinsic features of these alliances is the ambiguity of the relationship, which combines rivalry and cooperation simultaneously, forged between the allied companies. This ambiguity does not fail to raise specific management problems: too small a dose of collaboration may compromise the achievement of common objectives, but too much openness could undermine the competitive position of one or the other partner-cum-rival firm.

The nature of the relationship between allies has been interpreted in two totally opposing ways:

- For some commentators, all alliances between competitors should be considered as collusive behavior. They are assumed to eliminate competition between the allies and to collectively strengthen the partners' position in relation to their environment, i.e., other competitors, suppliers, customers, public authorities, etc. (Arndt, 1979).
- For others, alliances between competitors do not eliminate inter-partner rivalry, they only modify the forms that this rivalry takes. According to this perspective, alliances are a zero-sum game in

which one partner is bound to lose what the other gains (Hamel, Doz and Prahalad, 1989). Alliances are thus predicted generally to result in unbalanced outcomes.

In our opinion, it is equally mistaken to assert that all alliances between competitors are collusive as it is to claim, on the contrary, that they necessarily exacerbate rivalry between the allies. Our own research findings (Garrette and Dussauge, 1995) show that these alliances fall into three main categories and that, depending on the category to which they belong, alliances are more or less collusive or more or less competitive.

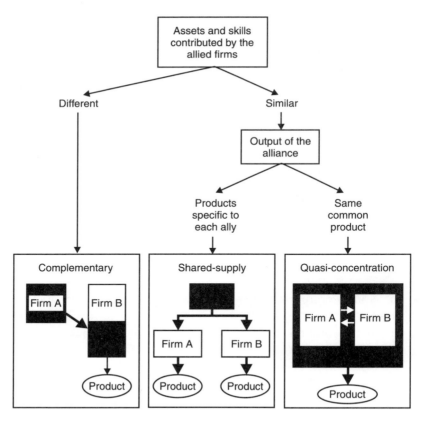

Figure 4.3   The three types of alliances between competitors

A Typology of Alliances between Competitors

Alliances forged by rival firms can take on three different forms that may be distinguished according to the classification rule presented in Figure 4.3. This classification is based on two criteria: the contribution made to the alliance by each ally and the alliance's "output".

The first distinction is based on the nature of the contributions made by the allies to the partnership.

When the assets contributed by the partner firms are different in nature (for example, a manufacturing plant on one side and a distribution network on the other), we have considered the alliance to be "complementary". The alliance that Chrysler formed with Mitsubishi to market Japanese-made cars in the USA was aimed at combining Mitsubishi's experience in designing and manufacturing small, fuel-efficient cars and Chrysler's distribution network in North America; it was therefore a complementary alliance.

When the assets contributed by the partner firms are similar in nature (for example, all allies contribute product development capabilities and manufacturing facilities), we distinguished alliances according to the nature of their output:

- First, the alliance may remain pre-competitive and cover only one stage in the production process. In this case, although the final products incorporate jointly produced inputs, they are nevertheless specific to each partner and the alliance is not readily apparent to the market. We have termed such agreements "shared-supply" alliances. IBM and Siemens have formed such a shared-supply alliance jointly to produce semiconductors which they then separately use in their respective product lines.

- Second, the alliance may cover the entire production process and result in the production of a common product marketed by all allies. In this case, the alliance is impossible to conceal from customers. Alliances of this type are clearly an alternative to mergers and acquisitions and we shall therefore refer to them as "quasi-concentration". The Airbus consortium, for example, is a quasi-concentration alliance that European aircraft manufacturers have formed jointly to develop a family of commercial jets; Airbus, which is not a real company but only an alliance of four different firms, is indeed perceived by customer airlines as a single supplier.

Our research, based on analysis of a sample of more than 200 alliances formed by rival firms from all the main regions of the world, shows that the three-category typology presented above encompasses most of the other significant criteria used to analyze alliances. Indeed, alliances in each of the three types identified share an extensive set of economic, strategic and organizational features, such as nationality of the partner firms, industry, scope of the agreement, allocation of tasks among the partners, etc. These three types therefore appear as three contrasted patterns of alliances, each defined by a coherent set of features and corresponding to a particular rationale.

In order to identify the specific features of each type of alliance, we have mapped all the characteristics of alliances taken into account in our study. This representation positions close together characteristics that are frequently present simultaneously in the same alliance, and positions far apart those characteristics that are rarely associated in the same partnership (Figure 4.4).

The map in Figure 4.4 is organized around two axes which summarize all the characteristics of alliances:

- The horizontal axis measures the symmetry of the alliance. Thus, the further the alliance is placed to the right of the diagram, the more it possesses characteristics signaling symmetry and balance between the partner firms. The allied companies come from the same region (intra-Europe or intra-USA alliances); they are comparable in size and have similar competitive positions; they contribute to the alliance by bringing assets of the same nature (shared-supply and quasi-concentration alliances). In contrast, alliances positioned to the left of the map are characterized by lack of symmetry and dissimilarity between the allies. The partner firms come from different areas of the world (Japan–Europe, Japan–USA or Europe–USA alliances); one of the allies is significantly larger and enjoys a stronger competitive position than the other; the contributions of the various allies are different in nature (complementary alliances) and one of the partners uses the alliance to expand the sale of its products in its ally's domestic market.
- The vertical axis measures the competitive impact of the alliance. Thus, alliances situated towards the bottom of the map substantially alter competition between the allied firms. These alliances

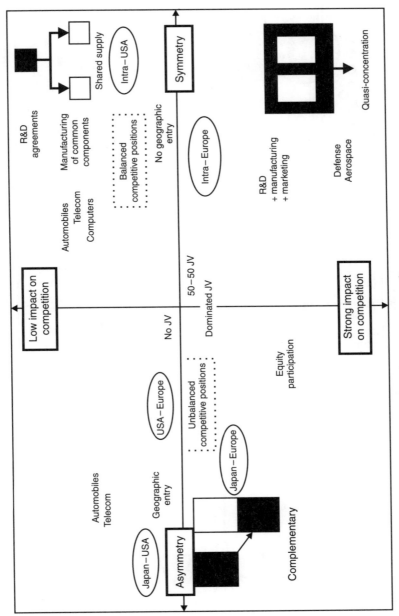

Figure 4.4 A mapping of strategic alliances between competitors

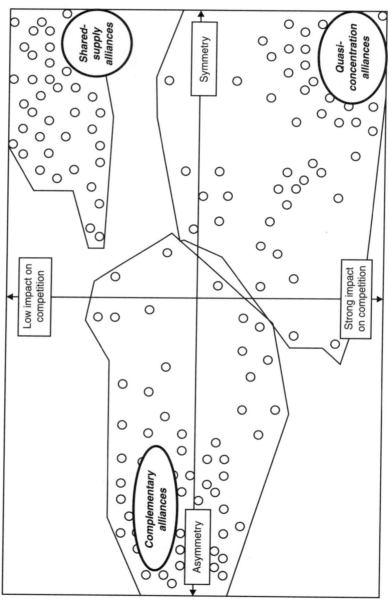

Figure 4.5 Clusters of intercompetitor alliances

cover all functions (R&D, manufacturing and marketing); a single product is produced and marketed by all partners (quasi-concentration alliances). In contrast, the further an alliance is situated towards the top of the map, the less it alters competition. These alliances are limited to R&D or to the production of common components (shared-supply type) and never involve any joint marketing.

Figure 4.5, drawn around the same axes, shows how the 200 or so cases of alliances included in our sample cluster on the map of alliances between competitors described above. It can be noted that three main clusters of alliances, corresponding to the three types, clearly emerge. Shared-supply alliances, positioned in the top right-hand corner of the map, are symmetric and pre-competitive. Quasi-concentrations in the bottom right-hand corner of the map, are also symmetrical, but strongly anti-competitive. Complementary alliances, on the left of the map, are primarily asymmetrical.

It may also be noted that, contrary to the commonly accepted view, the legal structure of alliances as well as ownership and control of joint ventures are not linked to most other alliance characteristics, as witnessed by the position of these criteria in the center of the map (see Figure 4.4). The legal aspect therefore appears to be only weakly discriminatory in alliances between rival firms.

After having presented the typology of alliances between competitors, we shall now describe one by one the three main types of alliances identified.

Shared-supply Alliances

Shared-supply alliances bring together companies which join forces to achieve economies of scale on a given component or on an individual stage in the production process. These shared elements are then incorporated in products that remain specific to each partner company, and that compete directly in the market. Shared-supply alliances are formed when the minimum efficient size at a particular stage in the production process is much greater than for the entire product, and when neither of the partners produces large enough volumes to achieve this critical size.

Volkswagen and Renault, for example, chose jointly to produce automatic gear boxes that they then used in their respective ranges of automobiles. Collaboration on this equipment was justified by the fact that, in Europe, no more than 8% of all cars were equipped with automatic transmissions in the mid-1990s. Demand for such cars was thus so low that neither Renault nor Volkswagen could produce this piece of equipment efficiently on its own. In North America, where demand for manual gear shifts is very low, manufacturers collaborate on this type of equipment while producing automatic transmissions on their own. Shared-supply alliances are primarily aimed at improving efficiency in production and have no impact on the marketing and sale of the final products. The fact that they were fitted with the same automatic gear box in no way prevented the Volkswagen Golf and the Renault Mégane, two similarly positioned models, from competing head to head with one another. Most customers were unaware that the same system was fitted on both vehicles and this in no way affected their choice. Thus, shared-supply alliances, by confining collaboration to a limited part of each ally's activity, do not noticeably alter competition between them.

Shared-supply alliances are characterized by transactions carried out between the joint activity and the allies themselves. For example, IBM and Toshiba both procure flat panel displays from their 50–50 joint venture, Display Technology Inc. (DTI). This joint venture was set up in 1985 to develop and produce active matrix liquid crystal displays for both IBM's and Toshiba's ranges of laptop

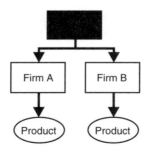

Figure 4.6 Shared-supply alliance

computers. DTI is managed in a fairly autonomous way and, although it sells its products exclusively to IBM and Toshiba, it is dealt with in a fashion similar to other suppliers. The diagram in Figure 4.6 provides a graphic representation of shared-supply alliances, stressing the transactions that take place between the partner firms and the joint venture.

Shared-supply alliances are usually formed between partners of comparable size. This is consistent with the goal pursued within the framework of these alliances: to benefit from economies of scale at one particular stage in the production process. If one of the allies were much larger than the other, the additional output resulting from the weaker partner's participation to the joint endeavor would be too limited to justify the creation of an alliance, and the economies achieved would be too small to cover the additional costs of managing the partnership.

Shared-supply alliances primarily involve R&D and manufacturing activities. When they focus on R&D, these alliances do not generally lead to the pooling of design departments, laboratories or research teams. Coordination of research activities between the partners makes it possible to optimize the resources used. All the findings, whichever ally's laboratories they originated in, are then shared and may be used in the products of either firm. If, on the other hand, the alliance sets out jointly to manufacture a component, manufacturing is generally carried out in a joint facility, the only way to benefit fully from the size effects and economies of scale.

Shared-supply alliances are particularly frequent in the automobile, electronics and data-processing industries; indeed, the cost of components and subassemblies is a very significant portion of total costs in these industries. These alliances are often formed by firms operating in the same zone; many of them are either intra-European or intra-North American alliances.

Quasi-concentration Alliances

Quasi-concentration alliances bring together companies that develop, produce and market a joint product. As in the case of shared-supply alliances, the assets and skills that the partner companies bring to the joint project are similar in nature and their goal is to benefit from increased economies of scale. But, unlike in shared-supply alliances, one common final product, shared by all allies, is produced and marketed. Thus, in the case of the Tornado fighter plane, developed, manufactured and marketed jointly by British Aerospace, DASA and Alenia, the aircraft leaving the assembly lines of any of the three manufacturers were too similar to be offered separately and competitively by the various partners to prospective customers. This could only have led to a price war—price being the only discriminating factor between identical products—which would have been detrimental to all partners.

A quasi-concentration alliance therefore inevitably eliminates open competition between the allies because it leads them to address the market in a concerted way. This does not, of course, preclude internal rivalry within the alliance, but for these disputes not to degenerate into mutually damaging competition in the market customer relations must be tightly coordinated. Airbus, for example, acts with its customers in the same way as an integrated aircraft manufacturer such as Boeing; this does not prevent the partners in the consortium from clashing violently over various strategic issues, such as the launch of new models or the creation of a second assembly plant at DASA's Hamburg facility (see Box 9.4 in Chapter 9).

Quasi-concentration alliances, unlike shared-supply alliances, are primarily characterized by transactions between the consortium of allies and the market. Inside the alliance, transactions between the allies are also carried out. Quasi-concentration alliances can therefore be represented by Figure 4.7.

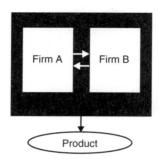

Figure 4.7 Quasi-concentration alliance

Quasi-concentration alliances generally cover all the main functions involved in carrying out an activity: R&D, manufacturing and marketing. Work within the alliance is for the most part organized on the basis of an allocation of development and manufacturing tasks among the partners. Within the framework of the ATR regional transport aircraft, jointly produced by Aerospatiale and Alenia, the French firm is responsible for designing and manufacturing the cockpit and wings while its Italian partner builds the fuselage of the plane.

With regard to marketing and sales, either they are split between the partners on the basis of geographic presence or they are carried out jointly by all partners via a shared organization set up specifically for this purpose. For CFM, the first option was chosen, with General Electric marketing the engine to airlines in North and South America and in Asia, and SNECMA marketing it in Europe, Africa and the Middle East (see Box 9.1 in Chapter 9). For Airbus, on the other hand, the second option was chosen, the joint Airbus Industrie subsidiary taking charge of marketing and after-sales for the entire world (see Box 9.4 in Chapter 9). In fewer cases, all R&D, manufacturing and marketing tasks are entrusted to a joint organization set up by the allies. Eurocopter, for example, is a joint venture resulting from the complete merger of the helicopter divisions of DASA and Aerospatiale. This joint venture is responsible for developing, manufacturing and selling all the helicopters produced by the two firms (see Box 9.3 in Chapter 9).

Quasi-concentration alliances are mainly found in the aerospace and defense sectors. In these industries, they account for almost 90% of all inter-firm alliances (Dussauge and Garrette, 1993a; Garrette and Dussauge, 1995). The majority of these quasi-concentration alliances are both intra-European and international, i.e., set up by companies coming from different European countries.

Complementary Alliances

Complementary alliances bring together companies which contribute assets and skills of different natures to the collaborative project. The most frequent case is when one of the partners has developed a product that is then marketed via the other's distribution network. In the pharmaceutical industry, Hoechst distributed in Europe cephalosporins—a particular strain of antibiotics—produced by Takeda in Japan (see Box 10.6 in Chapter 10). In the same way, Ford sold rebadged Mazda cars in the USA, just as Chrysler distributed Mitsubishi vehicles and General Motors Suzuki or Toyota models. In Europe, Renault marketed the Espace, a minivan developed and manufactured by Matra, via its dealer network and using its own brand name (see Box 10.3 in Chapter 10). The complementarity between the two partner firms was obvious: Matra had no distribution and after-sales network, but possessed exclusive expertise in the production of the vehicle's plastic bodywork.

For a complementary alliance to be formed, the product brought in by one of the allies must not compete directly with the products of the other partner. Indeed, a firm would have nothing to gain from facilitating the entry of a direct competitor to its market. This is why alliances of this kind are formed by companies whose products are highly differentiated, or by partners operating in different markets. Renault was willing to distribute the Espace only because this vehicle was specific enough to not compete with any model in its range; Chrysler only sold Mitsubishi cars that filled gaps in its product lines.

Transactions between allies are a central element of complementary alliances. These transactions are what make it possible to benefit from the complementarity in the partners' assets and expertise; to move on from one stage to another in the production and marketing process, the product is transferred back and forth from one

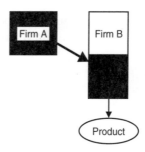

Figure 4.8 Complementary alliance

partner to the other. Thus, each partner can perform those operations for which it possesses the relevant assets and capabilities. In the Espace example, Matra first designed the minivan; Renault supplied mechanical parts that Matra incorporated in the vehicles that it assembled; the finished vehicle was then sold to Renault to be marketed through its dealer network.

Complementary alliances may thus be represented as in Figure 4.8.

Complementary alliances are usually formed by only two partner companies, while shared-supply alliances or quasi-concentration alliances more frequently unite multiple partners. Complementary alliances also bring together companies of very different sizes. The scope of complementary alliances is generally limited to marketing and sales or, more rarely, also includes manufacturing. The agreement between Chrysler and Mitsubishi, for example, initially provided for the simple import of cars manufactured in Japan; it was only in a second stage that the partners created the Diamond Star joint venture to assemble cars in the USA. This agreement never included R&D or design activities as the Mitsubishi models sold by Chrysler in the USA had been designed outside the alliance before it was established.

Complementary alliances are common in the automobile industry as well as in telecommunications. In that business, major competitors have formed numerous alliances of this type: AT&T teamed up with Philips to gain a foothold in Europe, while Ericsson joined forces with Matra to develop its presence in France. More generally, complementary alliances are often formed by Japanese companies with European or American firms.

To summarize, Table 4.2 compares the three main types of alliance between rival companies that we have presented in this Chapter, synthesizing the specific objectives pursued, their impact on competition, the organizations usually set up, as well as specific industrial or regional characteristics of each of the three types.

Table 4.2   Typology of alliances between rivals: a summary

	Shared-supply alliances	Quasi-concentration alliances	Complementary alliances
Definition	The competing firms develop and/or manufacture a common element which is then incorporated in their respective products	A consortium of rival firms develops, manufactures and markets a final product common to all partner firms	A firm distributes on its domestic market a product initially developed by a competitor
Objective	Achieving economies of scale on a particular input without turning to an external supplier	Achieving economies of scale on a complete product while avoiding conventional mergers and acquisitions	Taking advantage of the complementary skills and assets of the different partners without duplicating the corresponding investments
Impact on competition	Competition on the end products is unaffected	Competition on the joint product is eliminated	Direct competition is avoided due to differentiation of partners' products
Most frequent organization	Allocation of R&D work between the allies and manufacturing in a joint facility	The joint product is divided into subunits whose development and manufacture are allocated among the allies. Marketing may be entrusted to a joint venture	Each partner carries out the tasks corresponding to the assets it controls. Manufacturing or marketing can be entrusted to a joint venture
Most frequent industries and countries	Automobiles Computers Intra-Europe Intra-USA	Aerospace Defense Intra-Europe	Telecom Automobiles Japan–Europe, Japan–USA
Examples	PRV V6 engine Renault–VW IBM–Toshiba Siemens–IBM	Concorde Airbus Eurocopter ATR	GM–Toyota NUMMI Renault Espace Matra–Ericsson Hoechst–Takeda

5
International Expansion Joint Ventures

In 1992, *Playboy*, the world's most famous magazine for men, breaking for the first time with a long-standing tradition whereby its overseas development was carried out through licensing, decided to set up a 50–50 joint venture with VIPress, a Polish press group, to launch its Polish edition, which was also its sixteenth foreign edition and third in a former communist country.

In 1991, Chupa Chups from Spain, the world leader in lollipops, created the Neva-Chupa Chups joint venture with a Russian partner, the First Leningrad Confectionery Combinat. This joint venture, in which the Spanish company held a 75% stake, manufactured a million lollipops per day. Thanks to its partner's knowledge of the local environment and distribution networks, Chupa Chups rapidly gained a significant share of the Russian market and expected to become one of the dominant competitors in Russia in the very short term.

In 1990, the world's largest McDonald's restaurant was opened . . . in Moscow. A few months later it was serving 50 000 meals a day! The restaurant itself, in fact, was just the tip of an iceberg: the joint venture set up by McDonald's and the city of Moscow in 1988 controlled an entire industrial infrastructure including—among other things—a food-processing factory, several warehouses and a fleet of trucks. It also managed a network of local suppliers which, however, had to be given special training before they were able to produce meat and potatoes to McDonald's international standards. This enabled the joint venture gradually to phase out the costly imports on which the Moscow operation had had to rely during the first few months (Hertzfeld, 1991).

As illustrated by these three well-known examples, numerous joint ventures have been set up in Eastern Europe since the early 1990s and they have come to cover extremely diversified activities (Larçon, 1998). Fast on the heels of staple commodities and capital goods have come businesses related to culture, leisure and other services. The collapse of the communist system and the transition of Eastern Europe and of many previously state-controlled economies (such as Brazil, Mexico or India) to free markets have given a second wind to a form of partnership about which everything (or so it was thought) had already been said: the international expansion joint venture. Indeed, joint-venture formation peaked in the 1960s and early 1970s when such arrangements were widely used by American and European multinationals to penetrate new markets. Since then, the appeal of joint ventures had faded dramatically, and their use was restricted to certain developing countries such as China or Indonesia which required that all companies established on their territory have a local representative as their majority shareholder.

International expansion joint ventures are formed in order to enter new markets with the support of a local partner. In most cases, this local partner is a stranger to the business in which the joint operations are to be set up. This feature fundamentally distinguishes international expansion joint ventures from other forms of alliance, notably strategic alliances between competitors.

However, as far as management issues are concerned, the lessons to be drawn from the experience of international expansion joint ventures can, in general, be extended to all jointly owned subsidiaries, no matter what type of alliance led to the creation of the joint venture. Thus, most of the recommendations made in this chapter on how to manage jointly owned subsidiaries apply not only to international expansion joint ventures but to equity joint ventures in general.

WHY FORM INTERNATIONAL EXPANSION JOINT VENTURES?

The Joint-venture Paradox

When asked how they feel about international joint ventures, European and American managers tend to answer that they would much prefer to manage wholly owned foreign subsidiaries, but predict that their company is nevertheless very likely to enter into new joint-venture deals with foreign partners in the years to come (Killing, 1983). This reflects the conventional wisdom according to which joint ventures are a necessary evil. Indeed, until the early 1990s, joint venturing was made unavoidable by the protectionist regulations imposed by the governments of most developing or ex-communist countries. Paradoxically, however, even when these legal constraints are lifted, multinationals do not generally terminate the joint ventures they had previously set up and often continue forming new ones, as can be observed in Russia throughout the 1990s (Lawrence and Vlachoutsicos, 1993). This therefore suggests that multinationals do not merely use joint ventures as a form of "window dressing" in order to abide by host-country regulations. The formation of international expansion joint ventures is undoubtedly fostered by the policies implemented in many host

---

Box 5.1 Whirlpool's Joint Ventures in Emerging Countries

Whirlpool is the world leader in appliances. Headquartered in Benton Harbor, Michigan, USA, where it started as a family-owned machine shop, the company has manufacturing operations in 13 countries and markets products under 11 major brand names in approximately 140 countries.

Although Whirlpool's first international move was made in 1958, its international expansion did not really start until 1986, when David Whitwam was appointed CEO. The tactics followed by Whirlpool were basically the same in every market: create a joint venture with a local partner already in the home appliances business and then, if possible, take over completely after a few years. Initial successes led chairman Whitwam to title his 1994 interview with the *Harvard Business Review* "The Right Way to Go Global".

One of Whirlpool's first international moves was to purchase an equity stake in Brazilian Multibrás, later renamed Brastemp. Whirlpool further increased its involvement in Brazil by acquiring equity interests in Consul, an appliance manufacturer, and in Embraco, a producer of compressors. Other investments were made in Mexico in 1988 and Argentina in 1992. By the mid-1990s, Whirlpool was undisputedly number one in Latin America, with its main base in Brazil.

The next move into emerging countries was Eastern Europe. In 1992, Whirlpool formed a joint venture in Slovakia with Tatramat AS which commanded over 50% of the then Czechoslovakian market. According to the agreement, partly state-owned Tatramat traded its assets in the washing-machine business for a 56% stake in the new Whirlpool–Tatramat company. Whirlpool provided the joint venture with technology and equity funding in exchange for a 44% stake. The global value of the contribution in assets and intangibles was estimated at $13.7 million for both partners. Of the 1000 former Tatramat employees, the new venture hired 650, while the rest of the employees continued working for Tatramat's water-heater business, an activity not included in the joint venture. To signal further the separation between the activities included or excluded from the joint venture, Whirlpool built a concrete wall some ten inches thick and more than six feet high inside Tratamat's plant. Whirlpool's aim was clearly stated from the very beginning: bring the new venture up to Western European standards, and export Whirlpool-designed/Tatramat-made products throughout Eastern Europe. In this perspective, Whirlpool created a distribution subsidiary based in Hungary.

Whirlpool entered India in 1987 by forming a joint venture with a local partner, Sundaram-Clayton. Whirlpool increased its stake and became the majority partner in the venture in 1994 and, from then on, expanded throughout Asia very rapidly. In two years, Whirlpool spent $265 million to buy controlling interests in two more appliance companies in India and four in China. Its announced aim was to export products made in China throughout the Asian region.

With large operating losses in Asia in 1997, however, going global has been less than rewarding for Whirlpool. In that year, although insisting on an important commitment to its non-US operations, Whirlpool had to write off $350 million in assets to pull out of two of its four joint ventures in China. In particular, Whirlpool's worldwide product standardization policy seems to have failed, notably in China where a local competitor, taking into account the fact than most refrigerators in China are located in the living room, was very successfully offering products in 20 different colors and textures.

countries; however, they also seem to serve a strategic purpose for foreign multinationals, which suggests that, in many cases, the local partner is more than a "straw man". Whirlpool, for example, has long based its globalization strategy on initially forming joint ventures with local partners in host countries, even when this was not made mandatory by local regulations (see Box 5.1).

Political Constraints and Strategic Motives

Most developing country governments have been disappointed by traditional forms of technology transfer: the creation of local production bases through the acquisition of "turnkey" facilities did not succeed in stimulating the sustainable economic and industrial development that they sought for their countries. This is why they were led to encourage the entry of foreign multinationals which possessed advanced technology and know-how, while forcing these multinationals to form joint ventures dominated by local partners (Gomes-Casseres, 1990). From the host-country governments' point of view, requesting foreign investors to form joint ventures offers three main types of benefits:

- It forces the foreign multinational to become involved in the day-to-day running of the local operation rather than remaining in a "hands-off" technology-provider position. Because of its stake in the joint venture, the foreign partner will have a vested interest in making the operation a success. In contrast, in the case of a traditional technology transfer, as the multinational primarily profits from the straightforward sale of its technology, it has little incentive to make sure that this technology is well suited to local market conditions and may even be tempted to increase its revenues by deliberately transferring unnecessarily sophisticated processes.
- It limits the likelihood of the multinational partner's adopting opportunistic behaviors. Getting a local partner involved in the decision-making process is expected to prevent the foreign firm from behaving in a way that is too detrimental to host-country interests. In particular, as the local partner's gains are derived from the profits made by the joint venture, it makes it difficult for

the multinational to "export" much of the profit by manipulating internal transfer prices.

- It favors the host country's integration into the world economy by increasing "intra-firm" trade between the joint venture and other subsidiaries of the multinational partner.

Overall, the positive impact of joint ventures on industrial development is illustrated by the case of the newly industrialized countries in South-East Asia; the competitiveness achieved by such countries as Korea, Taiwan or Singapore in just a few years has been widely credited to their efficient use of joint ventures with multinationals.

Above and beyond the obligation to comply with local legislation, multinationals may deliberately choose to expand through joint ventures for two main reasons:

- The local partner may contribute skills and assets that will increase the likelihood of successfully entering the target country. The multinational can leverage its technology and product expertise by relying on its partner for skills that are specific to local market conditions (local customer behavior and preferences, legal aspects, labor relations, etc.). It is often argued that most of these skills could be acquired directly, in particular by hiring local managers, and that a wholly owned subsidiary would thus be as efficient as a joint venture. However, some of the partners' capabilities tend to be embedded in its organization and cannot easily be acquired or replicated simply by hiring a few people. The local partner may also possess assets (real-estate, a brand, a distribution network, etc.) that are not for sale on the market and are nevertheless instrumental to the success of the joint venture. For example, McDonald's chose to enter into a joint venture with the city of Moscow when it went into the Russian market because this partner controlled a strategic asset: real estate in the best possible locations.
- A good local partner often has a network of political and personal connections. Even if there is no legal obligation, giving a local partner a significant stake in a venture increases its acceptability by local political authorities, banks, distribution networks, suppliers, etc. A local partner's capital of personal contacts can substantially boost the chances of success of an investment made

in the country. It is also a fact that, in countries that do not enjoy a fully transparent political system or open and efficient markets, such relation-based entry strategies can be a *sine qua non* for the success of a local operation. The example of PJV (Perestroika Joint Venture, described in Box 5.2) illustrates how important it is to choose a partner who really has the right connections. This is often difficult because all would-be local partners claim to have the best possible relations with the most influential decision makers and, in addition, because subtle but frequent changes in the local political environment can all of a sudden dramatically reduce the value of privileged access to certain VIPs. PJV's success, as well as SNIT's failure, were largely due to the actual value of the political connections of their respective partners (see Box 5.2).

Because of the two motives for forming joint ventures presented above, selecting the right local partner is a critical issue when setting up international expansion joint ventures. A good local partner must substantially contribute to the success of the joint venture. Much too often, firms select a local partner on the basis of the

---

Box 5.2 Using Political Contacts in Moscow—the Case of PJV (Perestroika Joint Venture)

The end of communism in Russia was followed by the creation of numerous joint ventures associating Western companies and local firms. From the very beginning, one of the sectors in which foreign investors chose to form joint ventures was real estate. Indeed, in all major Eastern bloc cities, the lack of Western-standard office buildings generated a wealth of investment opportunities.

In March 1992, for example, a group of French and Russian property developers created a joint venture called SNIT. The venture's first project was to build a business complex on Moscow's Gagarin Square. SNIT's shareholders thought that the path had been cleared by signing a contract with the then mayor of Moscow, Gavril Popov. The mayor had signed the agreement on behalf of Mossoviet, the city council, responsible for the delivery of building permits. But as the foundation stone was being laid, members of Mossoviet demonstrated on Gagarin Square and had the construction project blocked, criticizing the profit-sharing agreement signed by the mayor and SNIT.

Several months later, the project was still blocked, and the French partners of the joint venture were left with no alternative but to pull out. Many other international construction projects in Russia failed for similar reasons: a Finnish company that had carried out the five-year-long renovation of one of Moscow's leading hotels, the Metropol, found out that it might never be paid, the Russian authorities arguing that, as a result of government reorganization, responsibility for the payment had been transferred to another entity.

Some joint ventures, however, have succeeded in this business, in particular Russian/American PJV (Perestroika Joint Venture). In 1987, Andrei Stroyev, the newly appointed chairman of Mosinzhstroi, the department within Mossoviet responsible for all the city's infrastructure, signed an agreement with the Worsham Group, a US family-owned real-estate company, which had developed over $1 billion worth of property, including the Hyatt Regency hotel in Miami and the Hilton Hotel in Fort Wayne, Indiana.

PJV was created as a joint venture owned by Worsham (54%), Mosinzhstroi (40%) and Glasmosarchitectura, Moscow's architectural commission (6%). Thanks to Stroyev's contacts among the city's *nomenklatura*, to Glasmosarchitectura's involvement in the project, which helped secure building permits, and to the presence on the JV's board of directors of Mikhail Posokhin, the city's chief architect, things went smoothly. The first project, the renovation of a seven-story building on Pushkin Square, only took seven months to complete. The building, called Pushkin Plaza, was an immediate success, leasing overnight to tenants such as BASF, Mitsubishi and London-based solicitors Baker & McKenzie. By 1992, PJV owned 12 buildings in Moscow valued at a total of $145 million.

However, PJV's very success bred internal problems: the parent companies found out that the American manager of the joint venture had been using contacts established with Moscow authorities for his own profit and had invested in a rival real-estate joint venture.

financial contribution it is willing to make; they can thus share the burden of setting up the venture and limit the risks associated with starting operations in a new country. Moreover, finding a local partner who is willing to invest is often used as a proof of the viability of the project: at the corporate level, investing in a new market will only be seriously considered if the managers in charge can come up with a deal in which a local partner makes a significant investment. However, it makes little economic sense for a company to form a joint venture, rather than set up a wholly owned subsidiary, simply to share the investment—because, in doing so, it will also end up sharing all future earnings while increasing the managerial and organizational costs of the local operation. Forming a joint venture is only justified if the local partner can add value to the operation.

The partner selection issue has determined the way in which Suez-Lyonnaise des Eaux has used joint ventures to expand internationally (see Box 5.3). To enter the German market, for example, it formed a joint venture with Thyssen, but refused to extend the scope of this partnership to neighboring countries. Indeed, Thyssen's main contributions in water distribution were its intimate

---

Box 5.3   The Role of Joint Ventures in Suez-Lyonnaise des Eaux's International Strategy

Suez-Lyonnaise des Eaux, one of the world's leading water utilities, has expanded internationally by creating a host of joint ventures with local partners. For example, it joined forces with the New World group to create Sino-French, a joint venture through which it opened up the water-distribution markets in Hong Kong, Macao and the People's Republic of China. Similarly, it teamed up with Thyssen in the Eurawasser venture in order to enter the German market.

New World, one of the 10 largest companies in Hong Kong with interests in construction, real estate, hotels, the management of port terminals, television, etc., was granted the concession for water distribution in Macao at the end of the 1970s. Lacking experience in this business, New World did not enjoy the success it expected, accumulated losses and produced a service of mediocre quality. The Chinese group decided to find a partner capable of providing badly needed know-how and technology. After contacting several leading companies in this industry, New World opted to collaborate with Suez-Lyonnaise des Eaux owing to the excellent personal relationship forged between the companies' chairmen. Sino-French, a 50–50 joint venture, was set up in 1984 and was entrusted with the distribution of water in Macao. In a very short time, the operation was turned around, the quality of service was considerably improved and the business became profitable.

When the market for water distribution in the People's Republic of China started to open up, Suez-Lyonnaise des Eaux and New World chose to expand their agreement and go after new concessions together. Suez-Lyonnaise des Eaux contributed its technical expertise while New World—whose senior managers are all Cantonese—provided its knowledge of the environment and its network of contacts. In 1998, Sino-French was managing the distribution of water in Tanzhou (100 000 inhabitants), had obtained the concessions for Nanchang (one million inhabitants), Zongchang (one million inhabitants) and Shenyang (three million inhabitants), and had signed a memorandum of understanding to supply Canton (six million inhabitants).

The same policy was adopted to enter the former East German market shortly after reunification. Suez-Lyonnaise des Eaux decided to team up with Thyssen, an iron and steel company which had diversified into telecommunications, oil refining and the management of shopping centers but with no experience in water distribution. In 1992, the Lyonnaise–Thyssen joint venture, Eurawasser, was granted the water-distribution concession in Rostock (600 000 inhabitants), which was the first contract of this type ever signed in Germany. In Eurawasser, employees on assignment from Suez-Lyonnaise des Eaux are in charge of all technical questions, while commercial, administrative and financial responsibilities are entrusted to former Thyssen employees. Thyssen suggested extending Eurawasser's activities to other countries in Eastern Europe, such as Poland or Hungary, but Suez-Lyonnaise des Eaux declined the offer, preferring to attack these markets in collaboration with local partners.

knowledge of the German political decision-making processes and, above all, its German nationality. In other countries, this knowledge of the German environment afforded no particular advantage. As for Thyssen's nationality, this could even have proved to be a handicap, for example in countries such as Poland.

Although it is more difficult to assess, mutual trust between partners is a decisive factor for the success of international expansion joint ventures. The substantial success enjoyed by Sino-French in the Chinese market is frequently attributed to the excellent relations forged by the senior managers of the two parent companies, Suez-Lyonnaise des Eaux and New World (see Box 5.3).

HOW TO MANAGE INTERNATIONAL EXPANSION JOINT VENTURES

Reconciling Diverging Partner Expectations

As discussed in Chapter 1, alliance and joint-venture success is often an ambiguous notion: should attention focus on the success of the joint venture itself—i.e., its survival, duration, growth and profits—or should it focus on the positive or negative consequences of the alliance for each of the parent companies? In the case of international expansion joint ventures, these two perspectives often seem to converge: the aim of the multinational company is to develop its business in the targeted country and the goal of the local partner is to derive adequate profits from its investment. To achieve their respective goals, both partners need the joint venture itself, as a separate business operation, to be successful and profitable. However, potential sources of conflict should not be under-estimated:

- The profitability of the joint venture is strongly affected by decisions made unilaterally by the multinational parent company. Indeed, in most cases, the multinational enterprise supplies the joint venture with technology, expertise, products, components or equipment. It is compensated for these services in a variety of ways (transfer prices, royalties, etc.). It can thus derive significant income from the operation even if the joint venture itself is not profitable. The local partner, in contrast, is totally dependent on the profits of the joint venture (Schaan and Beamish, 1988). In addition, the multinational can manipulate the profitability of the joint venture by increasing or decreasing the amount and price of the services it provides. The local partner is usually not in a position to assess properly whether such services are really needed for the joint venture to operate efficiently. For example, how could the local partner judge whether a sophisticated piece of equipment supplied by the other parent is absolutely vital or could be profitably substituted with a less elaborate and less expensive device?

- For the multinational parent, the joint venture is only one part in a much larger system which may include other joint ventures as well as wholly owned subsidiaries in a large number of different countries. The multinational firm will therefore manage its various operations in order to optimize the system as a whole, which, under certain circumstances, may entail decisions that are detrimental to the joint venture. A typical example of this is when a multinational parent decides to limit the exports of the joint venture towards a neighboring country because that local market can be more profitably supplied via a wholly owned subsidiary confronted with excess capacity. For the local partner, the consequence of such a decision is decreased sales and profits for the joint venture, which is not compensated by any other benefit. This lack of symmetry in the two partners' positions is further exacerbated when—as shown by a detailed study of joint ventures in India (Reynolds, 1979)—the joint venture is a major source of income for the local partner, sometimes its only industrial investment.

To avoid conflicts due to such diverging interests, the partner firms must set up a management structure capable of proceeding with day-to-day operations while respecting the aims and points of view of both partners. The two key elements to be defined when setting up such a structure are, first, the balance of power between the allies and, second, the role of the manager in charge of the joint venture.

The Balance of Power between the Partners: 50–50 or 51–49?

The specific management problems raised by joint ventures can all be traced back to the same cause: the fact that, unlike wholly

Table 5.1 Distribution of equity and performance of joint ventures in developing countries

	Successful JV	Unsuccessful JV
Multinational holding a majority stake	25%	75%
50–50	67%	33%
Local partner with a majority stake	75%	25%

Source: Schaan and Beamish (1988)

owned subsidiaries, they have more than one parent company. As discussed above, this imposes conflicting demands on the management of the joint venture. On the other hand, these parent companies do not behave as traditional shareholders in a public company: they get involved in the strategy-formulation process, may interfere with day-to-day operations and are not simply interested in earning an adequate return on their investment. This is why many potential partners insist on owning a majority stake in the equity; they believe that this will protect their interests while, at the same time, avoiding stalemate situations that 50–50 ownership might bring about. Since most firms considering joint ventures enter the negotiation room with such a request for majority ownership, many potential joint ventures fail before even being formed. There is some irony, however, in the fact that available research on the subject shows that the link between equity distribution and joint-venture performance is far from conclusive: joint ventures dominated by one partner are not necessarily more successful than 50–50 partnerships (Kogut, 1988). Research focusing on joint ventures formed in developing countries (Schaan and Beamish, 1988) shows that 50–50 joint ventures are indeed less successful on average than those in which the local partner holds a majority stake, but significantly more successful than those in which the multinational is the majority shareholder (see Table 5.1).

In addition, the distribution of equity in the joint venture does not necessarily reflect the influence that each partner firm wields in the management of the joint operation. Indeed, it appears that this balance of power has a greater impact on the performance of joint ventures than does ownership. In this respect, three types of joint ventures can be identified (Killing, 1982):

- Dominant parent joint ventures that are entirely managed by one of the parent companies, in the same way as a wholly owned subsidiary. In such joint ventures, the dominant parent appoints the general manager and senior executives. As for the board of directors, although it includes representatives from both parents, often in equal numbers, its actual function is to rubber-stamp decisions which are in fact prepared and made by the dominant parent.
- Shared-management joint ventures, i.e., those in which both parent companies jointly manage their common undertaking. In these cases, the managers of the joint venture are chosen by consensus and are often executives on assignment from the two parent companies. The board of directors usually plays an active role and is where consensus is formed or compromises are reached.
- Independent joint ventures in which the joint venture general manager enjoys a great deal of autonomy *vis-à-vis* the parent companies. There are relatively few of these independent joint ventures, as the way in which they operate is incompatible with the primary goal of an alliance, i.e., to leverage the complementary capabilities of the partners through collaboration. In these independent joint ventures, collaboration is limited to investing jointly and formulating long-term objectives. Under such circumstances, the partner firms merely act as investors and shareholders.

Research on international joint ventures (Killing, 1983) reveals that the balance of power within joint ventures has a significant impact on performance (see Table 5.2).

Table 5.2 Balance of power and performance of international joint ventures

	JV performance (as assessed by JV managers)			Number of terminated or restructured JVs
	Bad	Average	Good	
Dominant parent	23%	23%	54%	15%
Shared management	55%	20%	25%	50%
Independent JV	25%	0%	75%	0%

Source: Killing (1983)

However, identifying the category in which a particular joint venture belongs is not easy. This can only be done by examining how all key decisions—such as product design, technical choices, pricing, hiring, etc.—are made. The way in which these key decisions are allocated between the partners is indeed what determines the type of management (i.e., dominant parent, shared management or independent) implemented in the joint venture. The impact of management type on joint-venture performance suggests that it is more critical for the partner firms to work out how the decision-making power in all key areas is going to be allocated than to agree on a precise distribution of equity. Defining which partner will be in charge of R&D, manufacturing or marketing seems to have a greater impact on the likelihood of success than deciding who owns a majority stake in the joint venture. Indeed, while Table 5.1 suggested that 50–50 joint ventures were, on average, as successful as those with a majority parent, Table 5.2 shows that shared-management joint ventures tend to be significantly less successful than others. This supports the argument about the relative importance of management structure and equity distribution.

The relatively low success rate of shared-management joint ventures (see Table 5.2) undoubtedly has a great deal to do with coordination and negotiation problems induced by the balance of power within the partnership. Indeed, all major decisions require a consensus and, in addition, because of the allocation of key areas to each partner, must be tightly coordinated. However, despite its drawbacks, shared management is a sensible choice for those alliances that are aimed at leveraging synergies between the partner firms. In contrast, both dominant parent and independent joint ventures avoid the hassle of endless negotiation and difficult coordination, but cannot fully take advantage of the parents' complementary capabilities. Independent joint ventures will tend to create their own set of skills and resources almost from scratch, while dominant parent joint ventures will rely almost entirely on the managing parent's contributions. In our view, the study summarized in Table 5.2 does not do justice to shared-management joint ventures. By assessing joint-venture performance on the basis of manager opinions, it downplays the advantages of a management structure that creates confrontation, albeit positive and constructive confrontation. Independent or dominant parent joint ventures, in which few conflicts arise, create a much more comfortable environment for managers and are thus viewed more positively, even though in fact they may not produce such valuable synergies.

As for independent joint ventures, their above-average performance is somewhat difficult to interpret. Indeed, is the independence given to the joint-venture manager a cause or a consequence of the venture's good performance? One could argue that, by meeting or exceeding the partner firms' expectations, a joint-venture manager can gain a great deal of autonomy and reduce the incentive for the parent companies to become involved in the management of the venture.

The Key Role of the Joint-venture Manager

The success of any enterprise is strongly influenced by the quality of its senior management. This self-evident truth applies to an even greater extent in the case of joint ventures. If problems arise that the manager is unable to resolve on his or her own, this will encourage the parent companies to become involved. And this intervention, in turn, is likely to trigger a conflict between the partner firms that the joint venture manager will be in no position to control and arbitrate.

As the general manager of a joint venture once put it: "There are only three possible ways to manage a joint venture effectively: either it's partner A who takes charge, or it's partner B, or it's me." Another added: "The key factor for success in a joint venture is that success comes quickly." These opinions express the idea that it is vital for the manager of a joint venture to capture and preserve substantial autonomy *vis-à-vis* the partner firms (Killing, 1989). The best way for the joint-venture manager to avoid the parent companies' untimely interventions is to prove from the outset that giving the manager a free hand is a guarantee of success. In addition, in order to be in a position to mediate effectively between the parent companies, the manager of the joint venture must rapidly dissipate any suspicion that he or she might be more favorable to one of the shareholders.

Apart from maintaining a fair amount of autonomy, the manager of the joint venture must adhere to a second rule: manage each parent separately. All decisions requiring an involvement from both partners must be discussed and settled separately with each parent company before they are officially raised in joint meetings. Such meetings can then focus on working out the operational details of a decision on which a consensus has already been reached. Similarly, in board meetings, it is advisable to avoid votes on open questions, even when one shareholder commands a majority stake; it is preferable to treat each partner as if it held 50% of the equity and could veto all decisions of which it disapproved. Indeed, although it is possible, in theory, to force a minority shareholder to cave in—and to lose face—such behavior will generate bad feelings and compromise the future of the joint venture.

The choice of the general manager of the joint venture and, more generally, the staffing of the senior management team are thus critical decisions. These decisions should conform to the following guidelines:

- The manager of the joint venture must be chosen for his or her skills as a diplomat and for independence of mind. These two qualities are vital, as they will enable the JV managers to manage the parent companies subtly and maintain enough autonomy. This recommendation runs counter to the natural tendency of each parent company to try to bring in a manager who is a faithful servant and unconditional supporter of its own interests. In addition, the joint-venture manager must obviously be aware of the various cultures (both national and corporate cultures) that interact within the alliance.

- The multinational partner must accept the idea of appointing locals to senior management levels in the joint venture. This contradicts the conventional wisdom which leads many multinationals to send expatriates to manage their subsidiaries in developing countries. The rationale usually prevailing in multinationals is that the use of expatriates makes it possible to replicate tried and tested procedures and methods in the host country, while simultaneously facilitating communication—as well as control—between the parent company and its subsidiary. Relying on expatriates, however, implicitly denies any value to the contribution of the local partner, a contribution whose importance was emphasized in the first part of this chapter. In particular, in order to take advantage of the local partner's net-work of contacts—which very often represents a key asset in developing countries as well as countries in Eastern Europe—it is generally necessary to appoint a general manager from the local country (Lawrence and Vlachoutsicos, 1993). The ability to discuss with the local elites, such as bankers or politicians, calls for cultural and contextual skills that cannot be acquired in a few months. Moreover, surveys on this subject are categorical: joint ventures managed by a local CEO are significantly more success-ful than those run by an expatriate on assignment from the multi-national (Schaan and Beamish, 1988). This data further supports the idea that the multinational must not try to dominate its part-ner in the joint venture (see Table 5.1).

In summary, international expansion joint ventures should not be seen merely as a necessary evil imposed on multinationals by local legislation. Indeed, joint venturing offers an opportunity to leverage synergies between the specific skills contributed by both the local and the multinational partner. For this to happen, both partners should take part in managing the joint venture. However, shared-management joint ventures are precisely those that face the greatest risk of failure. Success then depends to a large extent on the joint-venture manager's qualities of openness, diplomacy and independence. This success also depends on the ability of the man-agement team to "localize" the joint venture and integrate it into the culture and environment of the country in which it operates.

These analyses and recommendations, which are derived from the observation of international expansion joint ventures, also ap-ply to other types of alliance which involve the creation of an equity joint venture. As discussed in Chapter 1, a joint venture created within the scope of an alliance is not to be confused with the alliance as a whole.

While this chapter examined a particular type of collaboration in which the joint venture overlaps to a great extent with the entire alliance, this will no longer be the case in the following chapters. When examining other types of alliances, we will focus on the specific issues they raise and will refer the reader to this chapter for observations concerning the management of joint ventures in general.

6
Vertical Partnerships

Since the early 1980s, a dominant trend in most manufacturing industries has been for major prime contractors to increase the amount of outsourcing while, paradoxically, reducing the number of their suppliers. This is particularly obvious in the automobile industry. Renault, for example, procured parts and components from about 700 suppliers in 1997; in 1980, it purchased from over 1800 vendors; at the same time, the proportion of purchased parts in the total value of an automobile increased from 40% to 70%. This trend developed in parallel with a radical change in supplier–buyer relations: carefully picked suppliers are required to invest in a long-term collaborative relationship with the customer and become "partners" rather than mere subcontractors. More and more industries are now organized on the basis of such vertical partnerships.

Vertical partnership can be contrasted to traditional supplier–buyer relations on the basis of the following attributes:

- the supplier participates in the new product design phase, almost from the very beginning, whereas in a conventional subcontracting relationship, it would only be called in at a much later stage;
- the buyer gives the supplier full responsibility for an entire subsystem of the product and for all the functions associated with it, whereas, traditionally, the supplier's job was limited to producing a basic component on the basis of a full set of specifications that were entirely drawn up by the buyer;
- the buyer enters into an exclusive relationship with the chosen supplier which becomes the sole source for the considered subsystem; in a traditional purchasing or subcontracting relationship,

the buyer would deliberately deal with several alternative sources of supply.

As demonstrated by the Intel–Hewlett-Packard alliance, vertical partnerships, when compared to traditional purchasing or sub-contracting, offer significant benefits: they improve the quality of the product by leveraging the supplier's expertise and capabilities while optimizing design and thus reducing costs (see Box 6.1). However, forming vertical partnerships is not justified in all cir-cumstances. The choice between purchasing, subcontracting and

---

Box 6.1   Intel and Hewlett-Packard—a Vertical Partnership in New-generation Microprocessors

Intel Corporation was, in the mid-1990s, the world's leading manufacturer of computer chips; it held a 90% share of the PC market, with a rising star product, the P5 Pentium chip. Hewlett-Packard (HP), already No. 2 in the USA and No. 3 worldwide in the PC industry was, at that time, striving to dethrone IBM and become No. 1. Even though it had developed a computer chip technology of its own, PA-RISC (Precision Architecture-Reduced Instruction Set Computing), HP had installed Intel-made computer chips in all its PCs.

In June 1994, Intel and Hewlett-Packard announced that they would join forces to develop a new-generation micro-processor, the P7, which used a new technology, VLIW (Very Large Instruction Word) computing, derived from HP's PA-RISC technology. The aim of the alliance was also to develop the operating system that would run PCs, servers and work-stations built around a P7 chip.

The two companies shared the estimated $500 million cost of developing the chip. No equity joint venture was created: all of the development work took place at Intel's facility, located 15 minutes away from HP's headquarters. Intel's role was to design most of the new chip, and HP engineers con-centrated on the operating system. While HP would produce PCs equipped with the P7, Intel could also sell the chip to other PC makers. The new chip, which was to be sold under the "Merced" name, was expected to be introduced in the summer of 1998.

vertical partnerships is influenced by the involved firms' strategic options as well as by the features of the parts and subsystems to be supplied.

The dominant trend towards vertical partnerships is likely to lead an ever-increasing number of firms, either on the buyer or on the supplier side, to enter, by choice or obligation, into such partnerships. In order to partake successfully in these collaborations, firms will have to redefine their strategic priorities and prepare their organization. This chapter will thus examine the strategic motivations for forming vertical partnerships, their organizational impact and their long-term consequences for the partner firms.

THE ORIGINS OF VERTICAL PARTNERSHIP IN THE JAPANESE AUTOMOBILE INDUSTRY

Although the use of vertical partnerships eventually spread to a great many industries, this particular supplier–buyer organization originally emerged in the automobile industry.

Simply put, the automobile industry has experienced two main revolutions in the course of its 100-year history. At the beginning of the twentieth century, American captains of industry such as Henry Ford and Alfred Sloan substituted job-shop unit production with mass, assembly-line manufacturing, which was soon known as *Fordism* or *Taylorism*. Then, beginning in the 1950s, Toyota invented "lean production" or *Toyotism*, which its Western competitors did not adopt until the early 1980s. This production system made greater use of outsourced parts and subassemblies, and changed the nature of the relationship between auto makers and their suppliers. Lean production made it possible to improve product quality dramatically while at the same time significantly reducing costs. In addition, lean production was a much more flexible form of organization; while in mass production huge volumes are required for costs to be contained, lean production makes it possible to manufacture shorter production runs with virtually no cost penalty (Womack, Jones and Ross, 1990).

Faced with this Japanese challenge, Western companies took a critical look at their model of industrial organization, based on mass production. By standardizing parts, components, subassemblies and complete products, mass production made it possible to maximize economies of scale and to move down the experience curve rapidly, thus achieving low unit costs, provided that volumes were large enough. This system eventually proved to be ill suited to satisfying the consumer's increasing expectations for quality and variety. In mass production, volume takes precedence over quality. As the watchword is "never stop the assembly line", quality controls and corrective operations are only carried out on the finished products. One of the key contributions of lean production was to reverse the order of priorities. In contrast to mass production, in lean production quality is monitored continuously and any worker may stop the assembly line whenever a problem is detected. The aim is to attain total quality by solving each problem at its root. As corrective operations at the end of the process are no longer needed, lean production turns out to be extremely cost effective.

The radical transformation in supplier–buyer relations and the spread of vertical partnerships in many industries is closely linked to the shift from mass production to lean production. To understand fully the true nature of vertical partnerships, it is helpful to compare supplier–buyer relations in both production systems.

Supplier–buyer Relations in Mass Production

In mass production, economies of scale can be achieved through both vertical integration and subcontracting.

Vertical integration is when a company is its own supplier and itself manufactures the parts and components used in its end products. While controlling the entire supply chain could, in theory, be an advantage, there is compelling evidence that vertical integration tends to make organizations very rigid and bureaucratic, thereby canceling out most of the expected benefits. General Motors, for example, suffered for many years from excessive vertical integration which made it one of the world's highest-cost producers in the 1980s. An anecdote often told within the company describes the mishaps of project managers who were not satisfied with parts supplied by a GM division and tried to place an order with an outside supplier. The story invariably ends with the manager of the supplying GM division running straight to headquarters and convincing top management that outsourcing the considered part would limit economies of scale and have a negative impact on all other GM cars using the same input (Womack, Jones and Ross, 1990). In a completely different industry, computers, the crisis undergone by IBM in the late 1980s has often been attributed to similar causes.

The drawbacks of vertical integration have led most firms, since the mid-1970s, progressively to increase the amount of outsourcing. In mass production, the dominant form of outsourcing is subcontracting. Subcontractors are suppliers that manufacture a specific part on the basis of specifications drawn up by the buyer. They are generally selected through a bidding process in which price and the ability to adhere strictly to the buyer's specifications are the two main criteria. If competition among potential suppliers is properly organized, subcontracting is usually less expensive than dealing with internal supplying units.

However, subcontracting also has shortcomings. It creates an adversarial relationship between the supplier and the buyer: provided that the specifications laid out initially by the buyer are met, the supplier has an incentive to lower costs as much as possible, even if this is detrimental to product quality and performance; conversely, there is no incentive for the supplier to suggest improvements in product design, as all resulting benefits would go to the buyer. In addition, subcontracting makes it difficult to ensure communication and coordination between suppliers of different parts. Each supplier's responsibility is confined to the basic part it manufactures, which may result in serious problems when it comes to integrating all the subcontracted components together in the finished product. Until recently, for example, General Motors produced virtually all car seats using 25 different parts manufactured by as many different subcontractors. Even though prototypes for each part were tested before mass production, numerous problems emerged at the assembly stage when the 25 parts were brought together; it was not rare to discover that they were impossible to assemble or that two of the materials used were incompatible. Lastly, subcontracting does not even guarantee the lowest possible cost. Unrealistic estimates frequently win the initial bid but, because of changes in specifications, quantities or scheduling requested by the buyer, the final price is subject to a host of subsequent revisions that, ultimately, lead to a higher price than that quoted in rival, rejected offers.

Supplier–buyer Relations in Lean Production

In a lean production system, supplier–buyer relations must be organized in such a way that they contribute to cutting production costs, shortening leadtimes, enhancing quality and eliminating inventories by taking better advantage of suppliers' capabilities. This resulted in a new model for supplier–buyer relations: vertical partnership.

In the Japanese automobile industry, supplier–buyer relations are organized according to three principles:

- Suppliers are organized in tiers, in the form of a pyramid. The prime contractor is at the top of the pyramid. The first-tier suppliers are the actual partners and they work in close collaboration with the prime contractor. Each of these suppliers then runs a network of second-tier suppliers which work with third-tier suppliers, and so on. There is a correlation between the position of the supplier in the hierarchy and the complexity of the tasks entrusted to it: first-tier partners produce complex systems that incorporate simpler parts procured from lower-level suppliers.
- The prime contractor holds a minority stake in the equity of the top-tier suppliers which, in turn, are linked in the same way to companies lower down. This creates a strong incentive for collective objectives to prevail over individual interests and protects against possible opportunistic behavior on the part of both suppliers and buyers.
- The suppliers of a particular prime contractor are organized into a *kyoryokukai*, i.e., a "club" of companies which swap personnel, information or technology. The strength of this system derives from the fact that, while remaining independent, the suppliers feel durably linked to their prime contractor.

In vertical partnerships, prices are calculated in direct reference to the market rather than on the basis of the supplier's costs. In other words, having adopted a target selling price for the final product, the prime contractor collaborates with its top-tier suppliers to work out the best way to meet this price objective, while at the same time giving profit opportunities to all partners. Together, they apply the *kaizen* method: they break down the total cost and identify possible sources of savings on each elementary part. When these savings stem from changes implemented by both the prime contractor and the supplier, the gains are shared. In contrast, the supplier is entitled to keep any savings attributable to its own actions. This system, which is based on a truly cooperative relationship between the parties, requires total openness on both sides.

This definition of vertical partnership introduces a fundamental notion not found in other forms of vertical relationships: the sharing of both information and profit. Transparency of this nature requires an atmosphere of mutual trust that distinguishes a true partnership from traditional subcontracting. Thus, partnerships are not imposed: they result from a strategic decision made on both sides.

TO MAKE, TO BUY OR TO COOPERATE?

True Vertical Partnership vs Subcontracting

While traditionally it was thought that by internalizing as many activities as possible firms could better control all the critical success factors in their business, the current conventional wisdom is that outsourcing extensively will make firms more flexible and nimble, and thus increase their competitiveness. This issue can only be resolved in practice by deciding, for each input in the production process, whether the firm should make or buy. The "make" option is quite straightforward: it implies that the firm will create an internal source for the considered input and thus become its own supplier. The "buy" option is in fact more ambiguous than is usually thought: it may imply that the firm will actually purchase an available part or component from an outside supplier, but, more often than not, it means that the firm will subcontract the considered input. Distinguishing subcontracting from purchasing is important, in as much as these two forms of outsourcing have a totally different impact on a firm's competitive position and offer very different opportunities for engaging in vertical collaboration.

Subcontracting is in fact a combination of make and buy. Indeed, in a subcontracting relationship, only manufacturing is bought from the subcontractor, while the design of the subcontracted part is made internally. One of the main drawbacks of such a relationship is that it does not take advantage of the supplier's expertise to optimize the design of the considered part; while the buyer is the best judge of the exact functionalities the component should have, the supplier is often more competent on how these functionalities can be achieved for the lowest possible cost. For example, an automobile manufacturer will best be able to determine the features of a car headlights, based on the vehicle's overall design, but a supplier of lighting equipment will know how to draw up exact specifications that meet the prime contractor's requirements while, at the same time, taking into account manufacturing constraints. However, as mentioned above, because of the adversarial relationship created in subcontracting, the supplier and the buyer have no incentive to leverage this complementarity.

Vertical partnerships are formed to overcome this problem: they favor close collaboration between buyers and suppliers on the design of certain inputs in order both to improve quality and performance and to reduce costs. While in subcontracting, design is carried out internally by the prime contractor, in vertical partnerships, design is carried out jointly by the partners. This in turn requires that the "supplier partner" is selected once and for all very early on in the product-development process. Though manufacturing is still outsourced, it is necessarily allocated to the selected partner that took part in the design of the part to be manufactured, and no competitive bids are considered. Indeed, in order to benefit from the supplier's full collaboration and involvement, the buyer must absolutely grant that supplier the production of the co-designed component. If the supplier suspects that manufacturing may be entrusted to a competitor, it will fear that all the ideas, innovations and technology it contributes at the design stage will be passed on to that competitor. It will thus refrain from sharing its best skills and solutions with the buyer during the joint development stage.

In summary, true vertical partnerships make it possible to take full advantage of a supplier's skills and technology and to leverage the supplier's and buyer's complementary resources and perspectives, but preclude choosing the cheapest manufacturer of the co-designed components through a competitive bidding process (see Figure 6.1).

Because of the extent of what is expected of them in vertical partnerships, the selection of those suppliers fit to become partners is absolutely critical. These supplier partners must of course be

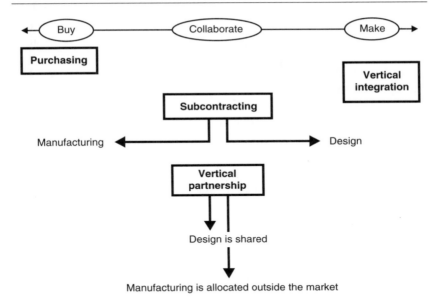

Figure 6.1 Vertical integration, purchasing, subcontracting and vertical partnership

chosen on the basis of their potential contribution to the design process and must therefore possess leading-edge technological skills. But they must also be efficient manufacturers capable of producing the relevant part competitively. In practice, prime contractors select their partners from among their best subcontractors on the basis of their innovativeness and proactive attitude in the relationship. Experience accumulated working with them also guarantees that they are cost-effective manufacturers. As only a few of all current subcontractors will be chosen to work as partners, the shift from subcontracting to vertical partnerships leads to a reduction in the number of suppliers with which large prime contractors work, and to concentration in the supplying industries.

When to Enter into a Vertical Partnership

In parallel with the formation of true vertical partnerships, a shift in vocabulary has been occurring: subcontracting has taken on a negative connotation and, as a result, all suppliers and subcontractors now tend to be called partners. This creates a great deal of confusion and implies that partnerships are "better" than other buyer–supplier relations, which is not necessarily the case. The choice between partnership, subcontracting or purchasing must be made carefully on the basis of a set of contextual factors.

First, when there is very little design involved in the transaction, i.e., when the input is a standard product that can be bought off the shelf and only requires minor, if any, adaptation, vertical partnership, as well as subcontracting, is to be ruled out. Thus, forming partnerships is only justified in the case of highly customized inputs.

Second, vertical partnership should only be considered if the benefits derived from collaborating on the design with a supplier significantly outweigh the costs of no longer using a bidding process to select the lowest-cost producer of the relevant components. Shifting from subcontracting to vertical partnership leads to a "fundamental transformation" (Williamson, 1975) in the competitive context in which the supply transaction takes place. Indeed, while the prime contractor initially had numerous subcontractors to

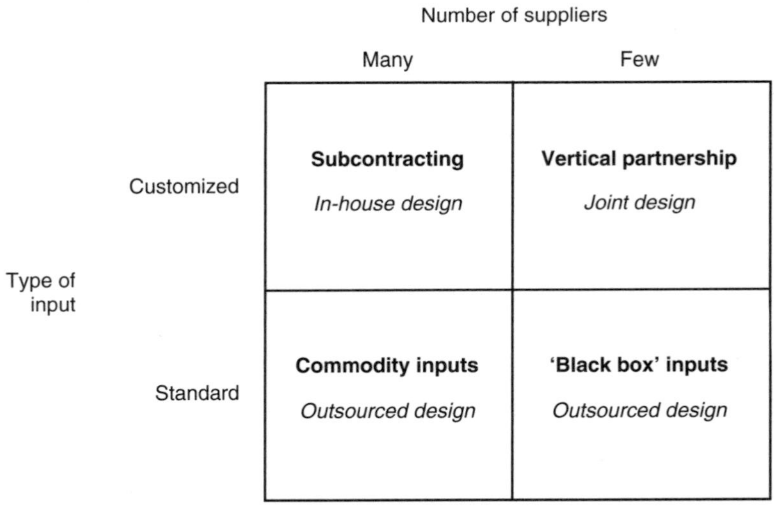

Number of suppliers

	Many	Few
Customized	**Subcontracting** *In-house design*	**Vertical partnership** *Joint design*
Standard	**Commodity inputs** *Outsourced design*	**'Black box' inputs** *Outsourced design*

Type of input

Figure 6.2 Types of supplier–buyer relations

choose from, by entering into a vertical partnership it deliberately reduces the number of potential suppliers and virtually gives the selected partner a monopoly position.

Figure 6.2 contrasts the various forms of supplier–buyer relations according to the factors discussed above.

For standard inputs, the optimal organization of the transaction is through the market. If there are numerous possible suppliers, which implies that the input is a commodity, the buyer has no incentive to favor one supplier over another; competition will drive prices down and reveal the most efficient supplier at any point in time. If, on the contrary, there are very few potential suppliers, which suggests that the considered input incorporates some proprietary features or technology, then it is the supplier that has no incentive to enter into a collaborative relationship. Indeed, it is in the supplier's best interest to serve as many customers as possible while protecting the proprietary nature of its technology.

For customized inputs, only the buyer is in a position to define the main features of the particular component. Therefore, the buyer is necessarily involved in the design process. Moreover, the only way to organize a bidding process among potential suppliers is to define precisely all the specifications of the input to be purchased. This leads the buyer to take on all the design work while confining the supplier to manufacturing. This corresponds to traditional subcontracting. Transitioning into the upper right-hand box in Figure 6.2 is a deliberate strategic move on the part of both the buyer and the supplier that will become a partner. Indeed, the small number of available suppliers is not a pre-existing circumstance which leads to the formation of partnerships but is in fact the outcome of the decision to collaborate on design. As mentioned above, making such a transition from subcontracting to partnership automatically implies that the market can no longer be used to allocate the manufacturing of the co-designed input. Prices can therefore no longer be determined through competition but must be agreed by both parties. Trust between the supplier and the buyer is thus a critical ingredient in the formation of successful partnerships.

The Sextant Avionique–Texas Instruments partnership illustrates the advantages that can be derived from forming vertical partnerships rather than relying on traditional supplier–buyer relations (see Box 6.2).

Box 6.2   The Sextant Avionique/Texas Instruments Partnership

In 1993, Traffic Alert and Collision Avoidance Systems (TCAS) were made mandatory in the USA for all commercial aircraft. These systems, which are produced by such companies as Bendix, Collins and Honeywell, comprise four main components: an aerial, a transmitter–receiver, a calculator and a screen. Following the enforcement of this new regulation, Sextant Avionique, one of the leading European aerospace equipment manufacturers specializing in visualization instruments, received orders from various airlines to supply them with over 3000 TCAS screens. These were to be delivered in less than eight months.

The initial studies carried out by Sextant Avionique's engineering department made it clear that it would be impossible to design and manufacture the whole product in-house owing to the short leadtime, the tight cost constraints and the innovative nature of the technologies required. To meet the specifications, Sextant needed a specific DSP (Digital Signal Processor), i.e., a very powerful graphic processor capable of carrying out a large number of operations in real time. Not only was Sextant unable to produce such a processor but, in addition, no adequate product was available on the market at that time. The only solution was for Sextant Avionique to turn to a microprocessor producer. Texas Instruments agreed to collaborate with Sextant on this project but, despite its expertise in microelectronics, was unable to develop an adequate processor on its own because of lack of in-depth knowledge of the customers' needs. It was only by working closely together that the two companies managed to meet all the technical specifications, as well as the time and cost requirements.

Cooperation between the partners had to be as extensive and transparent as possible. Texas Instruments could not consider itself a mere subcontractor but had to share in the financial and technological risks of the project. For Sextant Avionique, collaboration implied much more than simply placing an order with a supplier; it required the formation of a joint development team with TI. The two partners thus set up an integrated team and worked closely together up until the very moment the equipment was delivered to customers.

In addition to achieving its immediate objectives, this strategic partnership enabled both companies to strengthen their competitive position. Sextant Avionique managed to establish itself as a credible supplier of TCAS screens, to such an extent that certain producers of complete TCAS devices dropped their own visualization instruments to fit their systems with Sextant Avionique screens. On the other hand, the partnership gave Texas Instruments access to the attractive commercial aviation market. It also helped TI build a strong competitive position in DSP chips that have since been used for other applications.

Source: adapted from Bruel and Donada (1994).

THE MANAGEMENT OF VERTICAL PARTNERSHIPS

Selecting the Right Partner

The criteria generally used when selecting a subcontractor are inadequate when it comes to choosing a partner. These criteria are primarily measures of operational effectiveness, such as change-over time, inventory to sales ratio, productivity, track record of on-time delivery, etc., which only assess the manufacturing capabilities and the economic performance of potential suppliers. However, the most efficient subcontractors are not necessarily good partners. The selection process must therefore take into account more qualitative indicators in order to appreciate the quality and likely durability of the relationship to be established. Some of the factors to be taken into consideration include:

- the degree of mutual trust between the partners;
- the commitment to invest jointly for the long term, both in physical assets and in more intangible resources (know-how, time and effort to make the relationship improve and expand, etc.);
- the fit between the partners' strategies.

Overall, it thus appears that, in choosing the right partner, its commitment to the partnership is at least as important as its technical capabilities. This is why leading suppliers in a particular product area often do not turn out to be the best possible partners. Their dominant position creates less of an incentive for them to try to understand the buyer's specific needs and develop truly customized solutions. They will tend instead to adapt existing components and systems in order to barely meet the customer's requirements. Less powerful suppliers will have more to gain from investing in a long-term relationship with the customer and are thus more likely to collaborate innovatively in the design process.

Honda was one of the first companies to set up a formal procedure for choosing its partners. In particular, it shortlisted potential future partners and assigned permanent teams to those suppliers for relatively long periods in order to appraise their ability to become true Honda partners. Simultaneously, key executives from the potential partners would get deeply involved with Honda to obtain a clearer view of their customer's expectations and to judge whether these were compatible with their own objectives. It was on the basis of this mutual learning process that a decision to go ahead and form a partnership would ultimately be taken.

Organizing for Collaboration

Transitioning from a traditional subcontracting relationship to a true partnership requires a radical change in organization from both the buyer and the supplier.

On the buyer's side, the implementation of a partnership relation makes it necessary completely to redefine the role and authority of each major functional department involved in the relationship:

- Purchasing managers must change their attitude towards suppliers and refrain from exerting pressure on price without considering all the other aspects of the supplier's contribution. They must instead participate in the partner selection process and design pricing mechanisms that will encourage all parties to reduce costs while offering both sides opportunities for fair gains.
- The leadership and arrogance of the prime contractors' design departments must be challenged. Indeed, long used to having

the last say in the design of components and even in the way in which they are manufactured (either in-house or by a sub-contractor), engineers naturally tend to think that they have nothing to learn from their suppliers.
- For the methods department, whose role is to design and set up the manufacturing equipment, collaborating requires much earlier involvement and continuous interaction with the supplier partners, right from the product's initial design stages.

On the supplier's side, becoming a credible partner also requires significant changes in organization and may even lead the company to view its business from a totally new perspective:

- The sales function must be completely redesigned, as its objective is no longer to peddle the company's manufacturing capabilities but to come up with innovative ideas that will meet the buyer's needs, i.e., the final customers' expectations. This implies that, while traditional subcontractors can rely on the buyer to understand the customers' requirements and translate them into precise specifications, supplier partners must anticipate their buyers' demands by analyzing trends in the final market and therefore set up a real marketing function.
- In order to generate innovations that will add value to the buyer's products, supplier partners must set up a real R&D function that will collaborate with the prime contractor on design. This R&D function must partake in the product innovation stage rather than focus solely on optimizing the production process of a part entirely designed by the prime contractor.
- The innovations submitted by the supplier cannot be created within a particular function; they must emerge from collaboration between marketing, R&D and manufacturing. Indeed, the partner will create value for the prime contractor if it suggests innovative designs that better satisfy customer expectations while, at the same time, making manufacturing easier and less costly. Internal collaboration between the different functional departments of the supplier is thus a prerequisite for partnering efficiently with prime contractors.

Ultimately, to implement vertical partnerships successfully, both prime contractors and suppliers are led to redefine their organization simultaneously. Operations must be organized primarily around projects rather than around functions. At the very least, functional divisions must be complemented by a horizontal organization emphasizing teamwork. While project-based structures of this kind were adopted early on in such industries as aerospace, they are more of an innovation in many other industries. In the automobile industry, for example, the product-development cycle was traditionally divided up into successive phases, each dominated by a specific functional department. Thus, a new vehicle project would be passed on from market surveys to design, then to methods and tooling, to procurements, to manufacturing and, finally, to sales. With the introduction of project-based organizations, all the people involved in a project— both from within the company and from the supplier partners, irrespective of the function they represent—are involved right from the initial design phase. Thus, fuller account can be taken of their opinions, and problems that would normally arise at a later stage can be anticipated and solved right from the start. In addition, this process, known as concurrent engineering, enhances the overall unity and consistency of the product and improves its quality while reducing its cost.

In order to implement concurrent engineering more efficiently, prime contractors often choose to locate all the people involved in a project in the same facility. The case of the Chrysler Neon "platform" (Lewis, 1995) is a typical example of this organization (see Box 6.3). Such platforms provide working space to people from all functions, both from within the company and from the suppliers. The presence of each function or partner on the platform tends to vary over time according to the extent of their involvement in the different stages of the project. To improve communication between all parties, it is not uncommon for teams from the suppliers to be based for extended periods within the prime contractor's organization. In Japan, prime contractors and suppliers go as far as swapping personnel in order to facilitate the management of their vertical partnerships. In Europe, these practices are still uncommon but many senior managers of supplier companies are former employees of the prime contractor. Their understanding of the needs and organization of the buyer improves the efficiency of the partnership.

Box 6.3 Chrysler's Neon and CCV Platforms

When Chrysler introduced its Neon model in 1994, it impressed Japanese car manufacturers so much that Toyota had the car taken apart in a plant near Nagoya to reverse engineer it, the first time in 10 years that the company had done this with an American car. Neon's success has generally been credited to the new "platform teams" organization that Chrysler set up to produce the car. Chrysler did away with the organization traditionally used in the car industry. In the past, marketing, design, engineering, purchasing and manufacturing had been divided into separate, vertical departments, or "chimneys", as they have come to be called. For the Neon project, in contrast, Chrysler brought designers, engineers and executives from other functions, as well as representatives of selected suppliers, together into "Small platform development teams", and encouraged collaboration between them at every stage in the production process. Located at the Chrysler Technology Center in Auburn Hills, Michigan, the platform team had everybody working in one place. In the same location was the "pilot facility", a mini assembly plant where the platform team could make sure that the designs adopted would not lead to unforeseen problems at the manufacturing stage. Furthermore, during the whole development process, the Neon team was in permanent contact with the Belvidere (Illinois) assembly plant where the car was to be assembled. Designers thus had direct and immediate feedback on their ideas. With this method, Chrysler's new range of medium and small cars was produced in only 31 months, rather than in the usual four years. Development costs were also dramatically reduced: the Neon project was implemented with only one-third the number of engineers needed to produce Chrysler's previous range of cars.

In 1997, Chrysler was working on the CCV (Composite—or China—Concept Vehicle) project, a low-cost, plastic body vehicle aimed at markets in developing countries. The objective was to cut the variable costs of the car by 50% when compared to a typical subcompact like the Neon, by making the body out of four large, molded plastic parts. For the development of CCV, Chrysler implemented a platform organization similar to that of the Neon, involving suppliers to an even greater extent. Indeed, although Chrysler, like other car makers, already used plastics for a variety of small components, it did not manufacture large plastic body panels, having them supplied instead by subcontractors. A "body core team", which associated Chrysler engineers and staff from seven suppliers, was set up, as follows:

- Cascade Engineering Inc., which owned a 9000-ton injection-molding machine, one of the largest in the world, was in charge of molding.
- The material used for the body panels, a 15% glass-fiber reinforced plastic, which is tough, durable, totally recyclable and accepts color pigments, was developed by Ticona GmbH (Frankfurt, Germany).
- The molds were manufactured by Paragon Die & Engineering (Grand Rapids, Michigan); with the requested molds weighing up to 160 tons and being 14 ft long, 8 ft high and 6 ft deep, i.e., three times larger than previously used molds, Paragon had to change its production process and substitute six different segments for one big mold.
- Weber Manufacturing Ltd (Midland, Ontario) developed a nickel vapor deposition process that could be used to produce molds half the weight at 30% lower cost.
- Husky Injection Molding Technologies (Bolton, Ontario) supplied the machinery.
- Progressive Tool & Industries (Southfield, Michigan) provided the tooling and handling.
- Supply of the adhesive used to put the car together was entrusted to Ashland Chemical (Dublin, Ohio), which had previously provided Chrysler with adhesives for the Viper sports car program.

The Strategic Impact of Vertical Partnerships

Vertical cooperation substitutes a multitude of specialized subcontractors for a small number of selected partners with wider responsibilities. To adapt to this change, suppliers must therefore widen the range of their technical competencies and manufacturing capabilities. More particularly, it is vital for them to develop new skills in product design and engineering. The supplier partner, responsible for complete subassemblies rather than basic components, is increasingly led to work with second-tier suppliers and subcontractors. It must therefore learn how to work as a prime contractor and project leader.

If such changes favor those suppliers capable of adapting to them rapidly, they have a clearly negative impact on others. Unwilling or unable to take on extensive product-design work, some suppliers will be relegated to the position of lower-tier subcontractors and will have no contact whatsoever with the prime contractor. The weaker suppliers will quite simply disappear, a prey to industry concentration.

The frequent adoption of vertical partnership relations in lieu of traditional purchasing and subcontracting shifts the relative bargaining power of suppliers vs buyers. While prime contractors formerly dealt with a host of suppliers forced to compete with one another on price, they now tend to rely on virtually a single source of supply. The customer relinquishes extensive design work—and the capabilities that underpin it—to partners, and thus becomes dependent on these partners. In the long term, this can lead to a complete reversal of fortunes. This is how the IBM/Microsoft partnership—whereby IBM outsourced the development of the operating system for its PCs—was clearly dominated by IBM at the beginning yet turned out to benefit Microsoft in the end by allowing it to impose its standard worldwide.

This dependence is particularly strong when the buyer is no longer in a position to internalize the work done by its supplier partner because it has lost the corresponding skills. The use of electronics in many manufactured goods, for instance, has made manufacturers of such goods extremely dependent on their chip suppliers. The toy industry offers a blatant example: Texas Instruments, initially a mere supplier of electronic chips used in toys, went on to design its own range of electronic toys, marketed under the TI brand name. In the helicopter industry, the growing impact of electronic equipment has led helicopter manufacturers to involve their electronic systems suppliers in the design of their aircraft. The skills acquired by the latter have radically transformed the balance of power between the two industries. It is revealing in this respect that IBM, an erstwhile supplier of on-board electronic equipment, was chosen by the US Navy as the prime contractor for the development of the Sea Hawk helicopter. IBM then turned to Sikorsky, the world leader in helicopters, to produce the body and all the aerodynamic parts of the machine. This extreme example illustrates a situation where the subcontractor has become the prime contractor and uses its former prime contractor as a partner.

In a more general perspective, although partnership suggests understanding, mutual trust and balance, conflicting interests do not disappear all of a sudden; they are merely expressed in different ways.

7

Cross-industry Agreements

In the 1980s, most large computer manufacturers announced the creation of strategic partnerships with telecommunications equipment manufacturers (Pisano, Russo and Teece, 1988; Garrette and Quélin, 1994). This was notably the case for IBM with Rolm, for Olivetti with AT&T, for Honeywell with Ericsson and for Bull with Jeumont-Schneider. More recently, several major European banks have signed agreements with insurance companies. Thus, for example, Banque Nationale de Paris has teamed up with AXA-UAP and the Swiss Bank Corporation with Zurich-Assurance.

These cross-industry agreements between computer and telecommunications firms or between banks and insurance companies were formed at a time when these industries were also being swept by a wave of mergers and acquisitions. AT&T, for instance, took control of NCR in 1991 and IBM acquired Rolm after a short partnership before selling it to Siemens. GAN acquired 80% of the equity of CIC and, on this basis, developed "bank insurance" products, which include both risk coverage and participation in an investment fund.

These cross-industry agreements are not, however, a new evolution. As early as 1943, a chemical company, Dow Chemical, and a glass producer, Corning Glass, teamed up to create Dow-Corning, a joint venture which was to become the world's leading producer of silicon products. In 1973, Corning Glass implemented the same cooperative strategy, in partnership with Siemens, to start a fiber-optics business and created Siecor, a 50–50 joint venture that has since come to dominate the industry worldwide.

Cross-industry alliances form links between companies operating in different businesses; the partner firms are therefore neither competitors nor linked in a customer/supplier relationship. In addition, these alliances do not aim to facilitate the entry of one of the partners into a new geographic market. Thus, cross-industry agreements are founded on a rationale that is clearly distinct from that of international expansion joint ventures, vertical partnerships or strategic alliances between rival firms.

Cross-industry agreements can correspond to two main objectives. First, two companies can combine their competencies, either to create an entirely new business or because their respective businesses are converging and are expected to merge into a single competitive arena at some point in the future. Second, cross-industry agreements can provide a way for one of the partners to learn about the other partner's industry and help it diversify into this industry.

CREATING A NEW BUSINESS BY COMBINING FORCES

Taking Advantage of Converging Technologies and Capabilities

It sometimes happens that the combinations of skills and capabilities possessed by firms operating in completely different industries give rise to new business opportunities. When such an opportunity emerges, one way for a firm to take advantage of it is by forming an alliance with a partner that possesses the necessary complementary resources. Electronic trade is an example of such a new business. For this business to develop, it is necessary to ensure the security of transactions and payments carried out on the Internet. Designing an efficient, secure transaction technology requires advanced expertise in data processing as well as a great deal of experience in processing financial operations. This led Microsoft and Visa, two dominant players in their respective fields, to team up and jointly develop a software system that allows consumers to shop on the Internet using a credit card (see Box 7.1).

The alliance set up by SNCF, the French railway company, with American Airlines to develop a computerized reservation system adapted to railway travel is another example of a cross-industry agreement in which complementary assets and competencies are

Box 7.1   The Microsoft–Visa Alliance for Secure Electronic Transactions

One of the most important problems hindering the development of electronic trade is the security of data transmission on the Internet. As early as 1994, Microsoft offered bank-on-line services through its Microsoft Money 3.0 software which connected consumers with their checking, savings and credit card accounts. Money transfers through the Internet were still problematic, however, as the security of transactions and, more generally, of computer systems linked to the Net could not be guaranteed. As proved by a number of widely publicized scandals, clever hackers seemed capable of penetrating almost any system—including highly sensitive defense-related computers—of stealing mailbox IDs, of breaking private codes and of spreading lethal viruses.

In November 1994, Microsoft Corp. and Visa International Inc. announced that they would jointly develop a secure transaction software to give personal computer users more confidence in electronic shopping. With this technology, consumers would send an encrypted credit card number to a VisaNet payment system server, where buyers and sellers would be authenticated and where transactions would be cleared. The new technology could then be used to protect any data transmission, including telephone conversations and e-mail messages. The jointly developed software was released by October 1995. To ensure security, the Microsoft–Visa standard, called STT (Security Transaction Technology), uses both private-key and public-key encryption and has two layers of security: one between the consumer and the merchant, and one between the consumer and the bank, which, the partners claim, makes Web transactions more secure than telephone ordering. Included in Microsoft's Internet Explorer version 2.0, it offers PC users payment possibilities from Windows applications by clicking an icon and entering a card number. In the future, the system could include card readers connected to the user's PC, which would allow customers simply to swipe their credit card through for authorization.

The claimed goal of the alliance is to boost electronic business. However, as the Microsoft–Visa software only operates on Windows servers, critics have argued that Microsoft's aim was actually to create a Windows-based standard that excluded the technology developed by competitors, and thus in fact delayed the expansion of electronic trade.

The main competitor for Microsoft and Visa is another cross-industry alliance formed by Netscape, MasterCard, IBM, GTE Corp. and CyberCash Inc. These companies have developed a similar technology called SEPP (Secure Electronic Payment Process), incorporated into Netscape 2.0. By 1996, after a period of open war between the two dominating standards, a common compatible standard, Secure Electronic Transaction (SET), was released by Microsoft and Netscape.

---

combined to exploit new business opportunities (see Box 7.2). SNCF also formed an alliance with British Airways to operate the British section of the Eurostar high-speed rail link between London, Paris and Brussels; both companies can thus offer their customers combined air and rail travel.

The need to combine complementary skills and assets has also led to the formation of numerous alliances between small biotech companies and large pharmaceutical corporations (Pisano, Shan and Teece, 1988). More often than not, biotechnology firms are small, innovative organizations with no manufacturing capability or marketing resources. They consequently need a partner to help them develop applications in line with market needs, carry out clinical tests in order to get FDA approval, or its equivalent in other countries, manufacture products on an industrial scale and, finally, market these products widely. Large pharmaceutical companies possess all these complementary skills (Doz, 1988).

In contrast to the examples discussed above, cross-industry alliances set up by biotech firms and pharmaceutical companies are not aimed at starting operations in a business that is peripheral to the main activities of both partners. On the contrary, these alliances are at the very core of both the biotech firm's development and the pharmaceutical company's innovation process. More generally, innovations in biotechnology require complementary assets in their applications sector to be profitable. This is why biotech companies

---

Box 7.2 Resarail 2000—an Alliance between American Airlines and SNCF

SNCF, the French railway company, was a pioneer in developing high-speed trains and has played an active role in extending the network of high-speed rail connections throughout Western Europe. This has led it to compete directly with air travel on many routes. In order to capture an increasing share of the market, SNCF chose to implement a reservation system similar to those used by airlines but adapted to the specific needs of rail transport. It turned to American Airlines, which had developed Sabre, the leading computerized reservation system for airlines. Such systems, which first appeared in the early 1980s (the most famous of the others being Amadeus, Galileo and Apollo), enable travel agents to optimize the conditions and cost of air travel for their customers by giving them access to comprehensive information on all available flights. In parallel, these reservation systems make it possible for airlines to implement "yield management", i.e., to optimize income by modulating fares and maximizing flight occupancy rates.

On the basis of the Sabre system, SNCF and American Airlines jointly developed the Resarail system which SNCF has been using since 1993. In order to market their system to other railway companies, the two partners set up the Resarail 2000 joint venture. Continued collaboration between the two partners was necessary because adapting the system to the specific needs of foreign railways required the combined expertise of American Airlines and SNCF:

- American Airlines had developed extensive experience and knowledge in computerized reservation systems and yield-management techniques. This experience enabled it to customize such systems to a wide variety of applications.
- SNCF, for its part, contributed an in-depth understanding of railway services and of the users' needs, without which the American Airlines system would have been totally unsuited to use with railways.

This alliance was to open up an entirely new market for American Airlines' reservation system and it enabled SNCF to create a new activity derived from its core competency.

Box 7.3   SmithKline Beecham's Alliances with Biotech Firms

Genetic research has recently become a major field of research as well as a huge potential market for pharmaceutical
companies, giving rise to an increasing degree of cooperation
between small biotech firms and pharmaceutical giants.

The primary application of genetic research is diagnostics,
i.e., tests that will determine how a particular patient will respond to a given treatment. Genetic-based technologies are
expected to revitalize the diagnostics business (an $18 billion
industry in the mid-1990s).

To take advantage of this technology-driven opportunity,
SmithKline Beecham formed an alliance with a biotech firm,
Human Genome Sciences Inc., in 1993. SmithKline agreed to
pay HGS $125 million for exclusive access to its gene bank.
In return, HGS secured rights to all diagnostics applications
of its genes in the pact. This alliance allowed SmithKline
Beecham to become a leading player in this branch of
pharmaceuticals.

In 1997, SmithKline Beecham decided to make a further
move into genetic research and complemented its previous
alliance with HGS by creating a joint venture with Incyte Pharmaceutical Inc., a leading US biotech firm. Diadexus, the new
venture, was created on a 50–50 basis and inherited access to
two of the world's largest private libraries of genetic data,
Incyte's and the one developed by HGS and SmithKline
Beecham. In addition, SmithKline Beecham contributed the
marketing rights to five diagnostic tests for cancer and bone
diseases to the venture.

However, by 1998, Diadexus had not ventured into the actual manufacturing of diagnostics test kits, which suggests
that a third partner, capable of contributing suitable production assets, was still being looked for.

---

will form alliances with food-processing, agricultural products,
chemical and pharmaceutical companies, depending on the type of
application that their findings best fit. In genetic research, for example, a viable business can be built only by bringing together
complementary assets and skills possessed by different firms operating in various industries (see Box 7.3).

Alliances are, in cases such as this, much more effective than takeovers. Highly innovative individuals and teams usually react negatively to being integrated into large organizations. Acquiring small, innovative companies often proves disappointing; key executives and researchers tend to leave after the acquisition, thus destroying most of the innovation potential of the acquired firm.

Anticipating the Evolution and Consequences of Cross-industry Agreements

When new businesses are formed by combining skills and assets originating from several different industries, they may develop into a major new activity. More often than not, however, the expected growth of the business to be developed fizzles out and the alliance remains confined to a limited and marginal activity.

In the most successful cases, when a new business is actually created through the combination of the partners' contributions, all the necessary skills are assembled within the joint venture, which may then grow to be independent of its original parents. The joint venture is likely to become a fully fledged competitor in the new industry. Dow-Corning, for example, emerged as one of the world leaders in silicons and the two parent firms, Corning Glass and Dow Chemical, behaved as traditional shareholders in their dealings with this company rather than as industrial partners. This issue of Dow-Corning's status *vis-à-vis* its parents has taken on a critical importance since the company was sued by patients who allegedly suffered from various health disorders after receiving Dow-Corning silicon breast implants. Dow-Corning was held responsible and agreed to pay $3.2 billion in damages; as a consequence, the company filed for federal bankruptcy in 1995. Lawyers for the victims of these faulty breast implants were claiming that Corning Glass and Dow Chemical should be held liable for their joint venture's actions, while the two parent companies contended that they were merely shareholders in a limited liability company and were totally unaware of the potential hazards presented by Dow-Corning's products.

Despite the problems encountered by Dow-Corning, which incidentally were totally unrelated to the fact it was a cross-industry alliance, Corning Glass has made it something of a specialty to set up autonomous joint ventures of this kind. At the end of the 1980s, more than half of the company's earnings were derived from such cross-industry alliances. Siecor, for example, a joint venture with Siemens, has experienced considerable success and has come to dominate the optical fibers industry. In some extreme cases, the joint venture, bolstered by the development of the industry in which it operates, grows larger than the parent companies. Unilever, for instance, was created in 1929 as a joint venture by Lever Brothers from the UK, which dominated the British soap and detergent market, and Margarine Unie NV from the Netherlands, which had a strong position in Europe in oil and margarine; the two parent companies have since all but disappeared.

Experience shows, however, that most cross-industry agreements, like many new ventures in emerging businesses, do not live up to the expectations of the parent companies. The main reason for this is that the convergence of the parent firms' businesses is less extensive than initially planned and only creates small pockets of new activity. For example, many analysts had predicted that, in Europe, banking and insurance were two businesses that would rapidly blend into a new, extended financial services industry. To support this view, they pointed to the numerous mergers, acquisitions and alliances carried out in recent years by firms in these two businesses. However, despite these moves, the two sectors have remained essentially distinct and alliances formed on the premise that a whole new industry would emerge at the intersection of banking and insurance have not achieved their ambitious growth objectives. Indeed, the anticipated convergence did not encompass all segments of the insurance sector but only included life-insurance products, which are in fact a form of investment, like other financial products which are marketed by banks.

In addition, the synergies between banks and insurance companies in this segment should not be over-estimated, since life-insurance products are simple enough that banks could develop and market them on their own. Despite being allied to AXA-UAP (France's largest insurance company), Banque Nationale de Paris still chose to set up a wholly owned subsidiary, Natiovie, which offers products on its own in this area. As for the other segments in insurance—such as car insurance, home insurance, personal insurance, etc.—which do require skills specific to insurance companies (risk analysis, actuarial methods), they are of little interest to banks. Selling this kind of insurance through bank branches, which could benefit insurance companies by increasing their sales outlets and reducing their distribution costs, could even prove dangerous for banks. It creates a potential source of conflict with customers if, as is often the case, customers who have bought insurance from their bank are unsatisfied with the compensation paid to them after an accident.

Similarly, the technological convergence of computers and telecommunications has not led to a major restructuring of the two industries. Computer manufacturers and telecommunications equipment producers still operate in essentially distinct industries. A number of alliances set up to take advantage of the computer/telecom convergence have since been dissolved. This is notably the case for the alliances forged between AT&T and Olivetti, AT&T and Philips, IBM and Rolm. In parallel, firms that had chosen to merge or make acquisitions in order to address the same issue have also been led to back out; Siemens sold Nixdorf to Acer while AT&T separated from NCR.

Benefiting from the combination of complementary technologies possessed by prospective partners is often presented as the primary incentive for the formation of alliances. Alliances aimed at leveraging such synergies are said to blur the boundaries of existing industries and to partake in the creation of new businesses. Experience shows, however, that very few new businesses have been created through this process and that few cross-industry alliances have dramatically reshaped competition by redefining entire industries. In most cases, the new business which justified the formation of a cross-industry alliance remains a particular and limited segment of the previously existing businesses. The main benefits of combining complementary skills appear in fact to accrue within the boundaries of existing industries. This is why those alliances that produce a greater impact and have far-reaching consequences tend to be between competitors. Indeed, the technologies and capabilities combined in such alliances are closer and more easily compatible, while the new developments to which they lead are targeted at clearly identified markets. It is no surprise then that alliances between competitors are much more frequent than cross-industry agreements.

DIVERSIFYING THROUGH ALLIANCES

Why Use Alliances to Diversify?

Alliances are sometimes used by firms to enter businesses that are new to them. An alliance with an established player in the targeted industry makes it possible to acquire the necessary skills more rapidly. Thus, the Korean conglomerate Daewoo forged an alliance with General Motors to facilitate its development in the automobile industry. BMW teamed up with Rolls-Royce in order to enter the aircraft engine industry. In the same way, DuPont formed a joint venture with Merck to move into the rapidly growing pharmaceuticals industry (see Box 7.4).

Box 7.4   DuPont Merck Pharmaceuticals Co.

In July 1990, DuPont de Nemours and Merck announced the creation of a joint venture called DuPont Merck Pharmaceuticals. At the time, Merck was the world's largest pharmaceutical company with over $6 billion in sales. Over the previous five years, it had doubled its sales and had introduced 10 major new drugs. DuPont, the American chemical giant, was known for such breakthrough innovations as Nylon, Teflon and Lycra. Coming from the chemical sector, DuPont had been trying for many years to enter the fast-growing and highly profitable pharmaceuticals business but had encountered problems converting promising research into commercial products.

The new venture, located in Delaware adjacent to DuPont's headquarters, was equally owned by the two parents, each having equal representation on the board of directors. DuPont Merck Pharmaceuticals was created as a stand-alone company carrying out research, production and marketing activities. The research staff included 1500 people, with 400 doctoral-level scientists. The sales department employed 600 people. The company specialized in the development of drugs for treatments in four disease categories: nervous system disorders, cardiology, cancer and inflammatory conditions.

All of DuPont's assets in pharmaceuticals (patents, products under development, staff) were transferred to the joint venture, while Merck granted the joint venture a license to Sinemet, a medicine used to treat Parkinson's disease, and gave it marketing rights in Germany, France, Italy, Spain and the UK for Moduretic, a cardiovascular drug.

When the joint venture was created, the parent companies did not expect significant commercial results before the late 1990s. In 1995, however, DuPont Merck could already boast the introduction of Naltrexone, sold under the ReVia brand name, the first drug in nearly 40 years to win US government approval for treating alcoholism. In 1997, the venture achieved $1.3 billion in sales and employed a staff of 4200. Other leading DuPont Merck drugs included Coumadin, an oral anti-coagulant, Sustiva, a new class of HIV and AIDS drugs, and Cardiolite, a leading heart-imaging agent.

In May 1998, DuPont announced that it had agreed to acquire Merck's interest in the joint venture for $2.6 billion. The acquisition was expected to take place in July 1998. The co-operation between DuPont and Merck was nevertheless expected to continue in the development of drugs for the treatment of hypertension and for blood clot-preventing compounds.

While the entering partner's motivation is quite straightforward, it is not as clear why an incumbent firm would choose to assist a future competitor in entering the industry. A first motivation is financial profit. As demonstrated by the DuPont Merck example, the entering partner will, in one form or another, compensate the established partner for its assistance. Merck was paid $2.6 billion for its 50% share in a joint venture to which it had primarily contributed know-how and licenses. In addition, Merck expanded the distribution of those products for which it had granted marketing rights to the joint venture. This is another frequent motive for the incumbent partner in such alliances: by teaming up with a new entrant which is willing to invest in creating a distribution network, a brand name and a presence on the market, the established partner usually achieves expanded sales for its products at virtually no additional cost. A third motive driving certain established firms to team up with new entrants is opportunistic in nature. New entrants are often prepared to finance expensive and risky developments which established competitors would not choose to launch on their own, because these projects are not a top priority or because they are unlikely to generate adequate returns.

For example, Rolls-Royce, one of the world leaders in aircraft engines, agreed to collaborate with BMW on the development of a new family of small engines—under 20 000lbs of thrust—targeted at regional jets, because this segment was considered peripheral to its core business. In addition, Rolls-Royce decided not to enter this segment alone because the market for regional jets was very uncertain, many experts arguing that, on short-haul connections, the greater speed of jets over turboprop aircraft would not compensate for their higher cost. BMW, in contrast, was willing to commit significant resources to a risky project because it saw this as the price that had to be paid to enter the business.

The Outcome of Diversification Alliances: Creating New Competitors

When, in the mid-1980s, General Motors formed a joint venture with Daewoo to manufacture cars in Korea, it thought that this would help it achieve a significant position in the Asian market. In fact, Daewoo used the alliance to enhance its automobile technology and, by the time the partnership was terminated in 1994, had become a fully fledged player in the global auto industry. A few years later, in 1997, Daewoo beat General Motors in a bid to take over the Polish car maker FSO. Then, using its new base in Poland, Daewoo aggressively entered the Western European market, where it competed with GM by selling the Nexia model, which was in fact derived from a former Opel/Vauxhall model.

As this example demonstrates, the logical outcome of diversification alliances is for the entering partner ultimately to achieve its goal and become a competitor capable of operating on its own in the targeted industry. Such an outcome is often achieved by the entering partner taking over the joint venture. Daewoo, for example, took over GM's share in their joint venture in 1992. In the same way, DuPont acquired Merck's participation in DuPont Merck Pharmaceuticals, thus converting it into DuPont Pharmaceuticals (see Box 7.4).

How fast the entering partner will become capable of operating on its own in the targeted industry depends on how easily and rapidly it can acquire the necessary skills and capabilities. This is affected by three main factors (Hamel, 1991):

- The appropriability of the incumbent's expertise. All skills are not equally accessible. Some can easily be acquired by simply observing the activities carried out by the established partner, while others can only be captured through actually implementing those activities over long periods. It seems that more formalized skills are easier to acquire, whereas tacit skills, which are embedded in individual and organizational know-how, are much more difficult to replicate. In the case of the DuPont Merck alliance, for instance, it was probably easier for DuPont to learn how to develop new drugs than to gain the ability to market these new products to millions of physicians through a specialized network of sales representatives. New drug development is indeed based on fairly formalized technical capabilities which, in addition, are close to DuPont's expertise in chemicals; marketing pharmaceutical products, in contrast, is a capability developed through years of experience at both individual and collective levels, which is virtually impossible to codify.
- The openness and transparency of the incumbent firm. Certain companies are more able than others to protect their specific skills. This protection may result from special procedures such as the centralization of all kinds of information, extremely restrictive policies regarding training or exchanges of personnel, or a corporate culture that promotes secrecy. In certain cases, the national origin of the established partner and the working language used within the alliance may affect the ease with which learning can take place.
- The ability of the entering partner to capture and internalize new skills. When the knowledge base of the entering partner is not too distant from that of competitors in the targeted industry, learning will occur faster. In addition, certain companies manage to diffuse throughout their organization information gathered

from their involvement in cross-industry alliances. This aptitude, which derives from an internal organization and a style of management that facilitates lateral communications, the mobility of personnel, etc., greatly enhances their learning ability.

In summary, cross-industry agreements can serve two purposes: to position the partner firms favorably when converging technologies lead to the creation of a new business, or to help one of the partner firms enter into a new business with the assistance of the other ally. Overall, however, experience shows that these alliances seldom live up to the expectations of the companies that form them. When technologies or other capabilities originating from different industries are combined, they rarely develop into a major new business; in most cases, the core businesses of both partners remain distinct, while the new activities resulting from the combination of skills tend to remain peripheral and marginal. In the case of diversification alliances, the process often takes much longer than expected and the entering partner does not always succeed in becoming a credible competitor in the targeted industry. And in those cases where diversification is achieved, the incumbent partner has created a direct rival for itself.

8

Shared-supply Alliances

In 1994, for the first time, IBM and Apple both introduced a new line of personal computers driven by the very same microprocessor; the Power-PC. This chip was jointly developed by the two companies, in collaboration with Motorola. In the process, yielding to the market's demand for compatibility, IBM and Apple put an end to 10 years of bitter rivalry—with each firm seeking to impose its own specific standard in personal computing—and began collaborating on this major development.

Ten years earlier, in 1984, Siemens and Philips had decided to launch the Mega project which was to create a European source of memory chips, a key component for their respective electronic product lines. That same year, Siemens, Bull and ICL founded the European Computer Industry Research Center (ECRC), a joint research facility focusing on computer-assisted decision making. Both these alliances were aimed at challenging the domination of Japanese manufacturers in microelectronics and data processing. In the USA, the Sematech consortium was set up by 11 major American companies and the Department of Defense with a similar objective (see Box 8.3).

In the automobile industry, such alliances, aimed at jointly producing common components, date back to the early 1970s. Thus in 1971, Peugeot and Renault decided to team up in the development of a V6 engine and persuaded Volvo to join in. This PRV (short for Peugeot–Renault–Volvo) alliance pioneered what was to become a major trend in the European motor industry. For over 20 years, the PRV engine, produced in a joint plant, powered the top-of-the-range cars built by all three partner firms (see Box 8.5).

The chemical industry also provides examples of alliances set up by competitors in order to pool the production of compounds or chemical intermediates. DuPont de Nemours and Rhône-Poulenc, for instance, have created Butachimie, a joint European production facility for the manufacture of butadiene, a compound used to produce nylon (see Box 8.1).

All these examples fall into the same category of interfirm co-operation: shared-supply alliances. As discussed in Chapter 4, shared-supply alliances bring together rival firms that choose to collaborate on upstream activities while still competing head to head in the end market. Our research shows that most shared-supply alliances are formed between companies of comparable size originating in the same geographic region. Many shared-supply alliances are agreements binding European firms together, intercontinental alliances of this type being the exception.

WHY FORGE SHARED-SUPPLY ALLIANCES?

Cost-reduction Motives

Shared-supply alliances can be represented as in Figure 8.1. Their scope is limited to upstream activities, with the partner companies remaining direct competitors on the end products. The outputs of the alliance (technology, parts and components, subsystems) are shared between all allies, which subsequently incorporate them into their respective final products.

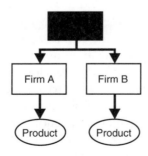

Figure 8.1   Shared-supply alliance

These alliances are forged "behind the scenes"; they are virtually invisible to customers. Each partner firm continues to market its own products which remain specific to it and compete against all other similar products, including those of the other partners in the alliance. This explains the ease with which public authorities give their blessing to such agreements, encourage them or even initiate them. Indeed, without hampering competition on the market, shared-supply alliances help enhance the competitiveness of all the firms involved. MITI in Japan, for example, has for many years been encouraging joint R&D programs between Japanese firms operating in the same industry in order to improve their competitive position relative to their foreign competitors. This model has been emulated in Europe, where joint technology-development programs have become legion since the early 1980s (Dumont, 1990). Initially reluctant, US authorities finally followed suit in 1984, when the National Cooperative Research Act was passed. This loosened up anti-trust regulations, made it legal for competitors to engage in cooperative R&D and made it possible to create so-called pre-competitive alliances. This new legislation was meant to level the field and provide American firms with the same advantages as those that their Japanese competitors had enjoyed for many years.

Paradoxically, the Japanese government only funded about 20% of the national R&D effort in the 1970s and 1980s, a figure considerably lower than government financing of technology in the West (approximately 50% in the USA or France and 40% in Germany or the UK). But MITI was nevertheless very successful at enhancing the technical capabilities and competitiveness of many Japanese industries (Collins and Doorley, 1991). It carried out this task not by substituting government R&D funds for corporate funds, or government laboratories for company-run research facilities, but rather by negotiating and coordinating the R&D work carried out by Japanese companies in order to avoid duplication and to direct all R&D efforts towards a set of common, clearly defined goals.

From the firms' point of view, the main incentive to enter into shared-supply alliances is to pool resources in an activity situated upstream from their main business. More precisely, a shared-supply alliance will be formed when the critical size in this upstream activity is greater than the volume of each partner's downstream business. Some technological developments, for example, are too expensive and too risky to be undertaken by a single firm, even if it is large and has a significant share of the market. Under such circumstances, it may make sense to form shared-supply alliances devoted to R&D. In other contexts, the problem may be cost-effectively to produce a component for which the minimum efficient size is greater than the individual requirements of each company involved. In this case, a manufacturing shared-supply alliance—for example, a jointly owned engine plant supplying several auto makers—may be an attractive alternative.

It should nevertheless be noted that the "size" factor mentioned above is only a necessary, not a sufficient, condition for setting up a shared-supply alliance. The critical size issue could indeed effectively be addressed through outsourcing. For example, in the case of the above-mentioned Philips/Siemens partnership formed to produce memory chips, the simplest, and probably cheapest, solution for both companies to procure these chips would have been to turn to one of the Japanese suppliers that, at the time, dominated the market. More generally, all the shared-supply alliances referred to in the introduction to this chapter could have been substituted by procurement contracts; each partner firm could have turned to an external supplier of its choice or, alternatively, one of these firms could have chosen to manufacture the component in question and supply it to the others. Opting for an alliance, therefore, is by no means the only option and is often not the best option.

In fact, considering that alliances between rivals are much more difficult to manage and have farther-reaching consequences than straightforward supply contracts, they should be avoided unless they offer significant advantages. In particular, mere cost-cutting objectives are not sufficient to justify the formation of shared-supply alliances. Therefore, it is only in a company's best interest to opt for an alliance of this type if it also enables it to achieve particular strategic objectives. An obvious motive for both European and American firms to form alliances to produce electronic chips was to reduce their dependence on Japanese suppliers that dominated the market to such an extent that this was thought to be threatening. In addition, the capabilities required to produce semiconductors were assumed also to be critical in downstream activities. And, last but not least, most of the Japanese suppliers of chips also competed in many of these downstream markets, thus making them simultaneously vendors and competitors, not an easy combination to deal with.

Strategic Objectives

As cost-cutting objectives alone do not justify entering into shared-supply alliances, firms must carefully assess the strategic advantages they expect to derive from collaboration to make sure that these advantages outweigh the organizational costs of the alliance and the risks it implies, in particular the risk of leaking valuable technological expertise to rival firms.

In the case of the alliance between Rhône-Poulenc and DuPont de Nemours (see Box 8.1), all the economic conditions for setting up a shared-supply partnership were fulfilled. Both companies wanted to produce nylon in Europe with a new technology that required the use of butadiene, an intermediate chemical, as an input to the process. However, the minimum efficient size of a butadiene plant was significantly greater than the requirements of either company. Combining these requirements made it possible to saturate the capacity of the plant to be set up in Europe, while procuring butadiene from the same jointly owned source in no way prevented DuPont and Rhône-Poulenc from competing in the downstream nylon market.

The size imperative in the production of butadiene did not, however, necessarily have to lead to the formation of an alliance. Rhône-Poulenc could have set up a factory of its own and supplied DuPont's European operations, or vice versa.

Entrusting Rhône-Poulenc with the production of butadiene, through a licensing agreement similar to the one signed many years previously for the production of nylon with the traditional process, would have been incompatible with DuPont's expansion strategy in Europe. Indeed DuPont, which was then only active in the European nylon market through imports as well as through a number of licensing agreements (with Rhône-Poulenc, ICI, BASF and Monsanto), wanted to establish manufacturing operations in Europe. For DuPont, in fact, implementing the butadiene-based process offered an opportunity to initiate this new European strategy, with

---

Box 8.1   Butachimie

Butachimie was set up as a joint venture by DuPont de Nemours and Rhône-Poulenc to supply both partner firms with butadiene, an intermediate chemical used in an innovative process for producing nylon. This process, an alternative to the original technique invented before the Second World War, was first implemented by DuPont in North America. It made it possible to decrease the production cost of nylon by cutting the cost of the raw material (butadiene was cheaper than benzene and propylene which were used in the traditional process). However, producing butadiene required large up-front capital investments. Thus, only large-volume production could make the butadiene process more efficient than the traditional process.

DuPont was able to implement the new technology profitably in North America, thanks to its dominant market share in nylon. However, its presence in Europe was not significant enough to support a local butadiene-producing facility. On the other hand, Rhône-Poulenc—one of DuPont's major European licensees for the traditional nylon process—had decided to expand its nylon production capacity and wanted to use this opportunity to acquire the new technology. However, Rhône-Poulenc's requirements were also below the minimum efficient scale for butadiene production.

The agreement to set up a jointly owned plant was signed in 1974. This agreement stipulated that Butachimie was to supply DuPont's and Rhône-Poulenc's European operations, with the output of the plant being equally shared between the two partners. The agreement did not encompass the production of nylon itself and the two partners continued to compete openly on the final market. The creation of the Butachimie joint venture did not affect DuPont's US activities; in North America, it continued to use its butadiene process autonomously. In 1998, Butachimie was still operating successfully.

---

the lower costs made possible by the new technology giving it a competitive edge over its rivals that used the traditional process.

The other alternative, a DuPont facility in Europe that would also supply Rhône-Poulenc, would have been particularly risky, for two main reasons:

- First, the new plant would have depended very heavily on Rhône-Poulenc purchases to achieve break-even. It was therefore essential that Rhône-Poulenc be bound through a long-term commitment; creating a joint venture in which Rhône-Poulenc had a 50% stake gave it a vested interest in the success of the venture and thus eliminated any temptation to behave opportunistically.
- Second, with no prior manufacturing experience in Europe, it was difficult for DuPont to start a large-scale operation from scratch. Forming a joint venture with Rhône-Poulenc made it possible to take advantage of the partner's knowledge of labor relations in Europe, its long-standing relationships with suppliers and subcontractors, etc.

As for Rhône-Poulenc, although it helped a major competitor strengthen its position in Europe, the alliance created the opportunity to acquire a new technology and gave it a significant advantage over its other rivals in Europe.

This DuPont–Rhône-Poulenc case illustrates the fact that, despite their pre-competitive nature, shared-supply agreements can have a long-term impact on the competitive positions of the partner companies. This impact is often overlooked, most companies focusing exclusively on the short-term economic benefits of entering into such shared supply partnerships.

Working with competitors on technology or components inevitably jeopardizes product differentiation. Indeed, the end products of all partners will incorporate common components or technologies derived from the alliance, which reduces the range of attributes on which they can offer specific features. For example, auto makers that join forces to produce common parts more economically are confronted with this problem: when two competing models are powered by the same engine, they can no longer differentiate themselves on the basis of horsepower, speed, fuel efficiency, etc. Therefore shared-supply alliances are primarily formed to produce low-visibility parts and components that go largely unnoticed by most consumers.

Such concerns about product differentiation led to the early termination of the alliance that Fiat and Saab had set up to jointly develop a platform for their up-market vehicles. As the project neared completion, Saab, which prided itself on its exclusive image, realized that pursuing collaboration beyond a certain stage would result in the production of visibly similar cars. The alliance was thus terminated earlier than initially planned. An informed observer, however, could notice a certain likeness between the Saab 9000 and the Fiat Croma, the two models derived from this temporary collaboration.

Even shared-supply alliances limited to pre-competitive research can have a major impact on the level of differentiation within the industry. When competitors from the same geographic region (Europe, for example) join forces to develop new technology, their initial aim may be collectively to strengthen their position relative to powerful foreign rivals (Japanese or American, for example). This, however, will impede each ally from developing individual innovations and finding specific market niches. Shared-supply agreements thus tend to level out the technology and innovation of the various competitors and to commoditize the industry. Consortia formed to define common standards in industries such as video recording, data processing and high-definition TV tend to "freeze" competition on technology and to shift rivalry in the industry to other factors such as costs, quality, manufacturing processes and marketing. At times, shared-supply alliances may even be used as a weapon to smother innovation in rival firms. In particular, by teaming up with smaller competitors, a market leader can lead them to concentrate on a given technology, thereby deterring them from exploring alternative, more original paths that might eventually challenge its dominant position. At the very least, pre-competitive R&D alliances tend to diffuse technological skills and innovations within the industry. The Sematech consortium mentioned earlier, which was set up to help the entire American electronics industry fend off Japanese competition, was blamed by the more innovative competitors for allowing other partners to keep a close eye on their innovations (see Box 8.3).

In summary, while sharing costs is indeed the primary objective of shared-supply alliances, firms considering the creation of such alliances should not focus solely on this issue. Clarifying why an alliance is the best possible option for achieving the desired cost reductions, anticipating all the likely side-effects of collaboration and scrutinizing what are the true agendas of the other partner firms are all critical. Even smoothly running shared-supply alliances raise difficult management problems; if hidden agendas interfere with the efficient operation of the project, the added costs of managing a complex organization are likely to outweigh the benefits derived from the partnership.

While all shared-supply alliances raise a common set of strategic issues, a distinction should be made, when it comes to implementation, between partnerships limited to R&D and alliances that involve manufacturing activities. Jointly managing manufacturing facilities in this second case raises specific problems that must be contemplated from the very beginning.

Our own research suggests that two-thirds of shared-supply alliances are R&D agreements, while only one-third involve manufacturing operations.

HOW TO MANAGE R&D AGREEMENTS

Setting up a Joint R&D Facility or Splitting up R&D Projects among the Partners

In most R&D alliances, research projects are divided up between the partners rather than carried out in a joint facility (see Chapter 4). The allied firms form the alliance to share R&D expenses and to take advantage of their complementary skills; however, as they are also rivals, it is critical that, despite collaboration, they retain their core know-how and avoid technological leakage. Setting up a joint facility to implement the project tends to externalize the technology that is developed and, in addition, creates opportunities for inter-partner learning. Thus, R&D alliances are often implemented through informal structures, such as steering committees, that meet periodically to coordinate the research activities carried out at each partner's facilities.

The JESSI alliance (see Box 8.2), a European Union sponsored research agreement in semiconductors is a good example of how such alliances are often managed. In JESSI projects, no common facility was set up and no legal structure was created. This organizational choice, by which all joint research work was avoided, made it possible to define and achieve joint research objectives while limiting undesired technology transfers.

Box 8.2   JESSI and MEDEA

Munich-based JESSI, the Joint European Submicron Silicon Program, was an eight-year European research program launched in 1989 to promote Europe's independence of the USA and Japan in semiconductor technology. The aim of the program, organized under the EUREKA (European Research and Coordination Agency) umbrella, was to favor cooperation between over 200 firms from 16 European countries. The agreement stipulated that research projects eligible for JESSI funding had to be submitted by consortia of firms that agreed to collaborate with one another. Approved projects were to be conducted directly by the partner companies in their own research facilities. Collaboration was thus limited to dividing up the research work among the partners and coordinating their activities. Results were then to be shared through licensing and patent agreements.

Four areas of research were covered by JESSI: semiconductor technology in dynamic random access memory (DRAM), static random memory, erasable programmable read-only memory (EPROM) and logic chips. The $4 billion cost of the program was split between the European Commission (25%), the national European governments (25%) and the partner companies (50%). All the companies participating in the program were European except for IBM, which was apparently looking for European alliances against Japanese manufacturers.

JESSI started with difficulties, however, and after a year and a half its credibility was flagging. On the companies' side, Philips had to reduce its commitment because of financial problems, while UK-based ICL was expelled from key projects after it was acquired by Fujitsu. On the institutional side, European funding was severely cut, which made JESSI combine or drop many of its 70 projects and reduce its $540 million 1992 budget by 25%. In 1993, EC funding only accounted for 12% of the total cost of the program, national governments filling in the gap and financing 38% of the budget. Despite JESSI, Europe still lagged far behind Japan and the USA in microelectronics; by 1992, the Japanese had developed prototypes of 64 Mb/s DRAM and held 90% of the market for memory chips, while the Americans held 80% of the market for processors.

Nevertheless, notable successes were achieved: by 1992, JESSI had yielded a 16 Mb/s EPROM, developed under the leadership of ST Microelectronics, and a 16 Mb/s DRAM, under that of Siemens. A new phase of the program began, concentrating on the development of chips for high-definition television (HDTV), on digital audio broadcasting, on digital cellular telephones, and on advanced integrated services digital networks (ISDN).

By the time the program was completed, at the end of 1996, JESSI was considered a success: the technology gap had been significantly reduced and three generations of CMOS technologies had been developed in Europe. Overall, the partners in the program acknowledged that JESSI had significantly lowered their research costs and improved the efficiency of their research efforts.

In 1997, a successor to JESSI was launched: MEDEA (Micro-Electronics Development for European Applications), which was more market driven than JESSI. A four-year project, MEDEA was endowed with a $2.7 billion budget, covered 35% by Germany, 29% by France, 19% by the Netherlands and the remainder by other European countries. MEDEA was expected to continue JESSI's work by fostering the development of new-generation CMOS processors. Seven companies were involved in the initial MEDEA projects: Siemens, Philips, ST Microelectronics, ASM International, Bosch, Alcatel and Bull.

Box 8.3   MCC and Sematech

MCC

In 1982, 16 computer and electronics companies formed MCC (the Microelectronics and Computer Technology Corporation), based in Austin, Texas. MCC was the first major collaboration between US corporations on long-term research and no foreign company was allowed to participate in the program. Bobby Ray Inman, former director of the National

Security Agency and deputy director of the Central Intelligence Agency, was appointed as MCC's first president. MCC's mission was to enhance the competitive position of the US computer and microelectronics industries by sponsoring and engaging in collaborative research programs, and by licensing the results of these cooperative efforts to its members.

By 1998, MCC had 19 shareholders (including General Electric, Hewlett-Packard, Lockheed, Motorola and Texas Instruments) and 11 associates (including Boeing, Intel, Lucent and NASA). Associates had the right to join existing projects and participate in new project selection, to share royalty distributions and to license technologies from any MCC program 36 months after final release. Shareholders added to these rights a seat on the board of directors and a share in MCC's equity.

MCC research projects only dealt with pre-competitive technology, i.e., technology with a time horizon of three to five years. In addition to collaborative long-term research, MCC also carried out single-client R&D projects, the results of which remained proprietary to the contracting member firm. A typical project had four phases. First, member requirements led to a list of R&D projects to be pursued. Second, consortial studies were conducted to establish technical feasibility. These studies were funded from membership fees—a $250 000 one-time fee or an $85 000 yearly fee for shareholders and $35 000 for associates. All members could participate in the four to six studies conducted annually. No intellectual property was generated at this stage. The third step was the consortial project itself. Such projects, aimed at the development of business-driven applications, were then funded individually by interested participants—usually four to five—and had an average duration of two to three years. This process was based on collaboration between the participating companies and MCC staff. Intellectual property resulting from the project was owned and controlled by project participants. The last phase was the return of technological and financial benefits to member companies.

Sematech

Created in 1987, Sematech is an alliance of 11 American companies (IBM, DEC, Lucent, Motorola, Texas Instruments,

Hewlett-Packard, etc.) and the US Department of Defense (Spencer and Grindley, 1993). The Sematech consortium operates its own R&D facilities, also located in Austin, Texas; by the mid-1990s, it employed over 700 people, including 220 employees on assignment from the partner companies, and had an annual budget of $200 million. While the operating cost of Sematech was initially shared by the member companies and the federal government, as of 1996 the whole cost was covered by member companies.

The partnership was formed with the aim of improving manufacturing technologies and processes in the American semiconductor industry. Sematech's primary objective was to improve collaboration between semiconductor producers and their equipment suppliers. From this perspective, one-third of the consortium's budget was devoted to the development of manufacturing equipment in partnership with the equipment suppliers. The testing and certification of new equipment to be used by the partner firms were carried out at Sematech's facilities in Austin. Centralizing decisions on the development of new equipment and carrying out testing in a joint facility substantially reduced costs by eliminating unnecessary duplication among the partner firms.

Since it was created, Sematech has facilitated the introduction of new manufacturing techniques in the production facilities of most partners. However, in order to carry out its mission, Sematech was forced to alter significantly its approach on inter-partner collaboration. The initial project was to create a collaborative structure in which the member companies could work together at jointly developing and improving their manufacturing technologies. It rapidly became obvious that the partner firms were reluctant to share what they perceived as being valuable know-how. The more technologically advanced members of the consortium feared that this collaboration would disseminate proprietary technologies to less advanced competitors. Thus, Sematech shifted its focus towards improving collaboration between the member companies and their equipment vendors. Sematech has in fact become a structure through which "vertical" cooperation is organized, rather than a consortium in which "horizontal" cooperation between competitors is carried out.

Despite its advantages, such a loose organization creates few incentives to focus efforts and resources on the jointly defined objectives. All partners tend to give higher priority to their own research projects while constantly pushing the collaborative work on to the back burner. Unstructured R&D projects thus tend to drag on and often result in somewhat limited and disappointing outcomes.

Some R&D agreements do lead to the creation of a joint R&D facility in which all the collaborative work is carried out. Two such cases are the notorious MCC (Microelectronics and Computer Technology Corporation) and Sematech (SEmiconductor MAnufacturing TECHnology initiative) alliances (see Box 8.3). In the mid-1990s, MCC employed several hundred full-time researchers, most of whom worked at the joint venture's premises in Austin (Texas); MCC owned patents and licensed its technologies, primarily to its parent companies. Sematech was an even larger operation with an annual budget of approximately $200 million, close to 1000 employees and its own state-of-the-art research facility, also located in Austin (Texas).

While setting up a joint research organization like MCC or Sematech creates an environment in which efforts are more focused and results oriented, it can also become a source of concern for those partners that possess valuable proprietary technologies and might fear that these technologies could be disseminated to competitors—albeit partners in the venture—if they are shared with the consortium. On the other hand, if the partner firms are reluctant to transfer their expertise to the joint operation, they may undermine the value of the collaborative research that is carried out, thus making the whole alliance pointless.

Improving the Efficiency of Joint R&D while Protecting Proprietary Know-how

For R&D agreements to be successful, a basic contradiction must be overcome. On the one hand, as success is often measured through tangible results, there is an incentive for all parties involved, i.e., the representatives of the parent companies as well as those in charge of the joint R&D project, increasingly to push the partnership downstream into applied research and product development. On the other hand, competitive concerns make it difficult for firms to collaborate openly and effectively if the project is not restricted to upstream knowledge creation, the impact of which is only long term; more applied research that is likely to have a significant competitive impact in the shorter term is seen as too sensitive to be shared openly with competitors.

In alliances organized on the basis of a distribution of research tasks among the allied firms, when it comes to applying the jointly developed concepts to prototypes or to product development, deciding which of the partners will do the job becomes problematic; indeed, entrusting a partner with an experimental project is tantamount to subsidizing a competitor's new product development process. In those alliances where a joint facility has been set up, entrusting this entity with product development tasks can result in externalizing strategic know-how and making it available to all partner firms. The evolution of Sematech over time illustrates this idea (see Box 8.3).

Thus, these competitive concerns strongly restrain the value of joint R&D projects. Only those projects that have little influence on critical aspects of the business are given the latitude to proceed smoothly, while potentially more interesting projects are often hindered by mutual suspicion. It often happens that the partner firms discontinue joint research rather than letting one of them derive greater benefits from it than the others. This unproductive outcome prevents most R&D agreements from leading to the development of more substantial new know-how that could result from "cross-fertilizing" the allies' competencies.

As some technological leakage is practically unavoidable if interesting joint R&D projects are to be carried out successfully, it is often more advisable to take advantage of this context to learn as much as possible than to adopt an overly defensive behavior and try to protect proprietary knowledge at all costs. For example, by simply analyzing the research topics suggested by the other partners, it is possible to gain a good understanding of their technical interests. This implies that extreme caution should be used when making proposals for joint research; more importantly, competitors' proposals should be monitored by experienced engineers, capable of interpreting the other partners' intentions. Lastly, a firm must not rely too heavily on the alliance for developing its technological base. On the contrary, skills acquired through the partnership must be internalized and combined with proprietary knowledge in order to enhance the firm's capabilities. Indeed, it has been shown that in order to benefit fully from collaborative R&D, a firm should invest heavily to develop internally advanced technical skills in the same area (Cohen and Levinthal, 1990; Mothe and Quélin, 1998). Without going so far as to duplicate the work entrusted to the alliance, which would be tantamount to writing off all possible benefits in advance, it is vital to maintain independent expertise alongside the jointly held technology.

HOW TO MANAGE MANUFACTURING SHARED-SUPPLY ALLIANCES

Beware of Organizational Inertia

Manufacturing shared-supply alliances, in which the partner firms jointly develop and manufacture a component or subassembly, frequently last a long time. Our research suggests that the longest-living alliances are to be found among these manufacturing shared-supply partnerships (Dussauge and Garrette, 1998). This could be interpreted as evidence of the greater success encountered by shared-supply alliances when compared to other types of alliances. Unfortunately, this observation is misleading; in the case of alliances, duration and survival are not reliable indicators of success. In many cases, longevity stems from the barriers preventing dissolution rather than from the performance of joint operations. Shared-supply alliances—more than other types of strategic alliances—are subject to inertia and may continue operating for many years after they have outlived their purpose.

By their very nature, manufacturing shared-supply alliances are inevitably plagued by the lack of flexibility typical of all vertical integration strategies. Indeed, these alliances result in the creation of an "in-house", albeit shared, supplier. The partner firms thus become captive customers of their alliance and isolate it from the harsh realities of the marketplace. In the long run, this often proves to be unsustainable. Even if changes in technology or in demand make the components manufactured by the alliance obsolete or

Box 8.4   The Peugeot/Renault Joint Ventures

The broad collaborative agreement signed by Peugeot and Renault in 1966 was the first of a long series of alliances subsequently formed in Europe by automobile makers. This agreement was implemented through several shared-supply joint ventures, many of which were still in operation in the late 1990s, despite the fact that the initial agreement was terminated as early as 1974.

The FM Engine Plant

When it started operating in the early 1970s, the FM (Française de Mécanique) plant was the largest engine factory in Europe; it had a production capacity of 5000 engines per day and employed over 6000 people. The aim of both partners was to optimize costs through increased economies of scale and the use of state-of-the-art technology. Investments and ownership were shared by Peugeot and Renault on a 50–50 basis. The FM plant was highly integrated and included a large foundry operation, tooling units and engine assembly lines. However, the scope of FM was limited to manufacturing. Engine development was carried out directly by the R&D departments of Peugeot and Renault. As far as day-to-day operations were concerned, FM was quite independent: the board members delegated by Peugeot and Renault would only get involved when productivity, quality and scheduling issues were discussed at the monthly board meetings.

Twenty-five years later, the success of this venture seemed indisputable: FM was still a 50–50 joint venture, it manufactured 6000 engines a day and employed 5500 people. Despite this apparent success, the evolution of the joint venture's activities over time suggests that its very purpose is questionable. Initially, it had been planned that FM would produce common engines that would be fitted on both Peugeot and Renault cars. In fact, only the very first engine produced at FM fitted this pattern. All other engines subsequently manufactured in the joint venture were specific to either Peugeot or Renault. Indeed, after their initial agreement, Peugeot and

Renault were unable to agree on common specifications and therefore chose to design their own engines. FM rapidly became a *de facto* subcontractor to which Peugeot and Renault entrusted the production of equipment specific to each of them. In this context, the economies of scale resulting from the joint venture, if any, were necessarily very limited.

The STA Automatic Transmission Joint Venture

Renault and Peugeot created STA in 1969; Renault owned 75% of the equity and Peugeot 25%. Very soon, Peugeot lost interest in this operation and never procured automatic gearboxes from it, relying instead on outside sources, such as ZF. Renault, which initially did procure automatic transmissions from STA, eventually chose to form another alliance with Volkswagen to produce large quantities of such equipment for its US operations (Renault acquired American Motors Corp. in 1979 to enter the North American market and withdrew in 1985). This agreement, however, did not lead to the creation of a joint venture; each partner manufactured some of the parts and both firms assembled complete gearboxes.

Despite its unsuccessful history, the STA alliance was revived in 1995 when Peugeot and Renault, anticipating an increase in the demand for automatic cars in Europe, decided to produce a new automatic gearbox.

Chausson

In 1972, Renault and Peugeot jointly acquired Chausson, one of their subcontractors. Their objective was to pool the assembly of short production-run vehicles, such as delivery vans, coupés and convertibles. Indeed, low-volume models could not be efficiently manufactured in their existing plants which were geared to mass production.

At the time it became a Peugeot–Renault joint venture, Chausson was the largest assembler of delivery vans in France and also produced a range of automotive parts. The company employed 17 000 people, operated six plants and ten foreign subsidiaries. By 1993, Chausson employed a mere 2900 people, operated two obsolete factories and had sold all its subsidiaries abroad as well as its automotive parts business; in September of the same year, the company filed for bankruptcy. In the wake of this, massive layoffs took place, the social climate deteriorated and strike followed strike until, finally, the company was dismantled.

Chausson's unfortunate fate can be traced back to Renault and Peugeot's declining interest in their joint venture. Indeed, both firms chose to produce most of their low-volume vehicles without collaborating with one another and without relying on Chausson:

- As early as 1976, Peugeot teamed up with Fiat to produce delivery vans (the Peugeot J5, Citroën C25, Fiat Ducato models) in a factory in southern Italy. In 1994, Peugeot and Fiat extended their alliance to the joint production of passenger minivans (see Box 9.2 in Chapter 9).
- In the meanwhile, Renault signed an agreement with Daf for the development of a new range of delivery vans (this agreement was never implemented because of Daf's bankruptcy). Renault also chose to collaborate with Matra-Automobile to produce its Espace minivan (see Box 10.3 in Chapter 10).

Disagreement between the allies over the management of Chausson degenerated into open conflict in 1993 when Peugeot refused to shoulder its share of the financial burden of the 1991 and 1993 redundancy schemes. Renault ended up suing Peugeot on this issue. Despite their lack of interest in Chausson and their total disagreement about how to manage the company, it still took the partner firms several years to terminate their joint venture.

uncompetitive, the partner firms are not in a position to stop purchasing from their joint venture, as their agreement usually includes a provision by which they commit to procure certain quantities of the components from it. This, in turn, tends to delay any corrective action concerning the features or conditions of production of the common components. The lack of flexibility generally induced by vertical integration is exacerbated in shared-supply alliances by the fact that, for corrective action to be taken, all partners must fully agree on what is to be done. The negotiation process that takes place between the partners inevitably slows down any attempt at fixing the problem. The long-term developments of the Peugeot/Renault joint ventures (see Box 8.4) provide a clear illustration of this difficulty.

It should be added that the way in which most manufacturing shared-supply alliances are organized makes them even less flexible by creating significant exit barriers. Indeed, the organization that appears to meet the initial objectives of the alliance best is to set up a joint manufacturing facility for the common components, thus making it possible to benefit fully from scale economies and experience. All alternative forms of organization—such as splitting production between the partners (as in the Renault/Volkswagen alliance for automatic gear boxes mentioned in Box 8.4)—are necessarily less efficient than concentrating production in a single plant, where all the expertise is available on site. But once a joint manufacturing facility has been set up, this makes it difficult to terminate the alliance because both the physical assets and the human resources committed to the partnership would have to be redeployed or abandoned.

The broad collaborative agreement signed by Peugeot and Renault in 1966 (see Box 8.4) led to the formation of several manufacturing joint ventures. Most of these joint ventures were still operating in the late 1990s, despite the fact that the Peugeot–Renault agreement was terminated as early as 1974. Most of these joint subsidiaries, which still employed over 7000 people in 1998, were no longer used for joint productions. Instead, in order to maintain a minimum level of activity, each partner provided them with a certain amount of subcontracting work. These joint ventures were no longer critical to the business of either partner and were not particularly efficient, but they were not restructured or closed down because Peugeot and Renault could not agree on the exact actions to be taken. The existence of jointly owned assets as well as the social cost of eliminating several thousand jobs have created major hurdles in the process of terminating these partnerships. In contrast, other Peugeot–Renault agreements that were organized on the basis of a division of labor and did not lead to the creation of separate joint entities were dismantled very rapidly after the overall alliance between the two firms fell apart.

Not all manufacturing shared-supply alliances necessarily encounter the fate we have just described. To avoid such an outcome, the allied firms must abide by two basic principles:

- First, it is vital that the partners make sure that their requirements concerning the component to be produced jointly are similar enough, and will remain so in the long term.
- Second, the partner firms must organize the alliance in an appropriate way. Our observations suggest that while it is preferable to divide technological developments between the partners, a concentration of manufacturing in a single facility is needed to achieve cost-effectiveness, which is the primary objective of the alliance.

Control for the Long-term Convergence of the Partners' Requirements

For manufacturing shared-supply alliances to be effective, it is absolutely critical that the partner firms maintain identical requirements in the long run. If at some point the allied firms can no longer agree on the exact specifications of the components or subassemblies they procure from their joint venture, the alliance loses its original purpose and slips into a downward spiral of failure, as described above.

While, at the negotiation stage, it is fairly easy for prospective partners to agree fully on the exact definition of the components to be produced jointly, this initial agreement frequently deteriorates over time. In particular, it is when the joint components or subassemblies have to be upgraded or redesigned that most problems arise. Indeed, as each partner firm implements its own specific market strategy, their respective product ranges are likely to evolve in different directions and, over time, will call for increasingly different components. When this is the case, the partners find it difficult to agree on new specifications for the new generation of their joint components. If a compromise is reached, there is a significant risk that the upgraded common components fail to meet the requirements of either partner adequately. If the partners fail to reach such a compromise and require different versions of the common components, the very purpose of the alliance is defeated. Evidence shows that manufacturing shared-supply alliances tend to last for long periods. It is therefore important for would-be partner firms to make sure that there is enough of a "strategic fit" between them, that their respective product lines will evolve in compatible ways and that the components they will need in the predictable future remain similar enough to justify the commitment of significant resources to the creation of shared facilities.

How durable the strategic fit between the partners may be depends on the industry in which the alliance is formed and, more specifically, on the stability of the technological environment of that industry. One of the reasons that the PRV joint venture operated quite successfully for over 20 years is the relatively slow pace of technical evolution in automobile engines (see Box 8.5); thus, the same basic engine was able to power three successive generations of automobiles, with only minor adaptations and upgrades. In contrast, in the case of MPI (see Box 8.6), computer disk drives have undergone such rapid change that the products manufactured by the joint venture rapidly became obsolete and the partners failed to agree about how to update them.

In addition to agreeing on the technical specifications of the components manufactured jointly, the partners must also require compatible volumes of these components over the long term. If the purchases of one of the partners increase too extensively, thus making it possible to achieve the minimum efficient scale for the production of the considered component, it could be tempting for this partner to pull out of the alliance and set up a fully owned production facility. In the case of the MPI alliance (see Box 8.6), when Control Data entered the minicomputer segment, its requirements for computer disk drives became so much larger than those of the other partners that its incentive to continue collaborating faded away. In addition to the specification problems mentioned above, this contributed to the demise of the alliance.

The IBM/Toshiba partnership in flat color screens for laptops provides an extreme example of just where the partners' diverging strategies can lead an alliance. In 1985, the two rivals decided to create DTI (Display Technology Inc.), a 50–50 joint venture located

Box 8.5   The PRV V6 Engine

In the early 1970s, Peugeot, Renault and Volvo needed a V6 engine to power their top-of-the-line sedans. However, in this segment, the sales that each of these car makers could hope to achieve were too small to allow for the efficient production of six-cylinder engines. Thus, in November 1971, the three firms created a joint venture—known as Franco-Suédoise de Moteurs–Peugeot Renault Volvo (FSM–PRV)—to produce a common engine that each partner could fit on its own cars. The joint venture's equity was equally shared by Peugeot, Renault and Volvo. Production began in 1974. The agreement was renewed in 1983. In 1989, Volvo decided to withdraw from the joint venture, while remaining a PRV customer.

The PRV engine equipped such models as the Volvo 760 and 780, Peugeot 505 and 605, Renault Safrane and Espace and Citroën XM. PRV engines were even sold to Chrysler. By 1995, more than 700 000 engines had been produced; 36% of these were supplied to Volvo, 30% to Renault, 22% to Peugeot, 10% to Chrysler and the remaining 2% to other car makers such as Lancia, Venturi, etc.

The development work on the PRV engines was split between the parent companies and carried out in their own R&D departments. The role of the joint venture was to coordinate the R&D activity and to manufacture the engine; it was also in charge of procurements and industrial investment decisions. More specifically, each new version or upgrade of the engine had to be unanimously approved by the partners and its development was then entrusted to one of the allies' R&D departments. Great care was taken to balance the workload among the three partners, while entrusting the development of a particular version of the engine to the partner that would end up being its primary customer.

Two committees, formed with executives from the parent companies, were created to define FSM–PRV's overall policy and to organize work within the joint venture:

- The PRV-Studies, Research & Development Decision Committee selected and allocated the research budgets devoted to PRV projects.

- The board of directors decided on FSM–PRV's production policy and investments. The chairman of FSM–PRV was chosen alternately from Peugeot or Renault; its managing director was appointed by Volvo.

Volvo's withdrawal from the alliance in 1989 was driven by the fact that the various versions of the PRV V6 engine all ended up being a compromise between the partners' different requirements. In addition, Volvo's increasing use of V6 engines in its product range, as well as the development of more flexible manufacturing techniques, made it economically viable for the Swedish car maker to produce its own engine. In contrast, Peugeot and Renault, whose purchases of V6 engines were more limited, decided to extend the alliance and develop an entirely new common six-cylinder engine.

Box 8.6   Magnetic Peripherals Inc.

The Magnetic Peripherals Inc. (MPI) joint venture was created in 1975 by Control Data, Honeywell and Bull. The distribution of equity reflected the value of the assets contributed by the different parent companies. Control Data, which had contributed most of the manufacturing assets, dominated the joint venture with a 75% stake. The goal of the alliance was jointly to produce disk systems to be incorporated in the mainframe computers manufactured by each partner. These systems accounted for up to 25% of the total cost of a computer and were subject to significant scale economies. This created very favorable economic conditions that allowed the partnership to work smoothly. In addition, the joint venture was clearly dominated and managed by one partner, Control Data, which eliminated most of the inefficiencies usually associated with shared management. Over time, however, significant problems arose, which eventually led Control Data to buy its partners out in 1987.

At the outset, the partners' objectives converged perfectly. Purchasing disk systems from MPI contributed to cost reduction and helped the partner firms compete successfully, notably against IBM, the industry leader. The objectives of the partners started to diverge, however, when Control Data decided to supply disk systems to other computer manufacturers, in particular to minicomputer and PC makers, two rapidly growing segments of the industry. This created new requirements that were not fully compatible with the internal needs of Bull and Honeywell. Also, the rationale for collaborating in the production of disk systems for mainframe computers tended to disappear over time; the industry had progressively de-integrated and there now existed a large enough number of low-cost and reliable suppliers. External procurements also offered a flexibility that the alliance could not provide. In addition, the way in which MPI was managed further contributed to the termination of the alliance.

Control Data's domination over the alliance increasingly led MPI to neglect the specific requirements of either Honeywell or Bull. In particular, the two minority partners felt that Control Data utilized the joint venture to implement its own R&D program, having the other two partners formally approve it while limiting their actual influence to a minimum. Convergence among partners was thus gradually "forced" by the dominant ally.

From an operational point of view, controlling costs and defining a consistent transfer price policy was complicated by the fact that the factories contributed to the joint venture by the various partners were based in different places: Heppenheim in Germany for Bull, Minneapolis for Control Data, and Oklahoma City for Honeywell. The plant which first started to manufacture a particular system rapidly managed to decrease its production costs thanks to the total requirements of the three partners. When the manufacture of that particular system was extended to another plant—in order to optimize capacity utilization and to bring the production of components closer to where they were to be used—costs were initially much higher at this new location. This created endless negotiations on transfer prices: if transfer prices were based on actual costs, partners purchasing from second-source plants felt that they were treated unfairly; if transfer prices were based on the average cost of the various factories, the partner purchasing from the initial source felt that it was penalized by the decision to relocate production, a decision which produced no benefit for it. Price and cost calculations were further complicated by the fluctuations in the currencies used by the different partners.

Tensions and conflicts progressively became so severe that the joint venture was eventually terminated and taken over by Control Data.

in Himeji (Japan), to manufacture liquid crystal screens on the basis of IBM's technology and Toshiba's manufacturing know-how. In April 1992, IBM launched a new laptop equipped with a screen manufactured by DTI. This computer, unfortunately, was more expensive, more bulky and less powerful than the latest competing model marketed by Toshiba. Indeed Toshiba, despite its alliance with IBM, had acquired licenses from Sharp that enabled it to produce smaller screens than those manufactured by the joint venture. In addition, the Toshiba laptop was based on a 486 microprocessor, while IBM used a 386. Nonetheless, IBM and Toshiba decided to extend their alliance to new generations of laptop screens; in 1995, they also started collaborating on the production of computer chips and organized their alliance on the DTI model, setting up another jointly owned plant.

Split R&D between the Partners and Concentrate Manufacturing

In manufacturing shared-supply alliances, development activities and manufacturing tasks require different organizational arrangements.

Development work should be split between the partner firms, with each partner being allocated a specific part of the entire project. As in the case of shared-supply alliances limited to R&D, this organization reduces the need for sharing valuable knowledge and thus limits technological leakage. In addition, as each partner participates directly in the development work, such an organization also ensures that the jointly developed components actually fit the needs of all the partners. In return, splitting the development work among the partners requires extremely close coordination in order

Table 8.1 The organization of tasks in shared-supply alliances

---

Organizations preserving the technological autonomy of the partners and favoring economies of scale:

JESSI

TASKS	ORGANIZATION
R&D	Distributed among partners

PRV-V6 engine

TASKS	ORGANIZATION
R&D	Distributed among partners
Manufacturing	Pooled in a joint facility

Organization unfavorable to the technological autonomy of the partner firms:

Sematech

TASKS	ORGANIZATION
R&D	Pooled in a joint facility

Organization unfavorable to economies of scale:

MPI

TASKS	ORGANIZATION
R&D	Distributed among partners
Manufacturing	Distributed among partners

---

to ensure the consistency of the joint developments. Choosing the alternative form of organization, i.e., entrusting all development tasks to a single R&D department (whether a separate joint venture or the R&D department of one of the partners), ensures the internal consistency of the joint development, but may disconnect it from the actual needs of those partners which were not directly involved in the R&D work.

Manufacturing, in contrast, should be concentrated in a joint facility; this is the only way to benefit fully from the increased economies of scale made possible by the alliance. It is the fact of concentrating manufacturing on a single site that makes it possible to create a larger, more efficient facility and to build up experience rapidly. As the MPI case clearly demonstrates, forming a manufacturing joint venture without rationalizing production only tends to make management more complicated; it does not produce economies of scale and reduced costs (see Box 8.6).

All in all, it would seem that the organizational choices made by the partners in shared-supply alliances play a decisive role in the future development of these partnerships and their ability to achieve the expected cost-reduction objectives. This conclusion applies both to pure R&D agreements and to manufacturing shared-supply alliances. Table 8.1 summarizes the available options for organizing shared-supply alliances, on the basis of examples mentioned in this chapter.

9
Quasi-concentration Alliances

In the early 1960s, Sud-Aviation in France and British Aircraft Corporation in the UK were working—separately—on plans for a supersonic transport aircraft. However, decision makers on both sides of the Channel soon came to realize that neither of the two companies possessed the financial and human resources needed to launch an aircraft of this kind alone, and gradually began to contemplate the idea of Franco-British cooperation on this project. Thus, even if political considerations also came into play at a later stage, it was primarily for financial reasons, to share the investment and to reduce costs, that Concorde was produced as an alliance. To claim that the results of this collaboration were financially disappointing would be an understatement. Budget and deadline over-runs were mind-boggling: the final bill for development expenses, estimated at $450 million in 1962, ultimately increased to more than $4 billion (Mowery, 1987). The plane, finally brought into service more than three years behind schedule, was produced in an extremely limited edition of only 14 aircraft instead of the 100 to 200 initially planned (Hochmuth, 1974). Not a single airline purchased Concordes; only Air France and British Airways, both state controlled at the time, were forced by their respective governments to operate the supersonic airliner without, however, actually purchasing the seven planes delivered to each. Yet, in the unanimous opinion of experts, Sud-Aviation (which later changed its name to Aerospatiale) and the British Aircraft Corporation (which became British Aerospace) learnt a great deal technically from their involvement in the program and, with the French and British governments absorbing most of the losses, actually strengthened their positions in the global aerospace industry thanks to the Concorde adventure.

Unlike Concorde, Airbus—another European alliance in aerospace—has unquestionably become a commercial and financial success (see Box 9.4). From Aerospatiale's point of view, however, this success has its downside: 30 years of involvement in successive Airbus programs have left the French company very dependent on the consortium and virtually incapable of developing, manufacturing and selling a commercial aircraft alone. At the same time, Airbus has allowed DASA, the German partner, which lagged far behind in technology at the beginning of the partnership, to catch up and become Aerospatiale's virtual equal; to such a point that DASA demanded, and obtained, to assemble one of the latest Airbus models, the A321, in Germany, a task hitherto reserved for Aerospatiale owing to the high level of expertise required for this work.

These two examples, Concorde and Airbus, illustrate two of the main problems which companies involved in quasi-concentration alliances have to face. In certain cases, the organization and day-to-day administration of the partnership are so inefficient, and the management problems created by collaboration are so serious, that the hoped-for economies never materialize, quite the contrary. In other cases, the organization of the alliance proves to be efficient but cooperation then leads to the loss, for the partner firms, of some of their vital capabilities.

WHY FORM QUASI-CONCENTRATION ALLIANCES?

Achieving Economies of Scale without Merging

When Aerospatiale and Alenia decided in 1980 to produce the ATR commuter aircraft, each of the two firms possessed the necessary competencies and facilities to launch the production of such a plane on their own. Both future partners had, in fact, developed plans for an aircraft of this kind which they intended to develop and manufacture alone. It was only when they realized they had similar projects that the two companies considered working together.

In this context, cooperation between Aerospatiale and Alenia on the ATR project was not intended to bring together complementary expertise or resources which, once combined, would have made it possible to carry out the project. The partnership, on the contrary, brought together firms possessing similar competencies, know-how and assets, in order to produce economies of scale. But, unlike shared-supply agreements examined in the previous chapter which create such economies on an particular component, the ATR alliance encompassed an entire family of products.

More generally, quasi-concentration alliances associate companies contributing similar capabilities and assets to the alliance in order to develop, manufacture and market a joint product. This relationship can be represented graphically as shown in Figure 9.1.

Firms forging quasi-concentration alliances try to benefit from the same advantages as those enjoyed by larger rivals without, however, having to merge with one another to reach this critical size. We have decided to call these alliances "quasi-concentration" to express the fact that they offer the advantages of concentration without actually leading to mergers, acquisitions and consolidation of the industry.

By forming a quasi-concentration alliance, the partner firms can first share the joint project's fixed costs—notably in R&D. In the ATR case, for instance, instead of shouldering all the costs of developing an aircraft of this type, Alenia and Aerospatiale each only had to finance 50% of the total bill. As development costs in aerospace add up to billions of dollars, it is easy to understand that the two partners were eager to share the burden.

Quasi-concentration alliances also make it possible to expand the potential market for the jointly produced product which benefits, in theory, from the sum of the partner firms' market shares. For

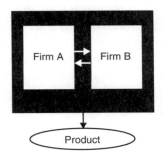

Figure 9.1 Quasi-concentration alliance

instance, the minivan manufactured in partnership by Peugeot and Fiat benefited from the combined distribution networks, brand equities and market shares of four makes, Peugeot, Citroën, Fiat and Lancia (see Box 9.2). Its production and sales volumes therefore substantially exceeded those that a similar vehicle launched by Fiat or Peugeot alone could have hoped to achieve. The increased economies of scale generated by the partnership's expanded presence on the market should thus enable the joint product to compete with products introduced by much larger rivals.

If the partners decide to form a quasi-concentration alliance rather than to merge, it is either for political reasons, or because they are only interested in joining forces on a limited portion of their overall business. In the aerospace and defense industries in particular, international mergers are fraught with difficulties owing to each country's concern for national independence. In other less sensitive industries, where no external constraint acts against a merger, it is the limited nature of the joint project that militates against a fully fledged merger. For example, it would be absurd for Peugeot or Fiat to merge, considering the substantial costs of such an operation, when all they want is in fact to collaborate on a single product line that accounts for only a minimal part of their business.

The Dangers of Internal Rivalry in Quasi-concentration Alliances

Conflicts between the vested interests of the partner firms and the collective interest of the joint project frequently arise in quasi-concentration alliances. These conflicts can usually be traced to two causes: first, the problem of using technologies developed by one or another of the partners within the framework of the joint project; second, the competition that occasionally arises between the joint products and other products developed by the partner firms on their own.

It is vital, in the interest of the joint project, that it benefit from the best technology that the partners can provide. On the other hand, as these partners more often than not remain direct rivals on other product lines, they are reluctant to let their most advanced technology become accessible to their partners. Experience has shown that this thorny problem can be solved in a number of different ways. In the case of the CFM-56 jet engine (see Box 9.1), the high-pressure core manufactured by General Electric was sealed before being shipped to SNECMA for assembly in the complete engine (Hayward, 1986). For the V2500, an aircraft engine that was jointly developed by Pratt & Whitney, Rolls-Royce, MTU, Fiat and JAEC and that competes with the CFM-56, the modular nature of the system enabled each partner to develop the part of the engine entrusted to it without having to know about the technology and processes used by the other partners. The problem with these procedures adopted to limit technology transfers is that they prevent the optimal use of the technical expertise possessed by the different partners; each sub-assembly only benefits from the know-how of the partner working on it. This is why, in the joint work carried out on Airbus, it was decided that any technology developed by one of the partners could be used by all the others within the framework of joint projects, but required prior permission, and would be subject to royalties, when used by another partner in pursuit of independent activities (Hayward, 1986).

A more critical problem, however, is that of competition arising between a product jointly developed within the scope of the alliance and one of the partners' own products. When one of the companies involved in a joint project independently offers a product that satisfies, even partially, the same needs and serves the same markets as the joint product, the danger is great that this partner will then systematically promote its own product over the one produced by the partnership. British Aerospace bitterly accused Dassault of compromising the export prospects of the Jaguar, a fighter-bomber jointly produced by both companies, by deriving a "ground support" version of its own Mirage F1 fighter. It should be mentioned that the criticism was probably not unfounded, considering that all export sales of the Jaguar (to India, Nigeria, Ecuador and Oman) were made by the British partner, with Dassault not managing to export a single aircraft. Similarly, one of the difficulties encountered in the V2500 cooperation stemmed from the fact that, for certain levels of thrust, both Rolls-Royce and Pratt & Whitney produced rival products on their own; and they obviously preferred to win deals in which they got all the revenues than contracts in which the revenues were divided between five partners.

Table 9.1   Forecasted and actual sales of helicopters jointly manufactured by Aerospatiale and Westland

	Puma	Gazelle	Lynx
Forecasted sales at the beginning of the partnership			
—Sales in France	130	170	55
—Sales in Great Britain	40	250	190
—Export sales	85	210	120
Total	255	630	365
Actual sales by the end of the program			
—Sales in France and Great Britain	217	521	234
—Export sales	462	517	76
Total	679	1038	310

Source: Hartley (1983)

A more extreme case is that of Aerospatiale, associated with Westland in the joint production of three helicopters (the Gazelle, Puma and Lynx), which went so far as to develop on its own, and almost simultaneously, its Dolphin helicopter, a machine that directly competed with the jointly produced Lynx. The sales of the Lynx suffered a great deal from this competition, as shown in Table 9.1 (Hartley and Martin, 1990). While the Puma and Gazelle both did substantially better than expected, only the Lynx, exposed to competition from the Dolphin, failed to reach its sales objectives. In addition, the shortfall can be attributed almost entirely to sales lost in export markets where competition from the Dolphin had a greater impact than in the protected UK market.

The organization set up to manage quasi-concentration alliances will make it possible to keep a more or less effective check on interpartner rivalry. This organization will therefore have a considerable impact on the effectiveness of cooperation.

HOW SHOULD QUASI-CONCENTRATION ALLIANCES BE ORGANIZED AND MANAGED?

Avoiding Duplication

In order to achieve the desired economies of scale, work within the alliance must be organized in such a way as to respect a number of specific conditions. If the same task—manufacturing, for instance—is carried out in parallel by each of the partner firms, the output of each partner will not be greater than the volume that each would have produced had it carried out the project alone. The size effect related to this manufacturing task would therefore be lost and the alliance would not, in this respect, be justified. More generally, such a *duplication of tasks* within quasi-concentration alliances cancels out the positive effects expected from collaboration.

In the case of Concorde, the aircraft's assembly suffered to an extreme extent from such duplication; two assembly lines were set up, one at Sud-Aviation in Toulouse, the other at British Aircraft in Filton. Investments in buildings and equipment were made twice . . . for the manufacture of a grand total of just 14 aircraft! What is more, owing to the experience curve effect, the unit cost of manufacturing an aircraft decreases significantly with each additional plane produced. By dividing up the assembly of Concorde between two different sites, the alliance wasted half the potential experience curve effect and failed to achieve all the theoretically possible cost reductions.

Despite their strong counter-productive impact, such task duplications are not uncommon in quasi-concentration alliances. In the aerospace and defense industries—two sectors that have witnessed the creation of a very large number of quasi-concentration alliances over the past 40 years—a duplication of tasks can be observed in approximately one-third of the alliances on record (Dussauge and Garrette, 1993a, 1995). Certain alliances have given rise to so many duplications that the chosen organization appears to be almost absurd. The production of the FH-70 motorized artillery gun, jointly manufactured by Vickers (UK), Rheinmetall (Germany) and Oto-Melara (Italy), involved the creation of three assembly lines at the facilities of the three partner firms. Worse still, the key parts and components used in the manufacture of this weapon were also produced independently in the three different countries. In all, the investments required for the production of the FH-70 gun, both for manufacturing the parts and for the final assembly, were carried out three times, and the production volume at each factory precluded the economies of scale and the learning curve effect that would have been possible had production been grouped together in the same place. In the organization of the

Concorde program—unanimously considered a poor example of efficiency—if the final assembly was duplicated, at least the production of each part and of each of the airliner's major subassemblies was carried out by one or the other of the partners on a single site.

Allocating the Tasks between the Partners

To ensure that quasi-concentration partnerships produce the expected impact, it is vital that each task carried out within the framework of the partnership should be organized to minimize investments while maximizing output and economies of scale. To achieve this, responsibility for each task should be attributed to a single operator. More often than not, this single operator will be one of the partners; we shall call this *distribution of tasks*. Sometimes, however, this single operator may be a specific structure, a joint venture, set up by the partners to carry out a series of tasks related to the alliance; we shall refer to this situation as the *pooling of tasks*. The most common organizational form adopted for quasi-concentration alliances is the distribution of all tasks between the partner firms.

The CFM-56 program (see Box 9.1) was entirely organized on the basis of such a distribution of tasks between the partner firms. The complete engine was divided into subassemblies; SNECMA on the one hand, and General Electric on the other, were entirely responsible for the design and manufacture of the parts of the engine entrusted to them. This system avoided duplication, since each basic part and each subassembly of the finished engine was only manufactured in one place, in Cincinnati (Ohio) for the General Electric parts, in Villaroche or Corbeil (France) for the SNECMA parts. In contrast, coordination between the partners for design of the engine, for technical integration and for production schedules, had to be extremely carefully managed.

The distribution of tasks between the partners is the form of organization that has also been adopted for marketing the CFM engines. General Electric and SNECMA divided up sales and after-sales activities on a geographic basis. If the distribution of tasks between partners is the dominant organizational form in CFM, the

---

Box 9.1   CFM-56—the General Electric–SNECMA Alliance

At the beginning of the 1970s, SNECMA wanted to launch a turbofan engine, in the range of 20 000 to 30 000lb of thrust, for short- and medium-haul 100- to 200-seat aircraft. Turbofan technology substantially reduced fuel consumption and noise levels, but was only used, at that time, on large engines fitted to 250- to 500-seat aircraft such as the DC-10 or the Boeing 747. SNECMA saw this as an opportunity to capture a share of a rapidly growing market, taking advantage of a technology that no other product incorporated at that time. In launching such a product, SNECMA lacked the necessary resources simultaneously to develop an entirely new engine and establish a commercial presence on the market for commercial aircraft in all the major regions of the world, notably North America which alone accounted for 50% of projected sales.

SNECMA therefore decided to seek a partner in order to produce its new engine. After consulting all major engine manufacturers, it decided to team up with General Electric. Pratt & Whitney was rejected because it demanded a dominant role in the partnership and wanted the new engine to be marketed under its own colors. In addition, P&W at that time was manufacturing the JT8D engine, based on older technology but aimed at the same market niche as the new project; SNECMA felt that rivalry of this kind within the alliance would be particularly harmful. As for Rolls-Royce, its catastrophic financial situation at the time prevented it from being a reliable and credible ally.

GE and SNECMA therefore signed a memorandum of understanding in 1972 for the joint production of the CFM-56 (CF for "commercial fan", the name of all the commercial engines manufactured by General Electric, M-56 because it was the 56th "Motor" project launched by SNECMA since its incorporation). The detailed agreement, signed in 1974 after intense negotiations, had not been subject to any fundamental change up to the late 1990s. It provided for a 50–50 partnership. The principle underlying this agreement was that both companies should divide the work and the risk equally. The agreement also provided for the creation of an equity joint venture, CFM-International.

The Role of the CFM-I Joint Venture

CFM-I was a small organization staffed with 30 people who were on assignment in equal parts from GE and SNECMA. The working language was English. Traditionally, the chairman of CFM-I was French. He was assisted by two vice-presidents who were the managers in charge of the CFM program at SNECMA and GE. CFM-I had no operating function; its role was mainly to coordinate dealings between the two partners.

The Organization of Development and Production

Each of the two allies was responsible for the design, development and production of a part of the engine, which was divided into modules: GE manufactured the high-pressure engine core and the combustion chamber; SNECMA produced the low-pressure parts, the fan and the lubrication and fuel systems (see Figure 9.2). Each partner manufactured in its own facilities the parts of the engine that it had developed. The final assembly of the engines was carried out in parallel by SNECMA in its Villaroche factory and by GE in its Cincinnati plant. Similarly, both partners had testing facilities where engines went after assembly and prior to delivery.

The Sales Organization

Unlike for other functions, the commercial side of the project could not be carried out by dividing the engine into modules; division in this area was based on geographic regions. Thus, GE was in charge of marketing the engine in North and South America, in the Pacific region, in South-East Asia and the Far East. SNECMA was responsible for sales in Europe, Africa, the Middle East and India. The sales personnel, irrespective of their sales areas and company of origin, acted on behalf of CFM-I. Each partner covered the costs of its salesforce. At the beginning of the partnership, SNECMA had no sales network and no sales experience with civilian customers. It was consequently obliged to build up its commercial position gradually, whereas GE already boasted its own salesforce which marketed its other models of engine. By the late 1990s, two-thirds of the engines had been sold in GE's sales region; in contrast, two-thirds of the customer airlines were based in SNECMA's territory.

CFM's first commercial steps were extremely disappointing. The initial sales were made to the military. In 1978, the American and French air forces chose CFM to supply new engines for their KC-135 tanker aircraft. In 1979, CFM-I finally recorded its first commercial order. This was from United Airlines, which was forced to re-engine its fleet of DC-8s in order to meet the new regulations on pollution and noise. The CFM-56-2, the first version of the engine, came into service in 1982. But sales only really took off with Boeing's 1981 decision to equip its B737-300 airliner exclusively with CFM-56-3 engines. The success of this medium-haul jet enabled CFM-I to record over 6000 orders out of a total of 14 000 received up until 1998. With a new version, the CFM-56-5, the company received orders in 1984 for the Airbus A320. The same engine also powered the A340.

By 1998, CFM had sold close to US$50 billion worth of engines to 160 different airline companies throughout the world. The CFM-56 was unanimously considered to be the most successful commercial engine produced to that date. It accounted for approximately 70% of SNECMA's sales and 25% of General Electric's business in aero-engines.

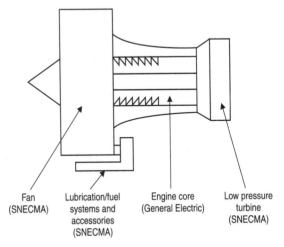

Figure 9.2 Work sharing on the CFM-56 engine

Source: based on Dussauge and Garrette (1993b).

allied companies have not entirely managed to avoid duplication, even in this very successful alliance. The final assembly of the engines—i.e., putting together the General Electric and SNECMA parts—as well as pre-delivery testing, are carried out in parallel by both partners. The managers in charge of the alliance point out that these tasks account for barely 1% of the total cost of the engine and that the impact of their duplication on the efficiency of the alliance overall is extremely weak. It remains true, nevertheless, that this duplication inevitably has a negative effect and we shall try to understand, in the following section, why the partners still chose to duplicate this work.

Carrying out Tasks together in a Joint Venture

Another form of organization adopted for quasi-concentration alliances—less frequent, however, than the distribution of tasks—is the pooling of tasks. For certain tasks, indeed, the partners may prefer to set up a joint structure that will carry out the job, instead of dividing up the work among them. In this case, the joint structure acts on behalf of the partner firms for those tasks entrusted to it.

Box 9.2   The Peugeot–Fiat Alliance for Minivans

In the spring of 1994, Peugeot introduced its 806 model, a new minivan destined to rival Renault's Espace (see Box 10.3 in Chapter 10). A few weeks later, Citroën (a division of the Peugeot group) also launched a minivan—the Synergy—a vehicle remarkably similar to the 806. Then came the Ulysses from Fiat, followed shortly by Lancia's Zeta (Lancia is a Fiat brand), both of which also bore a striking resemblance to the 806. All four models were, in fact, versions of the same vehicle; they only differed in detail (radiator grille, shape of the headlights, rear lights) and, above all, were sold under different brand names!

These four models resulted from a cooperation agreement signed by Peugeot and Fiat in 1988 to address jointly what was then a limited, yet rapidly growing, segment of the car

---

market in Europe. The limited size of this segment (fewer than 50 000 minivans were sold in Europe in 1988, 100 000 were sold in 1991, 160 000 in 1994 and 400 000 to 600 000 were forecast for 2000) made its access extremely difficult for a non-specialist car maker using traditional car-manufacturing techniques (metal stamping, automated production process, etc.). One solution was to adopt specific technology suited to short production runs, the option chosen by Renault and Matra for the Espace; short of this, it was virtually impossible for a model to be profitable if production failed to reach 500 vehicles per day, or approximately 120 000 vehicles per year.

It follows that a car maker could only break even on such a product if it captured about 30% of the European minivan market at the turn of the century. In the teeth of competition from Renault's Espace, Chrysler's Voyager, Toyota's Previa, Nissan's Serena and Prairie models, Mitsubishi's Space Wagon, Pontiac's TranSport, Ford's Galaxy and Volkswagen's Sharan, this goal seemed completely unrealistic, both for Peugeot, whose share of the European car market was 12% in 1994, and for Fiat, whose share was 11%. However, by teaming up to manufacture this vehicle, and by selling it under all the brands and through the various distribution networks of both groups, this target of 30% market share seemed more attainable. In forming this alliance, both Peugeot and Fiat sought to share the investment and development costs required to produce the vehicle and to expand its potential market.

To implement their alliance, Peugeot and Fiat created Sevel (for Société Européenne de Véhicules Légers, or European Light Vehicle Company), a 50–50 joint venture responsible for manufacturing the common minivan in a plant near Valenciennes in the north of France. The minivan alliance extended a similar agreement that Peugeot and Fiat had signed in 1978 for the joint production of small delivery vans in a factory located in the south of Italy.

On the minivan market segment, yet another alliance was to compete with the Peugeot–Fiat and Renault–Matra partnerships; in 1995, Ford and Volkswagen began jointly manufacturing their common minivan (sold as the Ford Galaxy and the Volkswagen Sharan) in Portugal. This alliance pursued the same goals as the Peugeot–Fiat agreement and was organized along similar lines.

Peugeot and Fiat, for example, created Sevel (see Box 9.2), a 50–50 joint venture, which owned the plant in which the minivans common to both partners were manufactured. In this alliance, manufacturing was pooled at Sevel while the design work was chiefly entrusted to Peugeot; marketing was duplicated, as both partner firms simultaneously marketed the vehicle through their respective dealerships.

Within the framework of the Airbus alliance, the partner companies decided to pool all the marketing, sales and after-sales activities; they therefore set up Airbus Industrie, a joint subsidiary fully responsible for dealing with customer airlines. The advantage of such a structure is that it enables the alliance to address the market in a coordinated way. In a global industry, when dealing with customers who enjoy a strong international presence, a joint structure ensures that the sales policy remains consistent worldwide. In contrast, when marketing activities are divided up between the partners along geographic lines, customers may be tempted to approach several partners in different regions simultaneously in order to play one off against the other; only very close coordination makes it possible to avert this danger.

In the case of Airbus, although marketing tasks were entrusted to a joint venture, R&D and manufacturing activities remained organized on the basis of a distribution of tasks among the partners. In certain quasi-concentration alliances, however, all the tasks related to cooperation are carried out jointly. In these cases, the joint structure is responsible for the entire business and has all the attributes of a fully fledged company.

Eurocopter, a joint venture of this type, was created in 1992 by Aerospatiale and DASA to manage, in an integrated manner, the helicopter businesses of both firms (see Box 9.3). The joint subsidiary received from both partners all their facilities and assets involved in the design, manufacture and sale of helicopters. Eurocopter resulted in fact from the merger of Aerospatiale's and DASA's helicopter divisions. Unlike in the case of Airbus, the partner firms relinquished all operational activities in the helicopter business and transferred them to Eurocopter.

Alstom (formerly GEC-Alsthom) and ST Microelectronics (formerly SGS-Thomson) offer further examples of quasi-concentration alliances where all the activities were pooled in a joint subsidiary.

Box 9.3 Eurocopter

In 1992, Aerospatiale and DASA (Deutsche Aerospace SA) decided to merge all their helicopter activities within a joint subsidiary, Eurocopter. As Aerospatiale's helicopter sales were approximately three times larger than DASA's, it was given a 70% share of the joint venture, with DASA owning only 30%.

Operationally, activities were integrated step by step. Marketing and sales were reorganized virtually immediately; all the helicopter models, irrespective of their origin, were marketed under the Eurocopter name, and the salesforces were merged. The manufacturing side was more difficult to integrate. Eurocopter had inherited facilities in France (at La Courneuve near Paris and at Marignane on the French Riviera) as well as in Germany (at Ottobrunn, Bavaria) and it was out of the question, for political and social reasons, to close any of these facilities down in order to group production together at a single site. It was decided, therefore, to have each factory gradually specialize; the Marignane plant, for instance, would manufacture large helicopters, Ottobrunn would produce small helicopters and La Courneuve would concentrate on the manufacture of certain components, such as rotor blades. Neither would the engineering departments be brought together in the same location; they would gradually specialize in technology, components or particular subassemblies so as to eliminate all redundancy between them.

Eurocopter's range of helicopters initially included all the old models sold by both DASA and Aerospatiale, and therefore lacked consistency. For example, the BO 105, originally from DASA, competed with the Gazelle and Ecureuil inherited from Aerospatiale; the same was true for the BK 117 (DASA) and the Dolphin (Aerospatiale). It was expected that as Eurocopter gradually renewed its range of models, the line of products offered would eventually become more consistent.

Encouraged by the success of their Eurocopter alliance, Aerospatiale and DASA had plans, toward the end of the 1990s, to merge their missile activities within a joint subsidiary, Euromissile, and their activities in satellites within a joint venture called Eurosatellite.

Alstom emerged from the 1989 merger of the electromechanical businesses of Alcatel-Alsthom from France and the corresponding division from the British GEC group. Equally owned by the two parent companies, Alstom became one of the world leaders in power generation systems and railway equipment. In the late 1990s, Alstom, known in Europe as the manufacturer of the highly successful TGV high-speed trains, had annual sales exceeding $10 billion and employed a total of 94000 people. In 1998, it was announced that Alstom would go public, 52% of the joint venture's equity being floated on the stock market and the partner firms each retaining only 24% of the shares.

Similarly, ST Microelectronics was a joint venture set up in 1987 by Thomson and STET—a subsidiary of the Italian state holding company, IRI—in order to combine their semiconductor activities. Realizing that they were too small and lacked the resources to survive on their own in this volume-driven and fiercely competitive

Table 9.2 The organization of tasks in quasi-concentration alliances

Airbus	
TASKS	ORGANIZATION
R&D and design	Distributed among partners
Manufacturing	Distributed among partners
Sales and after-sales	Pooled in a joint organization
CFM (General Electric–SNECMA)	
TASKS	ORGANIZATION
R&D and design	Distributed among partners
Manufacturing	—Subassemblies: distributed among partners
	—Final assembly and testing: duplicated
Sales and after-sales	Distributed among partners
Eurocopter, Alstom, ST Microelectronics	
TASKS	ORGANIZATION
R&D and design	Pooled in a joint facility
Manufacturing	Pooled in a joint facility
Sales and after-sales	Pooled in a joint organization
Peugeot–Fiat Minivan	
TASKS	ORGANIZATION
R&D and design	Distributed among partners
Manufacturing	Pooled in a joint facility
Sales and after-sales	Duplicated

industry, the two partners decided to combine forces. ST Micro-electronics was thus formed by the merger of Thomson's semiconductor division with STET's SGS Microelettronica subsidiary. Initially a 50–50 joint venture, ST Microelectronics has since opened its equity to new partners, including Thorn-EMI, France Télécom and CEA-Industrie. Overall, this alliance has made ST Microelectronics the largest European semiconductor company and the tenth largest worldwide, with close to 30000 employees, 1997 sales of over $4 billion, profits of $400 million and a share of the world market between 2% and 3%. Had they not formed this alliance, neither Thomson nor STET would have survived in the semiconductor industry.

In summary, Table 9.2 compares the organization of tasks adopted within several of the quasi-concentration alliances described above. The table clearly shows that the different possible organizations, i.e., distribution of tasks, pooling of tasks and duplication, can be combined in a relatively varied manner. In the following section, we shall examine the strategic consequences that quasi-concentration alliances may have for the partner firms. As we shall see, these consequences are strongly determined by such organizational choices.

TO SPECIALIZE OR NOT TO SPECIALIZE

If they are organized efficiently, quasi-concentration alliances lead almost inevitably to specialization by the partner companies. This specialization then makes the partners dependent on each other and reduces the competition that initially existed between them. In certain cases, quasi-concentration can even lead to a merger between the partners and thus produce actual consolidation in the industry.

Pressure in Favor of Specialization

In order to maximize efficiency and reduce costs, each of the tasks carried out within the framework of quasi-concentration alliances must be entrusted—as we have already seen—to a single operator. In certain cases, tasks are pooled and the operator is a joint structure; more frequently, tasks are distributed and the operator is one of the partners. In this second case, each ally sees its competencies reinforced in the areas entrusted to it but, simultaneously, loses its know-how in the areas entrusted to the other partners. The distribution of tasks—the dominant form of organization in quasi-concentration alliances—makes it possible to maximize the economies of scale and size effects associated with these alliances; what is more, by enhancing the skills of the various partners on those tasks entrusted to them, this type of organization increases the competitiveness of the alliance itself over time. But specialization caused by the distribution of tasks creates a growing interdependence for the partner firms. From this point of view, what is good for the alliance is also potentially dangerous for each of the allied firms.

Aerospatiale, for example, encountered considerable technical difficulties when, in the early 1990s, it was entrusted with fitting out the passenger cabin of the Airbus A340. This is an elementary operation for an aircraft manufacturer, merely consisting of attaching the seats to the floor, wiring the cabin and installing all the equipment that contributes to the passengers' comfort. Owing to the distribution of tasks within Airbus since the early 1970s, however, Aerospatiale had not had the opportunity to carry out this particular job for over 20 years (see Box 9.4). Because of this allocation of tasks, Aerospatiale had, over the years, lost some of the skills associated with this particular operation. Cooperation had thus insidiously led to specialization.

Box 9.4   Airbus

The idea of producing a wide-bodied, medium-haul aircraft within the framework of a European alliance was first seriously considered in the first half of the 1960s. But it was not until 1969 that the Airbus A300 was launched by Aerospatiale, by a consortium of German companies subsequently to be grouped together within DASA (Daimler-Benz Aerospace) and by Hawker Siddeley Aviation, which would be merged with other British firms to form British Aerospace (BAe). In 1970, the Airbus Industrie joint venture was created to coordinate collaborative activities and market the new aircraft. A short time later, the cooperation was expanded to include a Spanish partner, CASA (Construcciones Aeronauticas SA).

The shares of the four partners in Airbus were as follows: Aerospatiale 37.9%, DASA 37.9%, BAe 20% and CASA 4.2%.

It took almost 10 years for Airbus to meet with commercial success and it was not until 1978 that a second aircraft, the Airbus A310, derived from the A300, was launched. A third model, the A320, was launched in 1984, followed by the A321, the A340, A330 and lastly the A319. By the mid-1990s Airbus marketed a comprehensive range of aircraft with capacity ranging from 100 to more than 400 seats. The European consortium had become a serious competitor in the commercial aircraft industry, and was able to challenge its chief rival, Boeing, in almost all product segments and markets. By 1998, in 30 years of existence, Airbus had sold about 2500 planes for a total of approximately $100 billion.

This success was largely due to the organization of the alliance which made it possible to overcome most of the difficulties encountered in earlier European aerospace partnerships, such as Concorde. Research, development and production tasks were distributed among the partners, avoiding any duplication. From the very beginning, Aerospatiale was mainly responsible for developing and manufacturing the cockpit of the aircraft and for systems integration, DASA developed and manufactured the fuselage, BAe the wings and CASA the tail unit. For all the models of aircraft except one (the Airbus A321), final assembly was carried out in Toulouse (France) by Aerospatiale. The various subassemblies of the aircraft, which were manufactured in the UK, Germany or Spain, were delivered to the assembly plant using a fleet of giant Super Guppy air freighters. The cost of transporting parts between the different manufacturing sites was estimated at less than 0.1% of the total cost of the aircraft.

Unlike production, commercial activities were not split between the partners. Instead, all marketing, sales and after-sales operations were entrusted to the Airbus Industrie joint venture, which was the alliance's only interface with customers. To buy an Airbus, or to maintain their fleet, the customer airlines could not approach one or other of the partner firms directly, but had to deal with Airbus Industrie. In order to carry out this commercial function, in the mid-1990s Airbus Industrie employed 1600 people, some of whom were sent on assignment to the joint venture by the partner companies, but the majority of which (over 1000 employees) were hired directly into Airbus Industrie. The operating costs of Airbus Industrie accounted for approximately 2–3% of the aircraft's total costs.

From a financial point of view, Airbus Industrie was a virtually transparent structure. The joint venture invoiced customer airlines for each plane sold and paid each partner for its share of the work in producing the entire aircraft. The price paid to partners was calculated in such a way as to generate neither profits nor losses in Airbus Industrie's accounts. The actual profits or losses generated by Airbus were difficult to determine, because they only appeared in the accounts of the partner companies and were blended in with the partners' other activities. This system required that the partners agree about the relative value of their respective contributions. Negotiations leading to an agreement acceptable to all were inevitably difficult, because each partner would tend to over-estimate its own share of the work and under-estimate the shares of the others, in order to maximize the income derived from its participation in the Airbus consortium.

Despite the fact that it had no part whatsoever in the manu-facturing process, the role of Airbus Industrie should not be under-estimated. Being in contact with customers, Airbus In-dustrie *de facto* defined the alliance's product policy and elaborated the specifications of each new model of aircraft to be launched. What is more, Airbus Industrie tended to defend the point of view and interests of the alliance as a whole, even against the partner companies when the individual goals of the latter entered into conflict with the collective goals of the alliance. The role played by Airbus Industrie had become so important that the partners decided, in 1997, to turn it into a real manufacturing company. Thus, the factories and design bureaux involved in producing the Airbus aircraft were to be progressively turned over from the partner firms to their com-mon subsidiary. This new, integrated Airbus organization was expected to come into being by 1999. Such a transforma-tion was complicated, however, by the fact that the facilities in which Airbus aircraft were produced did not work ex-clusively for Airbus but were also used for other product lines specific to each partner. For example, Aerospatiale's facilities in Toulouse were used to assemble the ATR aircraft, while the BAe factories where the Airbus wings were manufactured also produced wings for 100% British planes.

Duplication: a Way to Avoid Specialization

Because of the specialization process under way in most quasi-concentration alliances, the allies may deliberately decide, in some cases, to duplicate certain tasks when organizing their partnership, despite the inefficiencies created by such an organization. In order to avoid losing skills that they consider vital, but that are associated with tasks entrusted to other partners, certain allied companies may choose to carry out these same tasks themselves and thereby impose on the alliance a form of organization that includes duplication.

In aircraft construction, final assembly is frequently deemed a particularly noble task giving the company that carries it out a great deal of visibility and involving a range of strategic competencies, notably systems integration and access to all the main components of the aircraft. Thus, it often happens that none of the partner firms is willing to give up this part of the work. This is why a great many quasi-concentration alliances in the aerospace and defense industries tolerate the duplication of final assembly, despite its negative impact on the overall efficiency of the alliance. For Concorde, in particular, assembly was duplicated because both partners demanded to carry out this operation; it even became a matter of national pride. Regarding the CFM-56 engine, as SNECMA was using this alliance to penetrate the commercial aircraft engine market, it considered it vital to deliver assembled engines to customer airlines and consequently appear in the eyes of the market as a fully fledged engine manufacturer. General Electric, on the other hand, already possessed assembly facilities which it used for the other engines it manufactured on its own and saw no reason for giving up this "noble" activity. The assembly and testing of the CFM engine were therefore organized on the basis of a duplication of these tasks, leading to diseconomies of scale and forcing SNECMA to make specific investments in order to set up its own assembly lines. This investment was not necessary from the point of view of the collaborative project itself, since similar facilities were already available in General Electric's factories.

Rotating Tasks to Preserve Industrial Versatility

In certain industries where numerous quasi-concentration alliances are formed, firms avoid specialization not through the duplication of tasks but by managing their involvement in several simultaneous alliances in a particular way. In order to preserve as wide a range of skills as possible, each company will try to be entrusted with different tasks in the various cooperative ventures in which it is involved. Each company will consequently accept apparent specialization in each of its alliances but, by choosing different specializations in each project, will in fact maintain its industrial versatility. An analysis of the network of quasi-concentration alliances formed in the European helicopter industry reveals the strategies adopted by the companies in this sector to avoid the specialization resulting

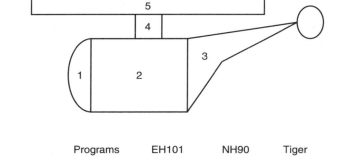

Programs	EH101	NH90	Tiger	Tonal
Companies				
Aerospatiale		1 + (5)	2 + 3 + 4	
Agusta	1 + 2 + 3	4 + (5)		(4) + 5
DASA		2	1 + 5	
Westland	4 + 5			1 + (4)
Others		3		2 + 3

N.B. The figures in brackets refer to the subassemblies of a program whose attribution was still subject to negotiation.

Figure 9.3 The distribution of tasks between partner firms in quasi-concentration alliances in the helicopter industry

from their involvement in increasingly large numbers of alliances (Dussauge and Garrette, 1992).

Figure 9.3 presents the distribution of tasks between partner firms for all the collaborative European helicopter programs being carried out in the early 1990s. The diagram above the table shows the main sections of a helicopter. Sets of critical skills, vital to the development and manufacture of a complete helicopter, are associated with each of these subassemblies. The numbers in the table refer to the sub-assemblies entrusted to each company in each alliance.

Figure 9.3 shows that all European competitors in the helicopter industry were trying to preserve their know-how and capabilities in all the major competency areas of their business. Indeed, the tasks they chose to carry out in the various projects in which they were involved embraced most of the key competency areas required for building helicopters. In other words, although none of these manu-facturers actually developed any new model alone, they in fact produced the equivalent of a complete helicopter by choosing to assume responsibility for different sections in different cooperative projects. This is why, in this kind of industry, the launch of each new project gives rise to intense negotiations to decide how the tasks will be divided up between the partners.

Rotating tasks and responsibilities over a series of quasi-concentration alliances is a way for each partner to maintain a complete range of skills without, however, impairing the efficiency of the partnership as much as when duplication is allowed. More specifically, the economies of scale made possible by cooperation are not jeopardized by the rotation of tasks, and the investments specific to each project are only made once. However, this task-rotation system is far from being economically optimal. The various projects carried out jointly would gain from deliberate specializa-tion of the partner firms. This would strengthen their skills in par-ticular technical subfields and, therefore, enhance the quality and value of their contribution to the joint endeavor.

Making Alliances more Efficient through Specialization

The drawbacks of task rotation explain why some quasi-concentration alliances continue unchanged for relatively long periods, are extended to cover new projects and always involve the same partners. These alliances lead to a high level of specialization among the various allies which, as specialization increases, progressively cease to be potential rivals and become complementary partners. As the allocation of tasks among the partners is maintained over long periods, each company implicitly accepts the loss of its know-how in areas entrusted to the other allies. By eliminating potential rivalry and enhancing complementarity, the specialization of skills in quasi-concentration alliances favors the stability and efficiency of the partnership as a whole. But specialization may also become a serious threat if one of the partners leaves the alliance, either to team up with an outside rival or to become a fully fledged competitor once again, provided that it has managed to preserve this ability despite the ongoing specialization process.

The gradual specialization of the companies in the commercial aircraft industry in Europe may be analyzed by examining, for all the collaborative programs in which they were involved, how the different tasks were divided up between the various companies (see Figure 9.4).

Specialization within the Airbus consortium is made obvious by the fact that the allocation of tasks among the partners has remained unchanged for three successive aircraft models—the A300/A310, A320 and A330/A340—which together span a period of more than 20 years. It is interesting to note that when the Airbus A320, the second model in the range, was launched in 1984, most of the partner firms wanted to change the distribution of tasks. British Aerospace wanted to design the cockpit, Aerospatiale wanted to build the wings and DASA wanted responsibility for final assembly (Hayward, 1986). It was Airbus Industrie which managed to persuade its shareholders, i.e., the partners, that a redistribution of roles such as this would have a catastrophic impact on the program's success. Indeed, this redistribution would have required a complete reorganization of the production process, considerable additional investments and exchanges of know-how, at a time when competition with Boeing was intense and Airbus could not afford the luxury of unnecessary additional expenses nor any loss in efficiency. Once three major successive programs had been carried out within the framework of the same division of labor and

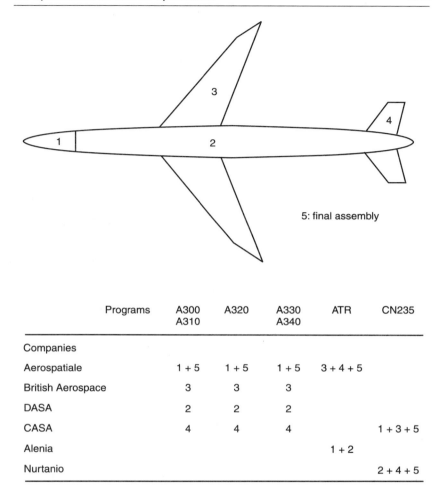

5: final assembly

Programs	A300 A310	A320	A330 A340	ATR	CN235
Companies					
Aerospatiale	1 + 5	1 + 5	1 + 5	3 + 4 + 5	
British Aerospace	3	3	3		
DASA	2	2	2		
CASA	4	4	4		1 + 3 + 5
Alenia				1 + 2	
Nurtanio					2 + 4 + 5

Figure 9.4 Specialization of skills following the creation of alliances in the commercial aircraft industry in Europe

over a relatively long period, it was unlikely that any major reorganization of the alliance would subsequently take place. The only exception to this *de facto* specialization within the Airbus consortium was the decision to have the A321—a lengthened version of the A320—assembled in Hamburg by DASA (in exchange for this concession, the fitting out of the passenger cabin of the A340 was entrusted to Aerospatiale, as mentioned above). This hotly disputed decision was taken under substantial pressure from the German partner, because it was in any case necessary to build a new assembly line and because Airbus's far better situation in 1990 made it financially possible.

It can also be noted in Figure 9.4 that, through its involvement in the ATR program in which it obtained responsibility for most of the tasks it did not carry out in Airbus, notably the design and manufacture of the wings, Aerospatiale has tried to avoid the consequences of specialization and to maintain, provisionally at least, a certain degree of industrial versatility.

The comparison between the two businesses examined above— helicopters and commercial aircraft—suggests that the question of whether an industry moves towards a system of stable alliances with partner specialization, or towards dispersion with the creation of multiple, unstable alliances forged between partners preserving their industrial versatility, is influenced by the intensity of competition in the industry in question. As long as they possibly can, all competitors will try to maintain their autonomy and preserve the full range of their competencies, and consequently will prefer forging project-by-project alliances. Stiffer competition may force alliances to seek greater efficiency, thereby imposing specialization on their partners . . . which, in turn, stabilizes the alliances in question.

In the commercial aircraft industry, where Airbus faced formidable competition—Boeing controlling over 70% of the market— European manufacturers could no longer afford to refuse specialization; it is only by achieving maximum efficiency and, therefore, by accepting the need to specialize that the European companies teamed up within Airbus could withstand competition from Boeing. In the helicopter industry, in contrast, competition was less focused, with three American manufacturers of relatively equal weight and four European manufacturers, one of which— Aerospatiale—ranked in second position worldwide (Dussauge and Garrette, 1993a). It could be added that the impact of military orders in the helicopter business, which accounted for approximately 70% of total industry sales, undoubtedly played a major part in maintaining versatile national manufacturers, supported by their governments.

The Emergence of Business-based Joint Ventures

The distribution of tasks inevitably raises major coordination problems among the allies. If different partners manufacture different parts of the same product, it is vital that the design of these parts as well as production schedules is perfectly coordinated. Similarly, if the partners sell the same product in several different parts of the world, their marketing and sales policies must also be closely coordinated.

In order to address these coordination issues more effectively, some quasi-concentration alliances have been organized on the basis of pooling of tasks. Pooling all tasks in a common entity provides a solution to coordination problems, as all the work is carried out within the context of the joint venture rather than directly by the different partners. In such an organization, the partners merely guide and monitor the activities of this business-based joint venture.

Once the partners have accepted the fact that their quasi-concentration alliance has become permanent, a business-based joint venture seems to be the most efficient form of organization. Economies of scale are maximized by pooling tasks within the joint venture and all duplication of work is avoided; investments are carried out just once, and if certain facilities or teams are already available in the partner companies, they may be used within the framework of the alliance via the simple transfer of assets or personnel.

While organizing quasi-concentration alliances as business-based joint ventures provides the greatest possible efficiency, it also raises a number of specific problems for the partner companies. Indeed, the partners no longer have direct control over the tasks and activities pooled in the joint venture and, consequently, lose the corresponding skills. In the case of Airbus, for example, the fact that all marketing activities are entrusted to Airbus Industrie has deprived the partner companies of all contact with customer airlines. Aerospatiale and British Aerospace, which both used to market their own aircraft (notably the Caravelle, Comet, Trident or VC-10), no longer have the sales teams necessary to do so, simply because these departments have been incorporated into Airbus Industrie. If one of these companies wanted to start manufacturing an aircraft alone once again, it would find it extremely difficult to market it.

In a more extreme way, the creation of Eurocopter deprived Aerospatiale and DASA of any direct presence and any operational involvement in the helicopter business. For some firms engaged in multiple business-based joint ventures, there is a risk of "hollowing out" the company, progressively converting it into a purely financial holding corporation. With all manufacturing work entrusted to joint ventures specializing in each area of activity, the partner firms will gradually lose their industrial substance and their very *raison d'être* will become questionable. By forming a host of business-based joint ventures over the years in all its major lines of activity, Aerospatiale was progressively handing over all operational tasks to these alliances and converting itself into a holding company with primarily financial responsibilities. GEC is another example of a company that relies heavily on business-based joint ventures and runs the risk of merely becoming a holding company.

10
Complementary Alliances

In the early 1980s, the automobile industry was swept by a wave of alliances formed by Japanese and American manufacturers (Chrysler with Mitsubishi, Ford with Mazda, GM with Toyota as well as with Suzuki). Japanese car makers were looking for ways to increase their penetration of the US market by circumventing import quotas, while American manufacturers wanted to add small, low-cost, fuel-efficient vehicles rapidly to their product ranges. By forming alliances, both sides were able to achieve their own specific objectives. Although they took various legal forms (acquisition of equity stakes, creation of joint subsidiaries, supply contracts), all these alliances were based on *complementarity* between the allies: the Japanese partner firms supplied models that complemented the products offered by their American allies in the small car segment; the US companies provided their Japanese counterparts with expanded access to the North American market via their well-established brands and distribution networks. Over the years, however, the initial complementarity has developed into cut-throat competition. Using their alliances as springboards, the Japanese car makers took advantage of their presence in the US market to launch large-scale operations in North America on their own and to develop an excellent image in the eyes of the consumer—to such an extent that when the same vehicle was sold in the USA with two different brands, one American and the other Japanese, it was not uncommon for the version with the Japanese badge to be able to command a higher price, and still capture a large share of the market.

Other industries—such as, for example, telecommunications equipment (public and private telephone exchanges, terminals,

etc.)—have experienced similar developments. The rapid expansion of alliances in the telecommunications industry, starting in
the mid-1980s, was triggered by two major developments. First,
deregulation—the most striking symbol of which was the disman-
tling of AT&T in 1984—opened up hitherto protected national markets to international competition. Second, the introduction of new
digital technology stimulated growth in this industry by creating
new telecommunications services and by speeding up the replace-
ment of older equipment throughout the world.

In this context, alliances (as well as takeovers) offered a way to
gain rapid access to foreign markets or to acquire new technologies. AT&T in particular, after losing its monopoly position in the
USA, chose to expand internationally by forming numerous alliances, notably with several of its European competitors. The APT
joint venture, set up with Philips in 1983 on a 50–50 basis, was an
important element in AT&T's strategy and was meant to enhance
the American firm's presence in the European market. Philips's
motives for forming the partnership meshed perfectly with this
objective. The Dutch company was having problems developing its
own digital switching system and was ultimately led to adapt the
ESS 5 exchange (the existing AT&T product) to European standards. Unfortunately, commercial results turned out to be very disappointing and Philips gradually withdrew from the joint venture.
AT&T then turned to another European partner, Italtel. After a
transitional period (1989–90) during which the subsidiary, renamed
AT&T-NSI, was jointly owned by AT&T (65%), Italtel (20%) and
Philips (15%), Philips finally chose to sell its entire stake to the
other two partners in 1990. With this withdrawal, it ended up completely exiting the public switching business, since all its assets and
personnel specializing in this area had been brought into the joint
venture and remained there despite Philips's withdrawal. This,
however, did not guarantee the success of the AT&T-NSI alliance;
in 1993, the two remaining partners announced that they were
terminating their partnership.

The cases presented above seem to suggest that complementary
alliances lead to highly unbalanced outcomes. As suggested by
these examples, by the end of the alliance the initial complementarity between the allies has often given way to increased competition and even, in some cases, to one of the partners withdrawing

from the business altogether. And these examples are far from being isolated cases. Nevertheless, complementary partnerships are frequently promoted as one of the best ways to access new technologies or to expand globally by taking advantage of potential synergies between the allied firms. This apparent paradox suggests that firms entering complementary alliances should manage them in such a way that they come out winning if the partnership does indeed result in an unbalanced outcome.

WHY FORM COMPLEMENTARY ALLIANCES?

Benefiting from Interpartner Synergies

In complementary alliances, the allies contribute different and complementary assets and capabilities to their joint endeavor, and thus benefit from the synergies created through the combination of their respective resources. In most cases, one of the partners contributes a product, a product design or a set of critical technologies, while the other provides the alliance with in-depth knowledge of the local market and access to it through an established sales network. Figure 10.1 offers a graphical representation of complementary alliances.

The globalization process that many industries have been undergoing is a strong incentive to the formation of complementary alliances (Yoshino and Rangan, 1995). Creating a complementary alliance enables one firm to use its competitors' commercial presence to penetrate new geographic markets rapidly. Our research

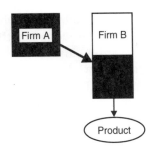

Figure 10.1 Complementary alliance

shows that almost 90% of all complementary alliances are set up to support the geographic expansion of at least one of the partners. In highly competitive industries undergoing accelerated technical change and a rapid globalization process, forming alliances makes it possible to focus resources and efforts on the business's critical success factors and core capabilities. Alliances thus appear as a means through which firms can enhance their competitive advantage; rather than scatter their investments in order to establish a presence simultaneously in many different markets on their own, they can devote most of their resources to creating and developing distinctive core competencies (Hamel and Prahalad, 1994), while global expansion is achieved through leveraging the complementary capabilities of partner firms.

Although the basic rationale for forming complementary alliances is similar to that of setting up traditional international expansion joint ventures (see Chapter 5), there is a big difference between these two types of partnership: in complementary alliances, the partner firms are both major players competing in the business in question, whereas in international expansion joint ventures, the local partner cannot compete in the business on its own. Potential rivalry between the partners—a distinctive feature of complementary alliances—inevitably has a decisive impact on the way in which these partnerships are managed. In a traditional international expansion joint venture, the local firm can only operate in the business in question with the assistance of its foreign partner. Therefore, the local company has nothing to lose from helping its foreign partner enter the host country through the joint venture. If successful, the joint venture will benefit both parties. In complementary alliances, in contrast, both allies cannot fail to realize from the very beginning that they are helping a competitor strengthen its position. In particular, a firm that facilitates the entry of a partner's products to its domestic market cannot ignore the implication that this partner is likely eventually to develop a permanent presence in this market, thus becoming a direct competitor. This is why, in a great many cases, the partners try to establish a second "reverse" agreement to counterbalance the initial complementary alliance.

The Pernod-Ricard/Heublein and Matra/Ericsson partnerships, described in Boxes 10.1 and 10.2, both included such reverse agreements to counterbalance the initial alliances. These cases

---

Box 10.1   The Pernod-Ricard/Heublein Alliance

In 1985, Pernod-Ricard and Heublein set up an alliance based on the complementary nature of their geographic presence and product ranges. Pernod-Ricard, which originally specialized in pastis, an aniseed-flavored spirit that is very popular in Southern Europe, had grown significantly to become one of the leading beverage companies in Europe. In the mid-1990s its Ricard drink was the third best-selling spirits brand in the world, behind Bacardi and Smirnoff. With the purchase of Wild Turkey, an American brand of bourbon, Pernod-Ricard acquired a strong position on the international whisky market. Heublein, building on its strong presence in the USA, had also initiated a process of international expansion, notably in Japan and Brazil. Heublein had become a world leader in vodka, through the acquisition of the Smirnoff brand.

The Pernod-Ricard/Heublein alliance included two agreements:

- Heublein was granted the exclusive distribution rights for Wild Turkey bourbon in the USA, enabling it to compete in a category where its position had previously been weak. Heublein acquired a 30% stake in the equity of Wild Turkey and sold a 30% share in its subsidiaries in Japan and Brazil to Pernod-Ricard. These subsidiaries were entrusted with the distribution of Pernod-Ricard products in their respective markets.
- Pernod-Ricard received the European distribution rights for Smirnoff vodka, which enabled it to complement its product range with a leading brand of vodka in its domestic market.

Unfortunately, the second agreement was terminated when Heublein was taken over by Grand Metropolitan. Indeed, Grand Metropolitan, with a strong position in Europe, was one of Pernod-Ricard's direct rivals in whiskies and other alcoholic beverages. Grand Metropolitan chose to distribute Smirnoff on its own and withdrew its concession from Pernod-Ricard.

As Pernod-Ricard did not possess a large enough distribution network to market Wild Turkey on its own in the USA, it did not break the first agreement even though the alliance had become extremely unbalanced. In order to reduce its dependence on a major competitor, Pernod-Ricard progressively set up its own sales teams in the USA for products other than those covered by the alliance. In the words of a senior manager at Pernod-Ricard, this presence in the USA, in parallel with the alliance, "created a healthy sense of insecurity in the partner" and helped to compensate for the imbalance in the alliance.

Box 10.2   The Matra–Ericsson Alliance

The telecommunications equipment industry has undergone dramatic change since the mid-1980s. Before then, the industry was organized on the basis of a series of national monopolies. In most countries, a state agency bought equipment from a dominant local manufacturer and, possibly, from a few minor competitors. Deregulation of the industry, initiated in the USA, quickly spread to Japan and Europe, completely upsetting this comfortable situation and opening the floodgates to foreign competition. At the same time, the development of digital technology generated new growth in the public switching market and created huge demand for private telecommunications systems (company switchboards, private radiotelephone networks, etc.).

These developments formed the backdrop to the alliance set up by Ericsson (Sweden) and Matra-Communication (France) in 1987. The alliance between the two companies was triggered, in fact, by the privatization of CGCT, a French state-owned company specializing in public telecommunications to which the French authorities had awarded 16% of the market for public exchanges in order to challenge the *de facto* monopoly of Alcatel, the dominant French producer of telecoms equipment. But CGCT, a former licensee of ITT, badly needed a new, up-to-date public telephone exchange system. As none of the French companies interested in acquiring CGCT (SAT, Jeumont-Schneider and Matra) possessed the necessary technology, and as the French privatization law limited foreign ownership to 20% of the equity of privatized companies, forming an international alliance appeared to be the only option. The Matra–Ericsson partnership, created for the occasion, was chosen over another consortium uniting SAT to AT&T.

Ericsson and Matra complemented each other very well. Ericsson had developed an excellent system, the Axe exchange, which merely had to be adapted to French standards, while Matra enjoyed excellent relations with the French purchasing authorities. The alliance was embodied in CGCT, which had become a joint venture in which Matra had a dominant stake. However, the negotiations between the two parties proved to be long and difficult. If Ericsson's interests and objectives were perfectly clear, i.e., gaining access to the French public switching market, those of Matra were more ambiguous. Why should Matra enter a business in which it had no competitive advantage, lacked the necessary technology and therefore risked being relegated to playing the role of Ericsson's foil?

Matra chose to complement the CGCT deal with a parallel agreement which would provide it with clearer long-term benefits. Matra demanded that Ericsson market Matra's PBXs internationally and pull out of this segment in France. In addition, Matra and Ericsson would work together on the development of a pan-European radiotelephone system. This second request was by far the most important, because it implied true technological cooperation and the acquisition of valuable know-how by Matra.

While the CGCT side of the alliance proved viable, the parallel agreements requested by Matra were never implemented successfully. Having established a foothold in the French public switching market, Ericsson had little incentive to help Matra become a stronger competitor in other telecommunications businesses. The cellular phone agreement was finally terminated in 1992 when Matra announced its decision to work with Northern Telecom on a European radiotelephone system.

By 1997, telecommunications markets in Europe were totally deregulated and Ericsson no longer needed Matra to operate successfully in France. On the other hand, Matra had little to gain from continued collaboration with Ericsson within CGCT. Thus, Matra decided to pull out of the alliance and Ericsson took over the joint venture completely.

Source: based on Ramanantsoa and Perret (1993)

highlight the fact that complementary alliances are unbalanced by nature and that, to offset this, the companies involved often forge parallel agreements in which their roles are reversed. The counterpart of the agreement whereby Pernod-Ricard entrusted Heublein with the distribution of a number of its products in the USA was a parallel agreement whereby Pernod-Ricard distributed a Heublein product in Europe. The counterpart of Ericsson's penetration of the French market thanks to Matra was a technological agreement in the area of cellular telephones (Ramanantsoa and Perret, 1993). But these two examples also show how difficult it is to maintain a balanced situation over the long term; in both cases, the reverse agreements came to an untimely end, and both Matra and Pernod-Ricard had to look outside their partnerships for alternative options.

Acquiring New Capabilities

As discussed above, the underlying rationale for complementary alliances is usually to swap access to a market for access to a product. Access to a particular market is made possible by the possession of a combination of specific knowledge and assets: in order to market the alliance's product, the host partner must know local customers and conditions well enough and, in addition, own the adequate distribution network, salesforce, etc. Conversely, to provide the adequate product, the entering partner must have developed the necessary technologies and capabilities and own the corresponding facilities. Complementary alliances are thus based on the complementary nature of the partner firms' assets and capabilities. The optimistic view of complementarity suggests that it is a basis for durable synergies between partner firms which are engaged in a long-term "symbiotic" or "win–win" relationship. But the very existence of synergies necessarily implies mutual dependence between the allies: each partner is dependent on the other's contributions to achieve the objectives pursued through the alliance. A more strategic view of complementarity would then suggest that, sooner or later, one of the allies may be tempted to reduce its dependence by acquiring the capabilities it lacks. This partner could then deliberately take advantage of the alliance to learn about the skills contributed by the other ally. Complementary alliances can thus be used to capture these skills progressively while simultaneously investing in the necessary assets in order eventually to be able to pursue the activities of the alliance autonomously. In this perspective, complementary alliances are often powerful learning tools.

The partnerships forged by American and Japanese automobile manufacturers provide an eloquent illustration of this, with the Japanese competitors using these alliances to acquire in-depth knowledge of the US market, an understanding of local labor relations and experience in dealing with American suppliers and subcontractors (Weiss, 1987; Womack, 1988). On the basis of the new capabilities they had captured through their alliances, they then gradually developed their own manufacturing facilities and marketing networks in North America. Toyota, for example, independently set up its own production units in the USA while continuing to work with General Motors within the NUMMI partnership (see Box 10.5). In contrast, evidence suggests that learning was not a priority for American auto makers engaged in alliances with Japanese partners, and that these alliances were merely used to fill a gap in their product ranges, in a segment that they did not perceive as being attractive. It was only when the compact car segment had grown into a major market that the American car makers started striving to make up the ground lost on their domestic market to their Japanese rivals. These developments should not, we feel, be seen as evidence of particularly Machiavellian behavior on the part of the Japanese allies, but rather as the outcome of two different uses of complementary alliances.

For complementary alliances to be formed, there must exist potential synergies in the respective resources, skills and assets of the two partner firms. Therefore, both partners seek to benefit from these synergies. Learning, on the contrary, is an additional aim which may not be shared by all partners. Indeed, in order to learn from an alliance, a firm must commit specific resources, both human and financial, to this goal, and make additional investments that would not be required in order merely to benefit from the expected synergies. This is why, in many complementary alliances, all partners do not have the same agenda: some partners focus on the economic gains made possible by interpartner synergies, while others are willing to invest in order to acquire new capabilities. It has been shown, however, that when the partner firms have different strategic intentions, complementary alliances tend to lead to unbalanced outcomes; primarily looking for synergies in the short term is a "losing" attitude if the other partner is using the alliance as a learning tool (Hamel, Doz and Prahalad, 1989).

HOW TO MANAGE COMPLEMENTARY ALLIANCES

The Trojan Horse

When potential synergies with a prospective partner have been identified, an obvious question to raise is that of the relative value of the contributions made by each ally. In other words, isn't helping a rival to secure positions on one's domestic market a rather high price to pay for access to a new product? The converse is equally relevant: is it worth strengthening a competitor in its own market by entrusting it with the distribution of a product only to gain access to that market? If an adequate balance can be found, by using "reverse" agreements or otherwise, the potential synergies made possible by the partners' complementary capabilities often argue in favor of forming an alliance.

However, because of the potential for interpartner learning created by complementary alliances, initially drawing up a balanced agreement does not guarantee a "win–win" outcome. Indeed, the way in which learning affects the evolution of many complementary partnerships over time should lead to a more cautious approach of such alliances. The metaphor which comes to mind is that of the Trojan horse, where one of the allies takes advantage of the alliance to capture its partner's most valuable skills and thus strengthens its position at that partner's expense. As, in complementary alliances, the partner firms are also competitors, they both have a strong incentive to reduce their mutual dependence by appropriating the capabilities they lack. Indeed, it is most uncomfortable to rely, for critical capabilities, on a rival. Moreover, the acquisition of new capabilities will not only tilt the balance of power within the alliance, it will also enhance the overall competitive position of the learning partner relative to other competitors in the same industry.

While partner firms in complementary alliances have strong incentives to reduce their own dependence, they also may be tempted to increase the dependence of the other partner. The more the other partner is dependent, the more a firm can influence the management of the alliance in order to serve its own interests. Maintaining the other partner in a state of dependence, or even increasing such dependence, is often easier than would be expected. Indeed, as the partner can benefit, through the alliance, from complementary capabilities it lacks without investing to develop them in-house, it is natural to rely, somewhat complacently, on the alliance. Investing to limit or reduce one's dependence on the alliance often appears as a counterproductive decision which defeats the very purpose of the partnership, i.e., benefiting from interpartner synergies. If an alliance fulfills its purpose profitably for one of the partners, that partner is likely to develop an "addiction" to the alliance; for example, the more and the longer a firm relies on its partner for particular technologies, the more difficult it will find it eventually to develop its own substitute technologies and reduce its dependence. The other partner can subtly take advantage of this trend to increase its control over the alliance, weaken the more dependent partner and even, in extreme cases, leave no other option than a full takeover. The evolution and outcome of the ICL–Fujitsu alliance has been interpreted by some in this way. After several years of collaboration with ICL marketing computers based on Fujitsu's technology, the alliance resulted in a complete takeover of ICL by Fujitsu.

The likelihood of a complementary alliance maintaining a "win–win" situation over the long term or, on the contrary, rapidly degenerating into a Trojan horse is determined by a set of underlying factors that, for obvious reasons, it is vital to identify early on:

- The appropriability of the respective capabilities contributed by each partner. Some skills are easy to capture by simply observing the partner's practices; others are too tacit or too complex to be understood easily and require extensive experience before they can be fully mastered. Some capabilities are directly linked to assets that are virtually impossible to replicate; distribution networks with outlets in particular locations or brand image and loyalty, for example, cannot be acquired by collaborating with a partner that owns them.

- The value and attractiveness for one partner of the capabilities contributed by the other. As mentioned earlier, one of the benefits of complementary alliances is that the partner firms can focus their resources on developing their core competencies while relying on their partner for more peripheral capabilities. In this perspective, the capabilities contributed by the other partner are not attractive enough to justify the efforts required to internalize them.
- The organization of the alliance. When the alliance is implemented by allocating different tasks to one or the other partner firm, the lack of day-to-day contact between the partners makes it difficult for significant learning to take place. If, on the contrary, certain tasks are carried out jointly in common facilities (a jointly operated research lab or plant, for example), a lot more learning will take place. Indeed, skills are acquired by people and organizational learning will occur more extensively if joint teams are formed and people work together on specific tasks.

Alliances in which firms contribute difficult-to-appropriate capabilities that are of little value to the other partner, and that are organized on the basis of an allocation of tasks between the partners, tend to lead to "symbiotic" relationships. On the contrary, if the capabilities are highly attractive and easily appropriable while the organization allows for extensive joint operations, then the alliance will rapidly turn into a "race to learn".

Managing Symbiotic Alliances

Symbiotic alliances are those in which the "win–win" label is most justified. The partner firms need each other's contribution but are either not interested or cannot capture the capabilities on which the other partner's contributions are based. In many cases, the symbiotic relationship is not an alliance between equals but unites a large global company to a small firm that possesses highly specialized skills. Such relationships are similar to symbiosis in the animal world: sharks and pilot fish need each other, as do rhinoceroses and oxpeckers. In such situations, capturing the other partner's capabilities is not an objective and protecting one's own skills is not an issue. What may in fact jeopardize the alliance is not the other partner's strategy but changes in the environment which reduce the value of one partner's contribution and therefore wipe out previously significant synergies.

For example, to expand internationally in the regulated European airline industry, British Airways formed alliances with local carriers, thus overcoming those regulations which restricted domestic operations to nationally owned companies; full deregulation in the late 1990s made these alliances pointless and led British Airways either to terminate them or to take over their partners completely. In France, BA had acquired a 49% stake in TAT, a local airline, and increased that stake to 100% as soon as restrictions on the foreign ownership of airlines were lifted. For virtually identical reasons, Ericsson took over its joint venture with Matra when the telecommunications market was totally opened up to foreign competition (see Box 10.2).

A typical example of a symbiotic, complementary alliance threatened by changes in the environment is the hitherto highly successful alliance between Matra-Automobile and Renault for the Espace minivan (see Box 10.3). When Matra approached Renault in the early 1980s with its "people carrier" project, the market for minivans in Europe was virtually non-existent. Matra's project would not compete with any existing Renault product and was destined to take a new and presumably very small niche in the automobile market. Matra's contribution to the alliance was vital, since its proprietary low-volume manufacturing technology made it possible to serve such a small segment profitably. This complementary alliance was obviously symbiotic. With an annual output of a few thousand cars, it was out of the question for Matra to set up its own distribution network and pull out of the alliance. Renault, on the other hand, whose primary business was the mass production of mainstream automobiles, had very little incentive to invest in acquiring a technology and facilities specialized in short production runs. The partner firms thus needed each other to produce and market the Espace. By the late 1990s, however, minivans had become a significant segment of the European automobile market and the Espace was being produced in such large volumes that Matra's SMC-based manufacturing process had become less cost-effective than the traditional metal-stamping process routinely used by Renault and all other major auto manufacturers. While three generations of the

Box 10.3   The Espace—a Matra–Renault Alliance in Minivans

The Renault Espace minivan was first introduced in 1984. Although initial sales figures were very disappointing (only nine vehicles were sold in the first month after the model was introduced!), the Espace went on to become an extremely successful car, rumored to be one of the most profitable automobiles produced in Europe since the Second World War. While estimates back in the early 1980s, before the product was launched, anticipated maximum sales of about 50 per day, in 1998 the third-generation Espace was still being produced at a rate of 350 per day (i.e., 75 000 per year). The success of the Espace was largely due to its exceptional features in terms of comfort and layout (versatile interior, movable seats, etc.) coupled with a road performance worthy of up-market sedans.

While it was sold in Renault dealerships using the Renault brand name, the Espace was actually designed by Matra-Automobiles. Matra also produced the body of the van using a specific technology: the body panels were made of SMC (or sheet molding compound, a resin and fiberglass mixture molded at high temperatures) and then glued on to a metal frame. Using a Renault platform and powertrain, Matra assembled the car in its own plant and sold the completed vehicles to Renault. Renault was in charge of all distribution and marketing tasks.

The value of Matra's plastic body technology had nothing to do with customer perceptions; if presented with a choice, most customers would have preferred a metal body vehicle. In fact, the advantage of Matra's SMC process was that it required investments two to three times smaller than sheet metal stamping which was traditionally used to manufacture automobile bodies. However, manufacturing SMC parts was 10 times slower than stamping metal body panels; variable costs were therefore much higher, making Matra's technology suitable only for low-volume production (up to a maximum of 450 vehicles per day).

Thanks to Matra's proprietary technology, the Espace dominated the passenger minivan segment in Europe for over 10 years. Until the mid-1990s, this virtual monopoly remained unchallenged (with the exception of the imported Chrysler

Voyager minivan which never managed to capture a significant share of the market) because, in such a small niche,
competing vehicles could not be produced profitably using
traditional automobile-manufacturing processes. However,
as soon as the European market for minivans had grown
large enough and competitors could reasonably expect to
achieve daily sales in excess of 500 units, the people-carrier
segment started to be attractive to other manufacturers using
conventional technology.

By 1998, all major European automobile manufacturers had
introduced direct competitors for the Espace (see Box 9.2 in
Chapter 9). At that point, Matra's SMC technology shifted
from being an advantage to becoming a drawback; well
suited to low production runs, it entailed a structurally higher
cost in a mass market. Because of this, Renault decided that it
would no longer collaborate with Matra on this kind of vehicle
in the future but would produce the fourth-generation Espace
on its own. As early as 1996, despite potential cannibalization,
Renault introduced the Scenic, a smaller, metal-body vehicle
derived from the people-carrier concept, which met with immediate success (daily sales in excess of 800 units). Matra, for
its part, was left with no other option than forming new alliances in which its proprietary technology and innovation
skills would once again become valuable contributions.

Source: based on Dumont and Garrette (1996)

Espace were produced over a 20-year period within the scope of a
highly successful alliance, the partnership was terminated when it
became obvious that it was in Renault's best interest to produce
minivans on its own (Dumont and Garrette, 1996).

Thus, even in cases where none of the allies has a hidden
agenda, a partner firm engaged in a complementary alliance must
monitor the way in which the value of its contribution changes over
time. No matter how good everyone's intentions are at the beginning, a symbiotic alliance will only last for as long as each partner's
contribution is valuable to the other. In order to succeed in symbiotic alliances, a firm must continuously improve its specific capabilities and, in this way, enhance the value of its contribution to the

alliance, while at the same time preparing itself for the possible termination of the partnership. In this perspective, it is advisable not to have all of one's eggs in the same basket and to keep exploring alternative options on which to fall back if circumstances so dictate.

How to Win the Race to Learn

In many complementary alliances, however, one of the partners may have a strong interest in capturing valuable capabilities contributed by the other. When the appropriability of the capabilities in question make such an objective realistic, the alliance is likely to degenerate into a "race to learn". When Nestlé and General Mills formed the Cereal Partners Worldwide alliance (see Box 10.4), neither of them could ignore the fact that their respective contributions were based on capabilities that were valuable and attractive to the other partner. Nestlé had previously tried to develop its own cereal business and had failed miserably while General Mills lagged far behind Kellogg's, its archrival in the cereal business, in all markets outside North America. It could be expected that Nestlé would eventually want to control a business of its own in cereals, one of the fastest-growing segments of the packaged foods industry; conversely, General Mills could not accept to rely on a joint venture for all its international operations, especially as most of the growth in the cereal business was driven by demand emanating from foreign markets.

All of the ingredients for a race to learn to flare up within CPW were thus combined. In this race, however, General Mills was at a disadvantage, since learning about breakfast cereal manufacturing technology is *a priori* easier and faster than developing a worldwide brand and the ability to deal with local distributors in many different parts of the world. Aware of this, General Mills requested that the agreement with Nestlé include a number of safeguards. First, Nestlé had to commit not to acquire General Mills, through a hostile takeover bid or otherwise, for at least 10 years after the joint venture was formed. Second, in the event of the alliance being terminated prematurely, Nestlé agreed to not enter the market for cereal in North America for at least 10 years. Finally, most products

Box 10.4 Cereal Products Worldwide—a General Mills–Nestlé Global Alliance

During the 1980s, the ready-to-eat cereal market experienced high growth, particularly in Europe, where habits were switching from more traditional breakfast foods to cereals, as well as in many other markets outside North America. The dominant player in this market was undisputedly Kellogg's, with market shares of 40% to 50% in all major markets.

In the late 1980s, General Mills was Kellogg's strongest competitor in the USA and had increased its market share from 21% to 27% between 1980 and 1989. This success was made possible by innovative products such as Honey Nut or Apple Cinnamon Cheerios. General Mills's presence outside the US, however, was extremely limited, leaving Kellogg's unchallenged worldwide.

Nestlé, the Vevey (Switzerland) based world leader in packaged foods, tried to enter the cereal market as early as 1983. Having met with limited success, it realized that it needed to improve its production process and also that it lacked the necessary technologies.

General Mills and Nestlé made the first contact in 1989 and agreed within 30 days to create Cereal Partners Worldwide (CPW), a 50–50 joint venture headquartered in Lausanne (Switzerland). The initial contract was for 10 years. By 1998, General Mills and Nestlé were estimated to have invested close to $1 billion each in their joint venture. Their aim was quite simple: to compete with Kellogg's everywhere in the world, except in North America where General Mills was already No. 2.

General Mills contributed a line of successful products with well-known brand names, as well as its manufacturing and technical expertise. Nestlé gave CPW access to its distribution and sales network throughout the world, and to its marketing skills in each country; Nestlé also granted the joint venture the right to use its two main brand names in cereal, Chocapic and Nesquik. Each of the partners appointed four to five executives to CPW's board of directors.

The first markets targeted by CPW were those where Nestlé had already established a presence in cereal products (France, Spain and Portugal). In 1992, CPW acquired a significant share of the British market (15%) by purchasing the cereal division of Ranks Hovis McDougall, which owned such brands as Shreddies and Shredded Wheat. In 1995, ahead of schedule, CPW reported its first pre-tax profit. Since then, CPW has also entered Asia, Latin America and Eastern Europe. By 1998, it was present in over 60 countries worldwide and was the second largest cereal company outside North America.

The difference in size between the two partners (Nestlé's annual sales were five times greater than those of General Mills) is speculated to have led them to include a "standstill" provision in the CPW agreement: neither partner would attempt to take control over the other during the alliance's first 10 years and, if a takeover were planned, an official announcement would have to be made at least 10 years before the actual purchase could take place.

introduced by CPW would carry trade marks owned by General Mills (such as Cheerios, Golden Grahams, etc.) which Nestlé could not continue using if the alliance were broken.

To control the transfer of valuable capabilities, partner firms engaged in complementary alliances can also choose organizational arrangements that limit or, on the contrary, favor learning in particular areas or fields of expertise. Indeed, the way in which tasks are carried out within the alliance has a strong impact on the transfer of know-how between the partners. For example, in alliances where manufacturing is pooled in a jointly operated factory, or where marketing and sales are entrusted to teams mixing managers from both partners, much more interpartner learning is likely to take place. More generally, all joint activities favor the transfer and acquisition of skills; by physically working together, teams from both partner firms will learn from one other. Organizing work within the alliance in an appropriate way can therefore allow one of the partners to acquire valuable capabilities from the other while limiting unwanted transfers in the other direction. More specifically, a partner should request joint management and joint operations in those areas where it wants to acquire capabilities, while arguing for a strict allocation of tasks between the partners in domains where it wants to protect proprietary skills.

In addition to all these factors (appropriability, value and attractiveness of contributed skills, organization of tasks within the alliance), the ability to take advantage of complementary alliances to acquire new capabilities also depends on the "absorptive capacity" of the firm (Cohen and Levinthal, 1990). To tap a wide range of skills as quickly as possible, the firm must, in particular, have an internal organization and culture that facilitate collective learning (Hamel, 1991; Doz and Hamel, 1998), encourages horizontal communication, favors the circulation of information and values openness and receptiveness to the outside world.

The influence of organizational choices on interpartner learning is particularly obvious in the case of the NUMMI joint venture formed by General Motors and Toyota (see Box 10.5). The organization of the alliance was deliberately designed to facilitate learning and skill transfers between the partners in specific areas, particularly in manufacturing, purchasing and human resource management. Had the objective of the alliance merely been to assemble and sell a few thousand Toyotas rebadged as Chevrolets, GM could have bought these cars from Toyota, or Toyota could have granted a manufacturing license to GM. The acquisition of new skills clearly motivated the decision to set up a jointly operated plant.

Box 10.5   NUMMI—a General Motors–Toyota Alliance

In 1984, General Motors and Toyota set up the NUMMI (New United Motor Manufacturing Inc.) joint venture. NUMMI was formed to manage one of GM's former plants, located in Fremont, California. This plant, which dated back to 1963, had been shut down in 1982 because of strained labor relations and poor productivity.

The NUMMI factory, although it was less automated than most other GM facilities and was staffed with rehired former Fremont plant workers, rapidly achieved higher productivity levels than other GM manufacturing facilities in the USA. Quality also improved substantially and the Chevrolet Nova assembled at Fremont turned out to be as reliable as its twin model—the Toyota Corolla—manufactured in Japan.

These achievements came with the manufacturing processes and management methods transferred to the joint venture by Toyota. Both partners explicitly intended to use

---

NUMMI as a tool for learning: GM would witness the Japanese manufacturing methods first hand and could then try to transfer them to its own production units, while Toyota would learn how to manage a factory in an American environment. Learning, for both partners, was focused on organizational skills linked to manufacturing. Because of the bilateral nature of the learning process, the NUMMI alliance had all the ingredients to turn into a "race to learn"; the first ally to achieve its objective would no longer need to collaborate. Time was of the essence as the Department of Justice, because of anti-trust concerns voiced by Chrysler, had mandated that the alliance be terminated by 1992. This time limit was eventually lifted and NUMMI was still operating in 1999; by that time, however, rumors of the Japanese partner exiting the alliance and possibly taking over NUMMI suggested that Toyota's learning objectives had been achieved.

As soon as the alliance was formed, GM had set up procedures to transfer new skills—or to "nummize", as GM jargon had it—its own manufacturing facilities. GM executives were assigned to the joint venture for three-year periods and worked with Japanese managers. A liaison office was set up at NUMMI in order to circulate all the information gathered (through videos, databases, documents, factory visits) within GM. However, while those managers that held lasting positions at NUMMI actually acquired new capabilities and were able to have an influence on GM's operations, it appeared that second-hand or more superficial exposure to the NUMMI experience had very little impact because the managers involved, although interested, remained skeptical about implementing the NUMMI methods in other plants.

In learning from NUMMI, GM faced a difficult challenge: only a handful of managers could be properly "nummized" while the valuable skills acquired in this process were to be transferred to the 100 or so manufacturing facilities that GM operated in North America. Toyota, on the other hand, only needed to train a few dozen executives in how to deal with the local environment in North America, in particular with labor and suppliers. These managers would then be used to staff Toyota's two North American facilities.

It thus appeared that, because its objectives were more limited, Toyota was more favorably positioned in its "race to learn" with GM.

Interpartner learning is a significant aspect in most complementary alliances. This often leads to earlier termination, as whichever partner has first captured the desired capabilities is likely to pull out of the alliance before learning takes place in the opposite direction. Research on alliances has also shown that complementary alliances are more likely to end with a takeover by one partner than are other kinds of alliances, which supports the idea that, when the race to learn is over, the winner can operate on its own while the loser is left with the alternative of either forming a new alliance or of pulling out altogether and selling its stake in the partnership (Dussauge, Garrette and Mitchell, 1998).

Deliberately Organizing the Transfer of Valuable Know-how

While termination of the alliance by takeover is often presented as a symbol of defeat for the selling partner, this outcome may in fact be planned in advance and openly negotiated by both allies. In such cases, a complementary alliance is formed deliberately to transfer capabilities that are vital to the efficient management of the business that will eventually be taken over. The alliance is thus used as a mechanism through which one of the partners assists the other in entering a new market. While the entering partner's motivations are usually quite straightforward, the host partner's motives are less obvious.

In many cases, this host partner intends to exit the business altogether by selling it to the entering partner; when Philips formed its alliance with Whirlpool, its deliberate objective was to sell its appliance division to its partner (see Box 10.6). An alliance which ended in a takeover was preferred to an outright sale because it created benefits for both Philips and Whirlpool. Whirlpool had no experience in operating in Europe and used the alliance as a tool for learning; Philips, on the other hand, used the alliance period to demonstrate the true value of its appliance business while selling its know-how of the European market.

In other cases, the host partner's motivations are more opportunistic: it derives financial benefits from assisting a foreign partner, albeit a competitor, in entering its domestic market. As knowledge

Box 10.6   Philips–Whirlpool

After several years of poor performance, Philips, the Dutch electronics giant, was engaged in a huge restructuring plan in the late 1980s. The new management of the company was streamlining operations, cutting the workforce by almost 20%, and refocusing the firm around its core electronics business. The appliance division was not judged to be part of this core.

At around the same time, Whirlpool, the US leader in appliances, was aggressively expanding internationally (see Box 5.1). One of its main objectives was to build a significant presence in Europe. In 1986, it had acquired a majority stake in an Italian manufacturer of compressors.

In January 1989, the two companies signed an agreement according to which Whirlpool acquired 53% of Philips's appliance business for $361 million. Through this move, Philips's former appliance division became a joint venture called Whirlpool International BV. The agreement stated that Whirlpool could buy Philips's stake in the joint venture as of January 1990, but that Whirlpool International BV could continue to use the Philips brand name until 1998.

In its first year, the joint venture, which employed 14 000 people, generated sales of $2.5 billion with an operating income of $75 million. The new strategy implemented by Whirlpool International was to "court the Euroconsumer" by promoting a standardized range of products across Europe, a market which was until then highly fragmented, consumers in each country requesting very different products (in terms of design, size, features). In addition, to create awareness of the Whirlpool name, which was unknown in Europe and considered as almost impossible to pronounce in any Latin language, this new range of products was sold under the Philips–Whirlpool brand.

The rapid recognition of the Whirlpool brand by European consumers led the partner firms to drop the Philips name in four countries (the Netherlands, the UK, Ireland and Austria) as early as 1992; conversion to the Whirlpool name was completed in all other countries long before the 1998 deadline. In order to continue benefiting from Philips's knowledge of the market, Whirlpool decided not to exercise its purchase option in January 1990 and chose instead to extend the life of the joint venture. By 1992, enough progress had been made for Whirlpool to buy Philips's 47% share in Whirlpool International BV for $610 million.

Although the initial response of consumers to pan-European product standardization was favorable, Whirlpool seems to have under-estimated the fragmented nature of the European market and many analysts reckon that it did away with the country-centered strategy and organization inherited from Philips much too hastily. By the end of the 1990s, Whirlpool was losing money in Europe and its acquisition of Philips's appliances was increasingly being considered a failure.

of the local market is an assest that is difficult to trade, a joint venture in which this knowledge is transferred from one partner to the other is formed. The host partner's efforts are rewarded through the profits made by the joint venture and through the sale of its stake in this joint venture once the transfer has been fully completed. Such a mechanism provides a strong incentive for the transfer of skills to be carried out efficiently; indeed, the host partner's compensation is directly linked to the performance of the joint venture and its value at the time of the sale. When the joint venture meets with sustained success, this signals that it has internalized the necessary skills and that the entering partner can now take it over and operate alone in the targeted market.

In such complementary alliances, while both partners fully agree on the ultimate fate of the joint venture, they may have different views on the timing of events; the entering partner often tends to seek total control as early as possible, while the host partner, on the contrary, can be tempted to delay the sale and reap a larger share of the profits. The Hoechst–Takeda alliance (see Box 10.7) is an illustration of how one of the partners can trade its contribution in knowledge and skills for cash, with the takeover of the alliance having been agreed right from the start.

In summary, it appears that the fundamental issue in complementary alliances is that of interpartner learning and skills transfers.

Box 10.7   The Hoechst–Takeda Alliance

In 1978, Takeda, a Japanese leader in the pharmaceuticals industry, set up a joint venture with Hoechst, a European giant in chemicals and pharmaceuticals, to market cephalosporins, a particular strain of antibiotics, in France. Through its Roussel-Uclaf subsidiary, Hoechst was one of the leaders in the French drug market; Takeda was in the process of globalizing its activities and sought to develop a presence in most major markets. When the alliance was formed, the partners each had a 50% stake in their joint venture, but had agreed that Takeda would progressively increase its share until it completely took over the venture. By the early 1990s, Takeda's share had grown to 95% and was expected soon to reach 100%.

Takeda's main objective in forming an alliance was to make its entry to the French market easier by learning how to deal with the specificities of this market from a partner that had accumulated a great deal of experience in France. In particular, getting approval for a new drug from the local authorities is a process that is totally specific to each country; it entails dealing with local health authorities, local physicians and accessing local distribution networks. Hoechst, in contrast, had little reason to help a new competitor enter a market where it had a strong presence. Only the financial benefits derived from this could justify forming the joint venture with Takeda. Hoechst initially invested very little in the joint venture but, by contributing its marketing know-how, significantly increased the value of the venture and cashed in on this value creation by progressively selling out to Takeda. Hoechst's rationale was that, sooner or later, Takeda would enter the French market and that it might as well reap some profits from this entry rather than let another local competitor do so.

As both partners had explicit and converging objectives and, in addition, had agreed on the final outcome of the alliance, the management of the joint venture did not generate major conflicts. One difficult issue, however, was the timing of Hoechst's withdrawal. Takeda tended to over-estimate its ability to do without Hoechst's assistance, while Hoechst emphasized the need for its continued support to the joint venture. This issue had managerial implications, as changes in ownership of the joint venture were paralleled by changes in the organization; executives initially assigned to the joint venture by Hoechst were progressively replaced by managers appointed by Takeda, often Japanese nationals. This managerial takeover of the joint venture was also a symptom of the skills transfer taking place within the alliance.

As discussed above, the extent to which such transfers will take place is strongly influenced by intrinsic features of the capabilities contributed by the allied firms: some skills are more attractive than others and some are easier to appropriate than others. While a firm considering a complementary alliance should definitely take these features into account before actually forming the partnership, there is not much that it can do to alter the nature of the capabilities contributed on either side.

In contrast, firms entering complementary alliances can decide on, or at least influence, other factors that also affect the likelihood of capabilities being transferred. First, a firm can enhance its absorptive capacity, i.e., its own ability to capture and internalize new knowledge; this requires the adoption of an open and flexible organization that facilitates lateral communication and the dissemination of information. Developing such an ability will increase the benefits that a firm derives from participating in virtually any complementary alliance. Second, partner firms can directly affect the transfer of skills that will take place in each particular alliance by organizing the partnership in an appropriate way; as mentioned above, joint work will increase the transfer of skills, while a distribution of tasks between the allies will limit interpartner learning.

On this basis, Table 10.1 contrasts the various organizations chosen for the alliances discussed in this chapter and points out their impact on interpartner learning and capability transfers.

The specific concerns raised by complementary alliances (interpartner learning and unbalanced outcomes) are frequently thought to apply to all partnerships between rivals. This is why, when negotiating a partnership agreement, managers often adopt a defensive attitude and focus on issues such as avoiding technology

Table 10.1 The organization of tasks in complementary alliances

Organizations unfavorable to the transfer of skills	

Matra–Renault Espace

TASKS	ORGANIZATION
R&D and design	Allocated to Matra
Production of mechanical parts	Allocated to Renault
Bodywork manufacturing and assembly	Allocated to Matra
Sales and after-sales	Allocated to Renault

Pernod–Heublein

TASKS	ORGANIZATION
Marketing in Europe	Allocated to Pernod-Ricard
Marketing in the USA	Allocated to Heublein

Organizations favorable to the transfer of skills

NUMMI (GM–Toyota) *(manufacturing skills)*

TASKS	ORGANIZATION
Manufacturing	Pooled in a joint facility
Sales and after-sales	Allocated to GM

Hoechst–Takeda *(marketing skills)*

TASKS	ORGANIZATION
Marketing in Europe	Pooled in a joint organization

leakage, guaranteeing a fair distribution of the gains and preventing unwanted outcomes (most notably a takeover). This widespread "paranoia"—which is hardly relevant in alliances which are not complementary, refer to Chapters 8 and 9—reaches a climax where alliances between Western and Japanese firms are concerned (Mankin and Reich, 1986). However, focusing in this way on the nationalities of the partner firms is misleading; if many alliances with Japanese partners end in unbalanced outcomes, including takeover, it is most likely because the vast majority of these alliances are complementary (see Chapter 4) rather than because of differences in culture and nationality.

11

Conclusion: Anticipating the Evolutions and Outcomes of Strategic Alliances

Being able to anticipate the likelihood of success of collaborative projects, long before any joint activity is actually carried out, is increasingly becoming a critical capability for many senior managers, as most of them will, at some point in their career, be confronted with the difficult challenge of dealing with strategic alliances. Indeed, only very few firms today can afford to develop all the new technologies they need on their own, or can market their products globally without the assistance of partners.

While many managers are pessimistic about the likelihood of success of strategic alliances and are therefore reluctant to enter into such arrangements, our own research shows that, in a majority of cases, these partnerships do in fact attain the explicit objectives for which they were set up. Airbus has turned out to be a major success despite having to coordinate the work of four different manufacturers from different countries with production facilities scattered around Europe. Ford and Volkswagen have managed jointly to produce a minivan which has become the most successful vehicle in its category in Europe. General Electric and SNECMA have jointly developed the world's most widely sold commercial aircraft engine and their alliance has generated close to $50 billion in cumulated sales. ST Microelectronics (formerly SGS-Thomson) has become one of the 10 largest semiconductor producers in the world and the only credible European competitor in this industry.

Siecor, a Siemens–Corning joint venture, is the world leader in fiberoptics. And these examples represent a mere fraction of all the successful alliances that could be mentioned. A more systematic analysis confirms this optimistic view in the particular case of aerospace-industry alliances (Dussauge and Garrette, 1995): more than 60% of the partnerships created in this sector are considered successful, or extremely successful, by a panel of independent industry experts.

It would seem, therefore, that companies usually manage to overcome the very real difficulties inherent in strategic alliances. The co-existence of multiple decision-making centers, the endless negotiations between allies, the constant temptation to seize short-term advantages at the partner's expense are specific issues that make cooperation a form of organization that is difficult to manage. Yet, provided that appropriate management methods are adopted, these problems are by no means insurmountable. This book has tried to highlight exactly what forms of management are most suited to each main type of alliance.

Making the collaborative project a success, however, does not necessarily imply that all partner firms will benefit from the alliance in the long term (Nakamura, Shaver and Yeung, 1996; Park and Russo, 1996). In the case of alliances, the very notion of success is indeed quite ambiguous; alliance success is usually assessed on the basis of the performance of the joint project or venture, but very rarely takes into account the impact that collaboration may have on the situation of the various partner firms. This issue is compounded by the fact that these partner firms may have very different reasons to collaborate and may pursue radically different strategic goals through the alliance.

For instance, the alliance formed in the late 1970s by Rover and Honda was probably seen as very successful by the marketing managers of both companies, given the large market share achieved by the jointly produced cars that were sold under both brand names. However, the senior management of both corporations should have been—and maybe was—concerned by the long-term consequences of the partnership. Wasn't Rover at risk of eventually becoming a mere subcontractor of Honda? Was Honda right to base its market penetration strategy in Europe primarily on its British partner, with most Hondas sold in Europe being assembled in the UK? All in all, even though the automobiles produced in

collaboration by Rover and Honda were commercially very successful, it is doubtful whether Rover saw its subsequent acquisition
by BMW as a positive outcome of the alliance. As for Honda, it may
have considered after all that penetrating the European market on
its own would have been a better strategy.

More generally, the two above-mentioned levels of concern can
be found in most interfirm collaborations. The operational managers of an alliance assess its success based on short- or medium-
term indicators such as the technical quality of the joint product, the
impact of cooperation on costs, profits made by the joint venture,
and the quality of collaboration between the teams from each partner firm. Senior managers at the corporate level, on the other hand,
should look beyond such short-term results of cooperation, and try
to anticipate the longer-term impact that an alliance may have on
the company's competitive position.

To better anticipate the evolutions, outcomes and strategic impact of alliances, it is necessary to distinguish between the main
types of alliances we have described and discussed in this book.

THE OUTCOMES OF ALLIANCES BETWEEN NON-RIVAL FIRMS

The three main types of alliance between non-rival firms follow
different development patterns.

The Outcomes of International Expansion Joint Ventures

International expansion joint ventures seem to enjoy high success
rates, provided that the selected local partner can make valuable
contributions to the joint venture's development and that the multinational parent gives this local partner enough latitude in the management of the joint subsidiary. International expansion joint
ventures suffer from a relatively high mortality rate in their first few
years in existence but, once they have passed a certain threshold,
they tend to be quite durable. The relative positions of the partners
does not, in general, change significantly as a result of cooperation;

the multinational partner maintains control over product technology and design, transfer of know-how is slow and the initial gap between the partners is seldom closed because of constant technological progress occurring at the industry level. From a wider perspective, international expansion joint ventures contribute to the globalization of the industries in which they are formed.

The Outcomes of Vertical Partnerships

Vertical partnerships benefit the partners who create them, both on the customer and the supplier side, and enhance the efficiency of the industry as a whole by improving product quality, cutting costs and promoting innovation. Vertical partnerships, however, lead to increased outsourcing by the buyer firms, which transfer a growing share of their activities to selected suppliers and specialize in overall system design and final assembly. These partnerships also induce a process of concentration in the supplier industries; in these supplier industries, weaker competitors find it difficult to make the move towards becoming reliable partners and are relegated to lower-tier subcontracting positions, or simply eliminated altogether. Suppliers that seize the opportunity to expand their skills and capabilities in order to become major partners can take advantage of the trend towards partnerships to enhance their competitive position in the industry, as well as their bargaining power *vis-à-vis* prime contractors.

The Outcomes of Cross-industry Agreements

Cross-industry agreements seem to enjoy a substantially lower success rate than other types of cooperation. This is due to the uncertainty inherent in the development of the new activities for which these alliances are formed. It appears that, in most cases, the growth of the new business to be created by combining the partners' complementary capabilities tends to fizzle out and that initial expectations are rarely fulfilled. In cases where the businesses in question really do take off, two main outcomes are possible: either the alliance acquires independent status in relation to the partners

Table 11.1 Outcomes of alliances associating non-rival firms

	Evolution of the alliance	Strategic consequences	Impact on industry structure
International expansion joint ventures	High mortality rate in their first years in existence followed by stability	Stability in the partners' relative positions	Globalization
Vertical partnerships	Long-term relationship between the partners	New division of the value added within the industry	Concentration of the upstream industry and changes in the relative bargaining power of suppliers and buyers
Cross-industry agreements	Results are frequently disappointing when compared to initial expectations	Joint venture becomes independent or intensification of competition between partners	Creation of new activities and arrival of new competitors

and becomes a fully fledged company, or one of the partners uses the alliance to diversify into the other partner's business, eventually leading to interpartner competition.

Table 11.1 summarizes the most frequent outcomes of the various types of alliances formed by non-rival firms, as well as their strategic consequences.

THE OUTCOMES OF ALLIANCES BETWEEN COMPETING FIRMS

In alliances associating competitors, the partner firms inevitably have conflicting objectives and interests, and must nevertheless be able to collaborate well enough to carry out their joint activity effectively. In such alliances, the benefits derived from collaboration by each partner are not directly linked to the performance of the joint project itself. Alliances between rivals, even if they often result in the success of the projects undertaken jointly, can in the long run have an unforeseen and, at times, undesirable impact on the competitive position of the companies involved. This is why we have chosen to examine the issue of alliance outcomes based on the way in which the relationship between the partner firms evolves over time, and on the strategic consequences that cooperation has for each partner, deliberately setting aside the question of the success or failure of the joint endeavor. We have also tried to evaluate the impact of alliances on the intensity of competition in those industries in which they are established. The analyses and conclusions drawn up here are derived from the study of a sample of over 200 alliances set up in a wide variety of industries, and on a worldwide basis.

Overall Outcomes of Strategic Alliances between Rival Firms

The outcomes of alliances can be analyzed on the basis of three dimensions: (i) the evolution of the alliance over time; (ii) the strategic consequences of the alliance for each partner firm; and (iii) the impact of the alliance on the intensity of competition (Dussauge and Garrette, 1998).

The Evolution of the Alliance over Time

Alliances associating competing firms can evolve in a number of different ways:

1. *The alliance comes to a "natural end"* once the objectives for which it was created have been achieved. For example, Dassault and British Aerospace, which had jointly designed and manufactured the Jaguar fighter aircraft, terminated their alliance once the program was over and no more planes were being ordered.
2. *The alliance is extended or expanded:* the partner firms choose to prolong their collaboration over successive generations of the joint product or expand it to new products or projects. Thus, Toyota and General Motors collaborated to manufacture several successive generations of automobiles within their NUMMI joint

venture, while the Airbus cooperation has been expanded to include a complete family of airliners.

3. *Premature termination*: the partner firms break up the alliance before the initial goals have been achieved. Matra-Harris and Intel, for example, broke up their Cimatel alliance in 1987, before any of the VLSI chips it was meant to produce were actually manufactured.

4. *The joint project is continued by one partner alone*, while the other partner pulls out before any tangible results have been achieved. Thus, Fairchild and Saab were designing a commuter aircraft (the SF-340) together when Fairchild, which was having problems of its own, decided to drop the project, which was continued by Saab (who renamed it the Saab 340).

5. *Takeover of one partner firm by the other*: the alliance comes to an end when one of the allies is acquired by the other. ICL, the British computer giant, was taken over by Fujitsu in 1990, after almost 10 years of collaboration in the area of mainframe computers.

The Strategic Consequences for each Partner Firm

One of the most important consequences of alliances between competing firms is the transfer of critical skills and capabilities from one partner to the other. Such skill transfers are very difficult to observe directly, but when a firm has been able to appropriate valuable capabilities from its partner, it usually leverages these capabilities to introduce, on its own, products that it had collaborated to produce in the past, or to enter its partner's home market on its own. The strategic consequences of alliances can thus be evaluated on the basis of how the scope of each partner's activities has changed over the time the alliance lasted. We therefore observed whether a partner had expanded or shrunk the product lines it manufactured and marketed on its own while the alliance was being implemented; in a similar way, we examined whether each partner had entered new markets or exited existing markets during the same timeframe. From this perspective, strategic alliances between competitors can have the following consequences:

1. *New capability acquisition*: when the alliance is over, all partners have expanded the scope of their activities; they have

developed new product lines or have entered new markets on their own. For example, Hitachi and Fujitsu formed an alliance in 1971, under the auspices of MITI, in order to develop a Japan-based mainframe computer business. The alliance was terminated in 1991, when each partner had a market share in this business in the Japanese market that was larger than that of IBM. Cooperation thus helped both Hitachi and Fujitsu become credible competitors in the mainframe segment.

2. *Mutual specialization*: when the alliance is over, all partner firms have reduced the scope of their activities and no longer produce certain product lines on their own or no longer operate autonomously in certain markets. After having collaborated to produce the Tiger military helicopter, Aerospatiale and DASA decided to merge their helicopter divisions, creating a jointly owned subsidiary called Eurocopter. Hence, neither of the partners can continue producing helicopters on its own.

3. *One-way skill appropriation*: when the alliance is over, one of the partner firms has captured new skills and capabilities and has expanded its product line or has entered into new markets, but the other partner has not gained the same benefits from the alliance. By the time that Chrysler and Mitsubishi terminated their Diamond Star alliance in 1991, with Mitsubishi taking over the jointly owned automobile assembly plant, the Japanese partner had been able to develop an extensive distribution network in North America and could operate in that market alone, while Chrysler still relied on Mitsubishi to manufacture the small cars that it was selling.

4. *No consequence*: when the alliance is over, the capabilities possessed by each partner remain unchanged, and none of the firms has either expanded or reduced the scope of its business.

The Impact on Competition

Alliances between rival firms can obviously have a strong anti-competitive impact, but they can also increase competition by favoring the introduction of new products to the market. The impact of alliances on competition can thus be assessed by examining the way in which alliances affect the diversity of products competing in a particular market:

1. *Increased diversity of competing products*: the number of competing products offered on the market by the partner firms has increased as a result of the alliance. The alliance formed by Toyota and General Motors ultimately resulted in a greater diversity of products being made available to US consumers, since Toyota began producing automobiles in North America and marketed them under its own brand with no help from General Motors; and those cars even competed in many cases with GM models.

2. *Decreased diversity of competing products*: for example, the Airbus alliance has limited competition in commercial aircraft to a two-way struggle between Boeing and Airbus; before the Airbus consortium was formed, the Airbus partners each produced their own aircraft.

3. *No impact on the diversity of competing products*: when the alliance is over, the number of competing products available on the market remains unchanged. The Philips–Whirlpool alliance in appliances, for example, ended with Philips transferring its entire appliance division to Whirlpool and withdrawing from the business entirely, while Whirlpool was able to enter the European market.

Table 11.2　The overall outcomes of alliances between competitors

Alliance outcomes	% of cases
Evolution of the alliance over time	
—Ongoing alliances	31%
—Natural end	9%
—Extension	23%
—Premature termination	16%
—Continuation by one partner	14%
—Takeover	7%
Strategic consequences for each partner firm	
—Ongoing alliances	31%
—New capability acquisition	1%
—Mutual specialization	4%
—One-way skill appropriation	26%
—No consequence	38%
Impact on competition	
—Ongoing alliances	31%
—Increased intensity of competition	13%
—Reduced intensity of competition	12%
—No impact on the intensity of competition	44%

For customers, the only change produced by the alliance was that former Philips products had been rebranded as Whirlpool products, but it was not the case that there were more competing products to choose from.

Table 11.2 presents the statistical distribution of intercompetitor alliances on these three outcome dimensions. The table reveals that the two most frequent outcomes of alliances between rival firms are either an extension of the alliance (23% of all cases, i.e., 33% of the cases for which the outcome has been identified) or premature termination (16% of all cases, and 23% of the cases with an identified outcome). Strangely enough, the outcome that might *a priori* be expected to be the most likely—that is, a natural end of the alliance once the objectives have been achieved—is in fact quite unusual (9% of all cases). Similarly, the most dramatic outcome on which many analysts tend to focus—takeover of one partner by the other—is found in only 7% of all cases.

Table 11.2 also indicates that, for almost half of the cases for which the outcome was identified, alliances had significant strategic consequences for the partner firms involved. This confirms that analyzing the success of alliances on the basis of the performance

Table 11.3 The evolution of alliances between rival firms

	Shared-supply alliances	Quasi-concentration alliances	Comple-mentary alliances	All alliances
	30% of the sample	30% of the sample	40% of the sample	Whole sample
Ongoing alliances	36%	29%	29%	31%
Natural end	14%	12%	4%	9%
Extension	7%	34%	26%	23%
Premature termination	28%	8%	14%	16%
Continuation by one partner	7%	10%	21%	14%
Takeover	8%	7%	6%	7%
Total	100%	100%	100%	100%

Table 11.4 The strategic consequences of alliances between rival firms

	Shared-supply alliances	Quasi-concentration alliances	Comple-mentary alliances	All alliances
	30% of the sample	30% of the sample	40% of the sample	Whole sample
Ongoing alliances	36%	29%	29%	31%
New capability acquisition	0%	2%	0%	1%
Mutual specialization	2%	12%	0%	4%
One-way skill appropriation	10%	15%	47%	26%
No consequence	52%	42%	24%	38%
Total	100%	100%	100%	100%

Table 11.5 The impact of alliances on competition

	Shared-supply alliances	Quasi-concentration alliances	Comple-mentary alliances	All alliances
	30% of the sample	30% of the sample	40% of the sample	Whole sample
Ongoing alliances	36%	29%	29%	31%
Increased competition	0%	3%	29%	13%
Reduced competition	9%	22%	6%	12%
No impact on competition	55%	46%	36%	44%
Total	100%	100%	100%	100%

of the joint venture or project alone addresses the issue in a very partial manner. It is interesting that very few alliances (1%) result in new capability acquisition for all partner firms. Alliances that lead to one-way skill appropriation outcomes (i.e., unbalanced consequences for the partner firms) are, on the contrary, quite common (26% of all cases, i.e., 38% of the cases with identified outcomes).

Finally, Table 11.2 shows that alliances between rival firms do affect the intensity of competition in the industries in which they are formed in about 36% of the cases. Alliances that increase competition are slightly more numerous than alliances that decrease the intensity of competition.

Tables 11.3, 11.4 and 11.5 show that the three main types of alliances formed by competing firms—shared-supply, quasi-concentration and complementary alliances—follow extremely different patterns.

The Evolutions and Outcomes of Shared-supply Alliances

Shared-supply alliances associating very similar partners that carry out R&D together or jointly produce parts and components are terminated prematurely more often than other types of alliances. Even when these alliances continue operating until their objectives have been achieved, they are rarely extended. This results from the difficult management problems raised by shared-supply alliances: the increased economies of scale they generate cannot compensate, in many cases, for the added complexity and cost of jointly managing R&D projects or production facilities. Over time, the partners tend to diverge on the exact specifications of the parts and components to be produced jointly or on the R&D programs to be carried out. Such differences may become insurmountable and lead to the sudden termination of all collaboration or, in less dramatic cases, they make managers reluctant to extend cooperation beyond what was initially agreed.

Shared-supply alliances also appear generally to produce similar results for all partners involved and very rarely have any significant strategic consequences. Thus, shared-supply alliances seem to be fairly unimportant ventures, with a limited scope and impact, that do not affect the long-term strategy of the firms participating in them.

It is therefore not surprising that shared-supply alliances have practically no impact on the intensity of competition in the industries in which they are formed. Indeed, they do not lead to either an increase or a reduction in the number of firms competing in a market and they have no impact on the diversity of products offered to consumers. Shared-supply alliances can thus be described as "pre-competitive", both from the point of view of their initial objectives and from that of the actual outcomes they produce.

The Evolutions and Outcomes of Quasi-concentration Alliances

Quasi-concentration alliances, which associate similar partner firms to develop, manufacture and market a common product, are very rarely terminated before the project for which they were created has been completed. Moreover, such alliances tend to be fairly frequently extended by the partners for the implementation of new projects. This stability of quasi-concentration alliances is produced by a set of converging factors. In the first place, the investment required to develop, manufacture and market the common product is so high that, once a significant portion of the resources has been committed, it becomes an exit barrier for all the partner firms. In addition, in most cases the alliance was formed because the partner firms lacked the resources needed to launch a similar product on their own. Under such circumstances, pulling out of the alliance or terminating it altogether would imply, for the partners, giving up any presence in the considered business or product line. For example, none of the partners in the Airbus consortium could continue operating in the commercial aircraft business on its own if it pulled out of the alliance. Finally, extending quasi-concentration alliances to subsequent products or new projects is encouraged by the fact that, over time, the partner firms learn to collaborate with one another more efficiently. Therefore, it becomes less difficult and less costly to cooperate with the same group of partners on each new project.

In the long run, however, such reiterated collaborations will produce increasing specialization for the allied firms: each partner will develop its skills and capabilities in those areas of the joint projects for which it is responsible (those sections of the product that it designs and manufactures, customer groups to which it sells, etc.), but will lose its skills in those areas allocated to other partner firms. This loss of capabilities implies that each partner firm will see its ability to compete autonomously decrease over time as cooperation continues. The partner firms thus tend to become increasingly interdependent. This is why it is in quasi-concentration alliances that the mutual specialization outcome is most often observed— that is, all partner firms see the scope of their activities reduced, and no longer produce certain product lines on their own, or no longer operate autonomously in certain markets. Although mutual specialization may appear to create an undesirable loss of autonomy for each partner firm, it is often the price to pay for survival and renewed competitiveness in the industry. Such quasi-concentration alliances can thus be interpreted as a milder and less painful form of restructuring the industry than mergers, acquisitions or outright competitor elimination.

As far as industry structure is concerned, quasi-concentration alliances tend to induce the formation of oligopolistic situations. Indeed, even though the apparent number of competitors operating in the industry may not have changed, the number of competing products available to consumers is reduced by collaboration, because several of the existing competitors produce only one product (or product line) together. In most cases, such oligopolies lead to reduced levels of competition; although, in some industries, the quasi-concentration alliances create stronger competitors able to challenge the dominant position of industry leaders. For example, Airbus has become the only competitor capable of resisting Boeing's domination.

The Evolutions and Outcomes of Complementary Alliances

Complementary alliances, which are formed in order for one partner to market a product previously developed by the other, are also quite frequently extended beyond what was stipulated in the original agreement. However, unlike the other two types of alliances, complementary alliances often end with one partner taking over the joint business alone. For example, AT&T eventually took over the APT (AT&T–Philips Telecommunications) joint venture that it had created a few years earlier with Philips in order to market in Europe switching equipment that AT&T had originally developed for the North American market. Such an outcome, which is typical of complementary alliances, results from the fact that the complementarity that initially existed between the allies, and that justified the very formation of the alliance, has progressively disappeared. When one of the partners develops the capabilities that were originally contributed by the other partner, cooperation is no longer needed and the joint activity can be taken over by one of the partners.

Unlike shared-supply or quasi-concentration alliances, complementary alliances often produce asymmetrical consequences for the partner firms: through the alliance, one of the firms captures new skills from its partner in such a way that it can expand the scope of its business, while this partner sees its position as unchanged. Indeed, regardless of the fate of the joint project itself, one of the partners often manages after some time to develop a similar business on its own, side by side with the cooperative venture. For example, most Japanese automobile manufacturers that formed alliances with their American counterparts in order to market their cars in North America took advantage of these agreements to set up their own distribution networks and even, in some cases, their own manufacturing facilities.

Complementary alliances thus tend to have an impact on competition that is the opposite of quasi-concentration alliances. By easing the entry of new competitors into the market and by increasing the number of products made available to consumers, they tend to increase the intensity of competition. Complementary alliances are, because of their strategic consequences and of their impact on competition, the only type of alliances between rival firms to which the Trojan horse metaphor actually applies.

Table 11.6 summarizes our conclusions on the outcomes of alliances between rival firms by contrasting the evolutions, the strategic consequences and the impact on competition of shared-supply,

Table 11.6 The evolutions and outcomes of strategic alliances between competitors

Alliance type	Evolution of the alliance	Strategic consequences for each partner firm	Impact on competition
Shared-supply	Natural end or premature termination	No consequence	No impact on the intensity of competition
Quasi-concentration	Extension	Mutual specialization	Reduced intensity of competition
Complementary	Extension or continuation by one partner	One-way skill appropriation	Increased intensity of competition

quasi-concentration and complementary alliances. While our research contrasts the evolutions and outcomes of different types of alliances, it does not make it possible to compare the impact of alliances with the consequences of other strategic options. Thus, our analysis can help managers anticipate the likely evolutions of alliances in which they are engaging, but it will not allow them to figure out whether an alliance is the best possible move. This is why those outcomes that may appear as detrimental to the firm (mutual specialization, one-way skill appropriation, or increased intensity of competition, to cite just a few) may nonetheless be more desirable than the consequences of avoiding alliances altogether. And correctly anticipating what to expect from a given alliance may make it possible for managers to minimize its undesired effects while taking best advantage of its positive consequences.

Bibliography

Argyris, C. and Schon, D.A. (1978) *Organizational Learning*, Reading, MA: Addison-Wesley.

Arino, A. and de la Torre, J. (1998) "Learning from Failure: Towards an Evolutionary Model of Collaborative Ventures", *Organization Science*, vol. 9, no. 3, p. 306–25.

Arndt, J. (1979) "Toward a Concept of Domesticated Markets", *Journal of Marketing*, vol. 43, p. 69–75, fall.

Barney, J.B. (1991) "Firm Resources and Sustained Competitive Advantage", *Journal of Management*, vol. 17, p. 99–120.

Beamish, P.W. and Banks, J.C. (1987) "Equity Joint Ventures and the Theory of the Multinational Enterprise", *Journal of International Business Studies*, vol. 18, p. 1–16.

Beamish, P.W. and Killing, J.P. (1997a) *Cooperative Strategies: North American Perspectives*, San Francisco, CA: The New Lexington Press.

Beamish, P.W. and Killing, J.P. (1997b) *Cooperative Strategies: European Perspectives*, San Francisco, CA: The New Lexington Press.

Beamish, P.W. and Killing, J.P. (1997c) *Cooperative Strategies: Asian Pacific Perspectives*, San Francisco, CA: The New Lexington Press.

Berg, S., Duncan, J. and Friedman, P. (1982) *Joint Venture Strategies and Corporate Innovation*, Cambridge, MA: Oegeschlager.

Berg, S. and Friedman, P. (1981) "Impacts of Domestic Joint Ventures on Industrial Rates of Return: A Pooled Cross-Section Analysis", *Review of Economics and Statistics*, vol. 63, p. 293–98.

Bleeke, J. and Ernst, D. (1993) "The Way to Win in Cross-Border Alliances", in Bleeke, J. and Ernst, D. (eds), *Collaborating to Compete*, p. 17–34, Chichester: John Wiley.

Bruel, O. and Donada, C. (1994) "TCAS", H.E.C. case study, Jouy en Josas: France.

Cainarca, G.C., Colombo, M.G. and Mariotti, S. (1992) "Agreements between Firms and the Technological Life Cycle Model: Evidence from Information Technologies", *Research Policy*, vol. 21, no. 1, p. 45–62, February.

Child, J. and Faulkner, D. (1998) *Strategies of Cooperation: Managing Alliances, Networks and Joint Ventures*, Oxford: Oxford University Press.

Coase, R.H. (1937) "The Nature of the Firm", *Economica N.S.*, vol. 4, p. 386–405.

Cohen, W.M. and Levinthal, D.A. (1990) "Absorptive Capacity: a New Perspective on Learning and Innovation", *Administrative Science Quarterly*, vol. 35, p. 128–52.

Collins, T.M. and Doorley, T.M. (1991) *Teaming up for the 90s*, Homewood, IL: Business One Irwin.

Conner, K.R. and Prahalad, C.K. (1996) "A Resource-based Theory of the Firm: Knowledge versus Opportunism", *Organization Science*, vol. 7, no. 5, p. 477–501.

Contractor, F.J. and Lorange, P. (1988) *Cooperative Strategies in International Business*, Lexington, MA: Lexington Books.

Curhand, J.P., Davidson, W.H. and Suri, R. (1977) *Tracing the Multinationals: A Source Book on U.S.-Based Enterprises*, Cambridge, MA: Ballinger.

Doz, Y.L. (1988) "Technology Partnerships between Larger and Smaller Firms: Some Critical Issues", in Contractor, F.J. and Lorange, P. (eds), *Cooperative Strategies in International Business*, p. 317–338, Lexington, MA: Lexington Books.

Doz, Y. and Hamel, G. (1998) *Alliance Advantage: the Art of Creating Value through Partnering*, Boston, MA: Harvard Business School Press.

Dumont, A. (1990) "Technology, Competitiveness and Cooperation in Europe", in Steinberg, M. (ed.), *The Technical Challenges and Opportunities of a United Europe*, p. 68–79, London: Pinter Publishers.

Dumont, A. and Garrette, B. (1996) "The Matra-Renault Espace Alliance and the European Minivan Market", H.E.C. case study, Cranfield: European Case Clearing House.

Dunning, J.H. (1988) *Explaining International Production*, London: Unwyn Hyman.

Dussauge, P. and Garrette, B. (1992) "The Helicopter Industry in 1990", H.E.C. case study, Cranfield: European Case Clearing House.

Dussauge, P. and Garrette, B. (1993a) "Industrial Alliances in Aerospace and Defence: An Empirical Study of Strategic and Organizational Patterns", *Defence Economics*, vol. 4, no. 1, p. 45–62.

Dussauge, P. and Garrette, B. (1993b) "CFM-International", H.E.C. case study, Cranfield: European Case Clearing House.

Dussauge, P. and Garrette, B. (1995) "Determinants of Success in International Strategic Alliances: Evidence from the Global Aerospace Industry", *Journal of International Business Studies*, vol. 26, no. 3, p. 505–30.

Dussauge, P. and Garrette, B. (1998) "Anticipating the Evolutions and Outcomes of Strategic Alliances between Rival Firms", *International Studies in Management and Organization*, vol. 27, no. 4, p. 104–26.

Dussauge P., Garrette, B. and Mitchell, W. (1998) "Acquiring Partner's Capabilities: Outcomes of Scale and Link Alliances between Competitors", in Hitt, M., Ricart, J.E. and Nixon, R.D., *Managing Strategically in an Interconnected World: 1997 SMS Best Paper Proceedings*, p. 349–71, New York: John Wiley.

Dussauge, P., Hart, S. and Ramanantsoa, B. (1992) *Strategic Technology Management*, Chichester: John Wiley.

Ebers, M. (1997) *The Formation of Inter-Organizational Networks*, Oxford: Oxford University Press.

Fiol, C.M. and Lyles, M.A. (1985) "Organizational Learning", *Academy of Management Review*, vol. 10, p. 803–13.

Franko, L.G. (1971) *Joint Venture Survival in Multinational Corporations*, New York, NY: Praeger.

Garrette, B. and Dussauge, P. (1995) "Patterns of Strategic Alliances Between Rival Firms", *Group Decision and Negotiation*, vol. 4, p. 429–52.

Garrette, B. and Quélin, B. (1994) "An Empirical Study of Hybrid Forms of

Governance Structure: the Case of the Telecommunication Equipment Industry", *Research Policy*, vol. 23, no. 4, p. 395–412.

Geringer, J.M. and Hebert, L., (1989) "Control and Performance of International Joint Ventures", *Journal of International Business Studies*, vol. 20, p. 235–54.

Gerlach, M. (1987) "Business Alliances and the Strategy of the Japanese Firm", *California Management Review*, vol. 30, no. 1, p. 126–42.

Ghemawat, P., Porter, M.E. and Rawlinson, R.A. (1986) "Patterns of International Coalition Activity", in Porter, M.E. (ed.), *Competition in Global Industries*, p. 345–66, Boston, MA: Harvard Business School Press.

Gomes-Casseres, B. (1990) "Firm Ownership Preferences and Host Government Restrictions: An Integrated Approach", *Journal of International Business Studies*, vol. 21, p. 1–22.

Grant, R.M. (1996) "A knowledge based theory of inter-firm collaboration", *Organization Science*, vol. 7, p. 375–87.

Gulati, R. (1998) "Alliances and Networks", *Strategic Management Journal*, vol. 19, p. 293–317.

Hagedoorn, J. (1993) "Understanding the Rationale of Strategic Technology Partnering: Interorganizational Modes of Cooperation and Sectoral Differences", *Strategic Management Journal*, vol. 14, p. 371–85.

Hagedoorn, J. and Schakenraad (1994) "The Effect of Strategic Technology Alliances on Company Performance", *Strategic Management Journal*, vol. 15, p. 291–310.

Hamel, G. (1991) "Competition for Competence and Inter-Partner Learning Within International Strategic Alliances", *Strategic Management Journal*, vol. 12, special issue, p. 83–103.

Hamel, G. and Prahalad, C.K. (1994) *Competing for the Future*, Boston, MA: Harvard Business School Press.

Hamel, G., Doz, Y.L. and Prahalad, C.K. (1989) "Collaborate with Your Competitors—and Win", *Harvard Business Review*, vol. 67, no. 1, p. 133–39, January–February.

Harrigan, K.R. (1985) *Strategies for Joint Ventures*, Lexington, MA: Lexington Books.

Harrigan, K.R. (1988) "Strategic Alliances and Partner Assymmetries", in Contractor, F.J. and Lorange, P. (eds), *Cooperative Strategies in International Business*, p. 205–26, Lexington, MA: Lexington Books.

Hartley, K. (1983) *NATO Arms Cooperation*, London: Allen & Unwin.

Hartley, K. and Martin, S. (1990) "International Collaboration in Aerospace", *Science and Public Policy*, vol. 17, no. 3, p. 143–51, June.

Hayward, K. (1986) *International Collaboration in Civil Aerospace*, New York, NY: St Martin's Press.

Hennart, J.F. (1988) "A Transaction Cost Theory of Equity Joint Ventures", *Strategic Management Journal*, vol. 9, no. 4, p. 361–74.

Hennart, J.F., Roehl, T. and Zietlow, D.S. (1999) "Trojan Horse or Workhorse? The Evolution of U.S.–Japanese Joint Ventures in the United States", *Strategic Management Journal*, vol. 20, p. 15–29.

Henzler, H.A. (1993) "Alliances in Europe: Collusion or Cooperation", in Bleeke, J. and Ernst, D., *Collaborating to Compete*, p. 265–68, Chichester: John Wiley.

Hertzfeld, J.M. (1991) "Joint Ventures: Saving the Soviets from Perestroika", *Harvard Business Review*, vol. 69, no. 1, p. 80–91, January–February.

Hladik, K.L. (1985) *International Joint Ventures: an Economic Analysis of U.S. Foreign Business Partnerships*, Lexington, MA: Lexington Books.

Hochmuth, M.S. (1974) *Organizing the Transnational: the Experience with Transnational Enterprise in Advanced Technology*, Leiden: The Netherlands, A.W. Sijhoff.

Hout, T., Porter, M.E. and Rudden, E. (1982) "How Global Companies Win Out", *Harvard Business Review*, vol. 60, no. 5, p. 98–102, September–October.

Itami, H. and Roehl, T. (1987) *Mobilizing Invisible Assets*, Cambridge, MA: Harvard University Press.

Jacquemin, A. (1991) "Stratégies d'entreprise et politique de la concurrence dans le marché unique européen", *Revue d'Economie Industrielle*, no. 57, p. 7–24, 3rd quarter.

Jarillo, J.C. (1993) *Strategic Networks*, Oxford: Butterworth Heinemann.

Jorde, T.M. and Teece, D.J. (1992) "Innovation, Cooperation and Antitrust", in Jorde, T.M. and Teece, D.J. (eds.), *Antitrust, Innovation and Competitiveness*, p. 47–81, New York, NY: Oxford University Press.

Kanter, R.M. (1994) "Collaborative Advantage: The Art of Alliances", *Harvard Business Review*, vol. 72, p. 96–108.

Khanna, T., Gulati, R. and Nohria, N. (1998) "The Dynamics of Learning Alliances: Competition, Cooperation and Relative Scope", *Strategic Management Journal*, vol. 19, p. 193–210.

Killing, J.P. (1982) "How to Make a Global Joint Venture Work", *Harvard Business Review*, vol. 60, no. 3, p. 120–27, May–June.

Killing, J.P. (1983) *Strategies for Joint Venture Success*, London: Croom Helm.

Killing, J.P. (1989) "Managing International Joint Ventures: After the Deal is Signed", Working Paper, the University of Western Ontario.

Kogut, B. (1988) "Joint Ventures: Theoretical and Empirical Perspectives", *Strategic Management Journal*, vol. 9, no. 4, p. 319–32, July–August.

Kogut, B. (1989) "The Stability of Joint Ventures: Reciprocity and Competitive Rivalry", *Journal of Industrial Economics*, vol. 38, p. 183–98.

Kogut, B. (1991) "Joint Ventures and the Option to Expand and Acquire", *Management Science*, vol. 37, p. 19–33.

Koza, M.P. and Lewin, A.Y. (1998) "The Co-evolution of Strategic Alliances", *Organization Science*, vol. 9, p. 255–64.

Larçon, J.P. (1998) *Entrepreneurship and Economic Transition in Central Europe*, Norwell, MA: Kluwer Academic Publishers.

Lawrence, P. and Vlachoutsicos, C. (1993) "Joint Ventures in Russia: Put the Locals in Charge", *Harvard Business Review*, vol. 71, no. 1, p. 44–54.

Lewis, J. (1995) *The Connected Corporation*, New York, NY: Free Press.

Link, A.N. and Bauer, L.L. (1989) *Cooperative Research in US Manufacturing*, Lexington, MA: Lexington Books.

Lorange, P. and Roos, J. (1992) *Strategic Alliances: Formation, Evolution and Implementation*, London: Basil Blackwell.

Lorenzoni, G. and Ornani, O. (1988) "Constellations of Firms and New Ventures", *Journal of Business Venturing*, no. 3, p. 15–22.

Lynch, R.P. (1993) *Business Alliances Guide: the Hidden Competitive Weapon*, Chichester: John Wiley.

Mankin, E. and Reich, R. (1986) "Joint Ventures with Japan Give Away our Future", *Harvard Business Review*, vol. 64, no. 2, p. 78–86, March–April.

Mitchell, W. and Singh, K. (1996) "Survival of Businesses using Collaborative Relationships to Commercialize Complex Goods", *Strategic Management Journal*, vol. 17, p. 169–95.

Moingeon, B. and Edmondson, A. (1996) *Organizational Learning and Competitive Advantage*, London: Sage Publications.

Morris, D. and Hergert, M. (1987) "Trends in International Collaborative Agreements", *Columbia Journal of World Business*, vol. 22, no. 2, p. 15–21, reprinted in Contractor, F.J. and Lorange, P. (eds) (1988) *Cooperative Strategies in International Business*, p. 99–109, Lexington, MA: Lexington Books.

Mothe, C. and Quélin, B. (1998) "How Firms Benefit From Collaborating Within R&D Consortia", in M. Hitt, J. Ricart and R. Nixon (eds), *Managing Strategically in an Interconnected World: 1997 SMS Best Paper Proceedings*, p. 321–47, New York: John Wiley.

Mowery, D.C. (1987) *Alliance, Politics and Economics: Multinational Joint Ventures in Commercial Aircraft*, Cambridge, MA: Ballinger.

Mowery, D.C., Oxley, I.E. and Silverman, B.S. (1996) "Strategic Alliances and Inter-Firm Knowledge Transfer", *Strategic Management Journal*, vol. 17 , p. 77–91.

Mytelka, L.K. (1984) "La gestion de la connaissance dans les entreprises multinationales", *Revue du Cepii*, no. 4, p. 9–17.

OECD (1986) *Technical Cooperation Agreements between Firms: Some Initial Data and Analysis*, Directorate for Science, Technology and Industry, Paris: DSTI/SPR/86–20, May.

Nakamura, M., Shaver, J.M. and Yeung, B. (1996) "An Empirical Investigation of Joint Venture Dynamics: Evidence from U.S.–Japan Joint Ventures", *International Journal of Industrial Organization*, vol. 14, p. 521–41.

Nohria, N. and Garcia-Pont, C. (1991) "Global Strategic Linkages and Industry Structure", *Strategic Management Journal*, vol. 12 (special issue), p. 105–24.

Ohmae, K. (1989) "The Global Logic of Strategic Alliances", *Harvard Business Review*, vol. 67, March–April, p. 143–54.

Park, S.H. and Russo, M.V. (1996) "When Competition Eclipses Cooperation: an Event History Analysis of Joint Venture Failure", *Management Science*, vol. 42, p. 875–90.

Penrose, E.T. (1959) *The Theory of Growth of the Firm*, Oxford, UK: Basil Blackwell.

Pfeffer, J. and Nowak, P. (1976a) "Joint Ventures and Interorganizational Interdependence", *Administrative Science Quarterly*, vol. 21, p. 398–418.

Pfeffer, J. and Nowak, P. (1976b) "Patterns of Joint Venture Activity: Implications for Anti-Trust Research", *Anti-Trust Bulletin*, vol. 21, p. 315–39.

Pisano, G., Russo, M.V. and Teece, D.J. (1988) "Joint Ventures and Collaborative Agreements in the Telecommunications Industry", in Mowery, D.C. (ed.), *International Collaborative Ventures in U.S. Manufacturing*, p. 23–70, Cambridge, MA: Ballinger.

Pisano, G., Shan, W. and Teece, D.J. (1988) "Joint Ventures and Collaboration in the Biotechnology Industry", in Mowery, D.C. (ed.), *International Collaborative Ventures in U.S. Manufacturing*, p. 183–222, Cambridge, MA: Ballinger.

Porter, M.E. (1985) *Competitive Advantage*, New York, NY: Free Press.

Porter, M.E. and Fuller, M.B. (1986) "Coalitions and Global Strategy", in Porter, M.E. (ed.), *Competition in Global Industries*, p. 315–44, Boston, MA: Harvard Business School Press.

Pucik, V. (1988) "Strategic Alliances, Organizational Learning and Competitive Advantage: the HRM Agenda", *Human Resource Management*, vol. 27, p. 77–93.

Ramanantsoa, B. and Perret, V. (1993) "Matra Communication", in Dussauge, P. and Garrette, B. (eds), *Stratégie d'entreprise: études de cas*, p. 281–302, Paris: InterEditions.

Reynolds, J.L. (1979) *Indian-American Joint Ventures: Business Policy Relationships*, Washington, D.C.: University Press of America.

Ring, P.S. and Van de Ven, A.H. (1994) "Developmental Processes of Cooperative Interorganizational Relationships", *Academy of Management Review*, vol. 19, p. 90–118.

Sachwald, F. (1992) *Cooperative Agreements in the World Automobile Industry*, EIBA, Proceedings of the 18th annual conference, University of Reading, December.

Sachwald, F. (ed.) (1994) *European Integration and Competitiveness*, Aldershot: Edward Elgar.

Schaan, J.L. and Beamish, P.W. (1988) "Joint Venture General Managers in LDCs", in Contractor, F.J. and Lorange, P. (eds), p. 279–300, *Cooperative Strategies in International Business*, Lexington, MA: Lexington Books.

Schmalensee, R. (1992) "Agreements Between Competitors", in Jorde, T.M. and Teece, D.J. (eds), *Antitrust, Innovation and Competitiveness*, p. 98–118, New York, NY: Oxford University Press.

Singh, K. and Mitchell, W. (1996) "Precarious Collaboration: Business Survival after Partners Shut Down or Form New Partnerships", *Strategic Management Journal*, vol. 17, p. 95–115, special issue on evolutionary perspectives on strategy.

Spencer, W.J. and Grindley, P. (1993) "SEMATECH after Five Years: High-Technology Consortia and U.S. Competitiveness", *California Management Review*, vol. 35, no. 4, p. 9–32.

Stopford, J.M. and Wells, L. (1972) *Managing the Multinational Enterprise*, New York, NY: Basic Books.

Stuckey, J. (1983) *Vertical Integration and Joint Ventures in the Aluminium Industry*, Cambridge, MA: Harvard University Press.

Teece, D.J. (1986) "Profiting from Technological Innovation: Implications for Integration, Collaboration, Licencing, and Public Policy", *Research Policy*, vol. 15, no. 6, p. 285–305.

Urban, S. and Vendemini, S. (1992) *European Strategic Alliances*, Oxford,: Blackwell.

Weiss, S.E. (1987) "Creating the GM-Toyota Joint Venture: a Case in Complex Negotiation", *Columbia Journal of World Business*, vol. 22, no. 2, p. 23–37.

Wernerfelt, B. (1984) "A Resource-based View of the Firm", *Strategic Management Journal*, vol. 5, no. 2, p. 171–80.

Williamson, O.E. (1975) *Markets and Hierarchies*, New York, NY: Free Press.

Williamson, O.E. (1979) "Transaction Cost Economics: the Governance of Contractual Relations", *Journal of Law and Economics*, vol. 22, p. 3–61.

Williamson, O.E. (1981) "The Modern Corporation: Origins, Evolution, Attributes", *Journal of Economic Literature*, vol. 19, p. 1537–68, December.

Womack, J.P. (1988) "Multinational Joint Ventures in Motor Vehicles", in Mowery, D.C. (ed.), *International Collaborative Ventures in U.S. Manufacturing*, p. 301–48, Cambridge, MA: Ballinger.

Womack, J.P., Jones, D.T. and Ross, D. (1990) *The Machine that Changed the World*, New York, NY: Macmillan.

Yoshino, M.Y. and Rangan, U.S. (1995) *Strategic Alliances: an Entrepreneurial Approach to Globalization*, Boston, MA: Harvard Business School Press.

Index

Index compiled by Liz Granger